THE CLASSICS
OF WESTERN
SPIRITUALITY

THE CLASSICS OF WESTERN SPIRITUALITY
A Library of the Great Spiritual Masters

BERNARD *of* CLAIRVAUX
SELECTED WORKS

TRANSLATION AND FOREWORD BY
G.R. EVANS

INTRODUCTION BY
JEAN LECLERCQ, O.S.B.

PREFACE BY
EWERT H. COUSINS

PAULIST PRESS
NEW YORK • MAHWAH

Cover art: Courtesy of the Mansell Collection, Ltd, London, England.

Library of Congress Cataloging-in-Publication Data

Bernard, of Clairvaux, Saint, 1090 or 91–1153.
    Bernard of Clairvaux : selected writings.

    Bibliography: p.
    Includes index.
    1. Spiritual life—Catholic authors.   2. Bible. O.T.
Song of Solomon—Sermons.   3. Catholic Church—Sermons.
4. Sermons, English—Translations from Latin.   5. Sermons,
Latin—Translations into English.   I. Evans, G. R.
(Gillian Rosemary)   II.   Title
BX2349.B39213   1987   282   87-20093

ISBN 0-8091-2917-5

Published by Paulist Press
997 Macarthur Boulevard
Mahwah, New Jersey 07430

Printed and bound in the United States of America

CONTENTS

Author of the Foreword and Translator of this Volume
GILLIAN R. EVANS, M.A., Ph.D., D. Litt., Litt.D., is currently Lecturer in History at Fitzwilliam College, Cambridge University, England. After receiving her degree at Oxford University in 1966, she was Lecturer in Theology at Bristol University, and is now British Academy Reader (1986–1988). She is the author of numerous scholarly works including *Anselm and a New Generation* (Oxford, 1980), *Augustine on Evil* (Cambridge, 1983), *The Mind of St. Bernard of Clairvaux* (Oxford, 1983), and *The Thought of Gregory the Great* (Cambridge, 1986).

Author of the Introduction of this Volume
JEAN LECLERCQ, O.S.B., a medieval historian, is a Benedictine monk. He has written some 70 books and 700 articles in a career of more than 40 years. He is presently a professor in the Institute of Religious Psychology, Gregorian University, Rome. His permanent residence is the Abbey of Clervaux, Luxembourg.

Author of the Preface of this Volume
EWERT H. COUSINS is Professor of Theology at Fordham University and Editorial Consultant for the Classics of Western Spirituality series. Editor and translator of the Bonaventure volume in this series, Professor Cousins is also General Editor of the 25-volume *World Spirituality: An Encyclopedic History of the Religious Quest*.

FOREWORD

The lifetime of Bernard of Clairvaux (1090–1153) coincided with one of the liveliest periods of monastic experiment in the medieval West. Adults of mature experience, men who had been soldiers and land-owners and their wives, were giving up their worldly positions to enter the religious life. Monasteries that had for many generations taken in the children given them by wealthy families and trained them now had to adapt to the demands of adult vocation and try to make monks and nuns of grown men and women, many of them unlettered and unprepared for the realities of the life they were entering.

Some of these converts founded communities of their own. Herluin, the first abbot of Bec early in the eleventh century, humbly took advice and designed his community along traditional Benedictine lines. Others had novel ideas. Some individuals went to live as hermits in remote places, or took a few friends with them and tried to live a life of apostolic simplicity. In this climate of change and experiment monks who had grown up in older Benedictine houses were attracted to similar ventures. We read of runaway monks who wanted to enter an Order which seemed to offer a surer road to heaven in a more austere and testing life.

Many of these attempts were short-lived. The most lasting and the most influential perhaps was the foundation of the Cistercian Order, whose monks aspired to live a simple and balanced life by the Rule of St. Benedict. Its success owes a very great deal to Bernard of Clairvaux.

The outward reform of life in the older houses that was stimulated by these adventurous individuals and challenging newcomers had a counterpart in a deepening of the inner life. Adult experience perhaps brought something to the long, steady, patient process of practice and improvement that had been the traditional way.

1

Bernard of Clairvaux did a good deal to shape these developments in monastic life and spirituality, both within the Cistercian Order and outside it. He had an influence greater perhaps than that of any other single individual. He joined simplicity of life and balanced observance of the Rule to ardor for God in the hearts of hundreds of new Cistercians and others. He did it by example, and by the powerful effect his preaching had on those who heard him. The books and sermons translated here convey that power with remarkable force and freshness, even removed as they are by the loss of gesture and tone of voice, and the delicate balance of Bernard's antithetical style, the near-rhymes and assonances to which his Latin lends itself. In his own day he appealed to all sorts of people because he spoke to the deepest level of common human experience. He does so still. The translations are made from the recently completed critical edition of Bernard's *Opera Omnia* by Leclercq, Talbot, and Rochais (LTR).

It has seemed important to include those of Bernard's treatises that trace the path of upward aspiration in the spiritual life. A small number of sermons from the series on the Song of Songs is given space. All these sermons deal more or less directly with the development of the spiritual life in the individual, but Bernard's opening sermons perhaps set out his ideas most clearly. One or two sermons from later in the series can be found here, too, and a few of Bernard's letters.

The working principle of the translation has been to remain as close to the Latin and to retain such marks of Bernard's style as readable English permits. Frequently used terms have been translated consistently as far as can be done without forcing the sense.

Translation of texts from the Bible follows Bernard's text, which is normally that of the Vulgate. Sometimes he gives the Old Latin version and occasionally his memory fails him and he alters the Vulgate.

THE TRANSLATIONS

Bernard did not write a treatise on the spiritual life, but in a sense all his writings take the spiritual life as their subject. As he puts his mind to the task of living the monastic life, of learning humility, of loving God, of converting others to God ("On Conversion"), or to preaching on some passage of Scripture, he always has before him the need to bring his readers or listeners to know God, and he falls again and again into an account of the best practical method of doing so. This single overall purpose gives a unity and interconnectedness to his writings over several decades. Themes are repeatedly taken up. The imagery of divine love recurs—especially that of the Song of Songs.

The texts translated here are arranged in the order of the spiritual pilgrimage: conversion (*De Conversione*); patient progress in humility (*De Gradibus Humilitatis et Superbiae*), treated ironically by Bernard as a sketch of a man's descent the other way into pride; learning to know God (Book V of the *De Consideratione*); loving God (*De Diligendo Deo*). Some of the sermons on the Song of Songs follow, and a selection of letters in which Bernard speaks of the spiritual life.

PREFACE

In the history of Christian spirituality, Bernard of Clairvaux holds a distinguished place. He played a decisive role in the monastic reform of the twelfth century, stimulating the development of the newly founded Cistercian Order and infusing into its spirituality his own dynamic vision. He defended the autonomy of spirituality against what he thought was the destructive rationalism of Peter Abelard and the emerging Scholasticism, which in later centuries would drive a wedge between spiritual experience and rational consciousness. He gave impetus to two devotions that flourished in the later Middle Ages, becoming major forces in subsequent spirituality: devotion to Mary and to the humanity of Christ.

In a century that was unique in Western history for the cultivation of love, Bernard towered above his contemporaries. In his eulogies of human love, he echoed the troubadours, trouvères, and the writers of romance; but unlike his secular counterparts, he saw this love as a symbol of the soul's love for Christ, and he charted a journey through love to union with God. His achievement was so great that he has become the classic guide for those who follow the path of love in Christian spirituality. It is not fortuitous, then, that Dante chose Bernard as his spiritual guide at the climax of *The Divine Comedy*. After the love of Beatrice had drawn Dante to the highest heaven, Bernard took over the role of guide, leading him first to Mary and then to a vision of God that united him to "the Love that moves the sun and the other stars."[1]

The emergence of a spirituality of love, however, was not confined to Christianity in twelfth-century France. Quite the contrary! As has

---

1. *Paradiso*, xxxiii, 1.145.

been observed by Richard Payne, the developer of the Classics of Western Spirituality, that was a great century for the spirituality of love in the world's religions.[2] In various traditions and in diverse geographical areas, love was cultivated as a spiritual path with an intensity and a creativity that was unprecedented. In Judaism, for example, rabbis turned with new vigor to compose mystical commentaries on the Song of Songs. In the latter part of the twelfth century, the Kabbalah emerged in France and Spain. This complex mystical tradition provided a theoretical framework and practical techniques for activating the energy of love in the spiritual life. It highlighted the *Shekhinah*, or feminine aspect of God, and saw the integration of male and female energies as central to the spiritual life. This led, in the thirteenth century, to the composition of the *Zohar*, the classical Jewish mystical text expressing the love of God in the Middle Ages. In this context, the sexual union of husband and wife on the Sabbath gradually became a sacred ritual that participated in the union of the male and female aspects of God.

In Islam love also flourished—for example, in the writings of the Sufi masters 'Aṭṭār, Ahmad al-Ghazāllī, and Ibn 'Arabī. They highlighted the theme that God is lovable in his divine beauty, which he has manifested through the beauty of creatures. With consummate literary skill, the Muslim authors turned to lyric poetry to express this spirituality of love, often addressing a beautiful woman as the manifestation of the divine Beloved. This tradition reached a peak in the thirteenth-century mystical love poetry of Rumi.

In Hinduism the way of love or devotion (*bhakti*) attained a stage of development that established it as a major Hindu path throughout subsequent history. Inspired several centuries earlier by the Ālvār and Nāyanār love mystics of southern India, the path of love was given a philosophical-theological foundation in the twelfth century by Ramanuja. It was at this time that the love tradition spread to northern India, becoming a dominant force in Hindu spirituality. It was at this time, too, that the *Gīta Govinda* was composed, the Hindu counterpart to the Song of Songs, which celebrates erotic love as a symbol of the spiritual journey. Although of earlier origin, the Tantric traditions reached full development in this period, focusing on the feminine aspect of God,

---

2. Richard Payne, "A Mystical Body of Love" (paper delivered at the interreligious dialogue conference on the theme The Spirituality of Love in the Twelfth Century and Today, held at Nantes, France, June 1–4, 1986).

drawing on erotic experience, and incorporating ritual into the spirituality of love.

In Buddhism similar Tantric developments occurred in northern India, Nepal, and Tibet. In Japan in the twelfth century Honen established the school of Pure Land Buddhism. He and his disciple Shinran taught that it was not the strict discipline of Zen but the benevolent love or compassion of the Amida Buddha that leads to enlightenment. This tradition has become a major force in Japanese Buddhism.

In the context of world spirituality, then, Bernard of Clairvaux has played a special role. At a time when love was being cultivated in the world's religions in a new and creative way, it was Bernard who emerged in Christianity as the spiritual master of the path of love. Since, among the world's religions, Christianity gives preeminence to love, it required a master of exceptional talents to bring this central theme to a new level of self-consciousness and to chart a path that would lead Christians from the first stirrings of love to union with God. In the twelfth century Christianity was gifted with such a master in Bernard of Clairvaux.

Yet Bernard did not stand alone. In Christian Europe in the twelfth century, love was cultivated in both secular and religious circles. It flourished in the court and in the cloister. In southern France before the twelfth century, troubador poets had begun to awaken a romantic strain, singing the glories and the sorrows of the love between man and woman. In the twelfth century this love poetry flourished, and its themes were further developed in the genre of romance. Storytellers recounted the tragic love between Launcelot and Guinevere, between Tristan and Isolde. Through the romances of Chrétien de Troyes, written not far from Bernard's abbey, knights and ladies of the court were instructed in the gentle manners and sophisticated emotions that became part of the mystique of courtly love. This secular movement, which has contributed so much to the myth of romantic love in Western culture, did not produce an explicit spirituality of love. Yet it did contain the seeds of such a spirituality, which later blossomed in Dante.

In twelfth-century France, it was the cloister rather than the court that produced a spirituality of love. Were there influences between the two? Scholars still debate this point. Whatever the influences, mutual or not, this much is clear: As the century progressed, love became the central theme in the spiritual writers of the period. Like Bernard, many turned to producing commentaries on the Song of Songs, for example, William of St. Thierry and Richard of St. Victor. These two writers

also composed theological treatises interpreting the Trinity in the light
of human love. Aelred of Rievaulx composed a treatise entitled *On Spiritual Friendship*. Like the Platonists of Chartres, Hildegard of Bingen
situated love in a cosmic setting. In this flourishing of the spirituality
of love, Bernard played a leadership role, influencing this milieu by the
power of his personality and position as well as by the depth of his spiritual wisdom.

As is characteristic of the twelfth century, Bernard bases his spirituality on experience. At the outset of his third sermon on the Song of
Songs, he bids his monks examine their own experience. "Today," he
says, "we read the book of experience." From the context, and throughout his writings, it is clear that he is concerned with religious experience, specifically the experience of affectivity, covering the entire
spectrum from the initial awakening of love to mystical union with the
Beloved. It would be wrong to see this as as a mere evoking of emotion
or sentimentality. Bernard and the major spiritual writers of the twelfth
century drew from the deepest levels of affectivity—from those
wellsprings of the spirit where affectivity and intellect are conjoined.
Moreover, Bernard is acutely aware of the dynamics of love as a spiritual path. It is this path that he charts with intellectual brilliance. In
his introduction to this volume, Jean Leclercq observes that Bernard's
"unique and definitive distinction is due to his method of reconciling
personal, subjective experience with universal, objective teaching." Far
from ignoring or denigrating intellect, the twelfth-century spiritual
writers achieved a new level of intellectual self-consciousness precisely
in the realm of religious experience. For example, Bernard's contemporary Richard of St. Victor is credited with founding the discipline of
speculative spirituality or speculative mysticism. The excitement that
followed upon this new burst of intellect into the realm of spirituality
led Richard to seek for "necessary reasons" for the Trinity—an out-
reach of intellect that the more hesitant Aristotelian theologians of the
thirteenth century refused to pursue.

Not all of Bernard's spiritual writings deal directly with love, but
in the total corpus of his works love is by far the dominant theme. Since
he presents the climax of the spiritual journey as union with God in
love, all of his writings can be seen as delineating stages in this process.
Hence Evans has arranged the selections in this volume according to
the order of the spiritual pilgrimages: "On Conversion," "On the Steps
of Humility and Pride," "On Consideration," which deals with con-

templation, "On Loving God," and "Sermons on the Song of Songs." The volume closes with a selection of letters, where the theme of love is also prominent.

It is in "Sermons on the Song of Songs" that Bernard's spirituality of love receives its most comprehensive expression. The central theme of these sermons is intimacy: the intimate love between the Bride and the Bridegroom, between the soul and Christ. The sermons begin with a longing for intimacy expressed in the first verse of the Song of Songs: "Let him kiss me with the kiss of his mouth." In Sermon 7, Bernard delivers a eulogy on the love between man and woman as the most intimate of human loves. Why does the Song of Songs use the image of bride and bridegroom? Because they are lovers and, as Bernard will explain, the most intimate of lovers. With great subtlety, he distinguishes the basic attitudes that constitute various relationships. Fear motivates a slave toward his master, desire for gain that of a worker toward his employer, knowledge that of a pupil toward his teacher, respect that of a son toward his father. But the one who asks for a kiss is a lover. "This affection of love," Bernard says, "excels among the gifts of nature, especially when it returns to its source, which is God." Because of the intimacy of their love, no names can be found that better express the love between the Word and the soul than those of Bridegroom and Bride. For they hold everything in common. "They share one inheritance, one table, one house, one bed, one flesh" (I.2).

Through the images of the bride and the bridegroom, Bernard describes at great length and with extraordinary sophistication the movement of the soul toward union with the Word. He does this with the full power of his passionate rhetoric as he orchestrates sensuous imagery to draw his hearers toward the heights of mystical affectivity. In the later sermons he describes, with remarkable delicacy and candor, his own intimate experiences of union with the Bridegroom.

In his symbolic interpretation of the Song of Songs, Bernard situates himself in an ancient tradition, which in its Christian strand goes back to Origen in the third century. In the prologue to his commentary on the Song of Songs, Origen states: "This book seems to me an epithalamium, that is, a wedding song, written by Solomon in the form of a play, which he recited in the character of a bride who was being married and burned with heavenly love for her bridegroom, who is the Word of God." Origen then proceeds to distinguish two allegorical meanings of the bride. "Whether she is the soul made after His image or the Church, she has fallen deeply in love with Him."[3] Although Bernard emphasizes the meaning of the bride as allegory of the individual soul, he also develops the second meaning, the bride as allegory of the Church.

In the patristic and medieval periods, allegory was looked upon not as a flight of fancy, but as a method of penetrating into a deeper level of the sacred text, based on the structure of reality and the very nature of the psyche. According to this perspective, God, in creating the universe, imprinted certain spiritual meanings into physical symbols, which could be discerned by a heightened spiritual sensibility nourished by Scripture and tradition. No wonder, then, that Bernard sees in the bride and bridegroom the most appropriate symbol for the soul aflame with love for the Word. The love between the bride and the bridegroom is a natural symbol—that is, structured into the very nature of reality—for the intimate love between the soul and God. As Bernard has eloquently expressed, no other human relation can achieve more intimate love than that of the bride and the bridegroom.

Moreover the two levels of the allegory—the soul and the Church—are not arbitrary. One can detect in this distinction the basis of a philosophy and theology of interpersonal and community relations. Of course, in this context the Church should be interpreted not as an institution, but as the community of believers. What is it, then, that makes such a community possible? The fact that the same Word is the Bridegroom of each individual soul. Thus the Word provides the basis of interpersonal and community relations since all are already related by being grounded in the same Word. It is this ground that is the ontological presupposition that makes interpersonal and community relations possible, and it is this ground that is awakened when these relations are activated.

These brief observations merely highlight some of the richness of Bernard's spirituality. The readers who explore this volume will be moved by the depth and sophistication of his teaching, as they will be

---

3. Origen, *Commentary on the Song of Songs*, prologue; English translation by Roland Greer, *Origen: An Exhortation to Martyrdom, Prayer, and Selected Works*, The Classics of Western Spirituality (New York: Paulist Press, 1979), p. 217.

carried along by his passionate eloquence, which shines through the translation. They will perceive those qualities that entitle him to a place of eminence not only in Christian spirituality in the twelfth century, but within the entire scope of its history and within the larger horizons of world spirituality.

INTRODUCTION

Bernard of Clairvaux, as a monk of the Middle Ages, is a distant figure to most people today. History has sometimes judged him harshly; yet he is still read, translated, and debated by those interested in the spiritual life. His message actually transcends the time and place in which he wrote; it is perennial and particularly relevant for our time, making him close to twentieth-century man for several reasons. First, he is fully human and has never denied the human dimension in himself or in others. The candor of his analysis—or psychoanalysis—of his own ego is appealing to us, if at first a bit surprising. In describing his ego, he speaks of our own; what takes place in him also goes on in each of us. In recognizing ourselves in him, we can identify with him and follow him on his journey from the finiteness common to all humanity to union with the infinite God. He gives us confidence in ourselves: his path can become our own. We too can go to God without losing our personal identity; God accepts us and draws us to himself as he has made us and experience has fashioned us.

St. Bernard belongs to the twelfth century, the highpoint of the Middle Ages from the point of view of spirituality. It was the age when the West achieved an integral and balanced humanism. As a result of the barbarian invasions, a new type of person came into being who combined the experience of the old Greco-Roman culture, which had been handed down especially by the Church Fathers, with the eager vitality of a youthful generation. This new, elite generation, especially those in monastic Orders, had slowly assimilated the whole legacy of the Ancients; they had faithfully passed it along but without reviving it very much. Medieval man was reaching maturity in the second half of the eleventh century, as the worth of the individual grew more evident.

Until that time, social structures had been the predominant influence. In the twelfth century a whole new secular and religious literature developed, which was devoted to a study of human feelings, especially love. It was the time that saw the development and clarification of the theology of marriage, as well as the growing prestige and popularity of the novels of courtly love. It was also the age of those spiritual writers whose masterpieces nourished the most religious people of the day, influenced others in society, and shaped the future. The greatest of these writers is Bernard of Clairvaux. The importance that he places on the state of the soul, both in his life and in his works, shows him to be a man of modern outlook. Yet he never engages in a superficial sentimentality, but is solidly based in traditional doctrine. He achieved the first great synthesis in the West between all of scriptural and patristic theology on the one hand, and the totality of human experience on the other. He left his mark on all who wrote on the spiritual life in the twelfth century, and after him the way was open for new syntheses. In the next century a whole new philosophical thought was coupled with this strong, interior zeal. By the thirteenth century, the time was ripe for, among others, St. Bonaventure, who, according to recent research, owed much to St. Bernard.

This evolution of thought continued with the great spiritual figures of the fourteenth and fifteenth centuries and, later on, with those of the Renaissance and of the Protestant and Catholic reformations; each insisted more or less on a certain aspect of theological consideration or mystical experience. But the point of origin for the synthesis of thought and experience is St. Bernard, the voice of the twelfth century.

Bernard's unique and definitive distinction is due to his method of reconciling personal, subjective experience with universal, objective teaching. In his life and work, Bernard's experience is the result of situations that history handed down or assigned to him; doctrinally, he receives the Christian tradition and accepts it in its fullness, but he also brings to it his enriching experience of genius and grace. Factually, people exist and events take place independently of him. He does not allow himself to be controlled by these facts; these, too, he accepts and at the same time tries to transform them. In himself, he must also accept the limitations that are part of the finite human condition; in accepting them, he also interprets them to make sense of them.

Experience and thought are the two guidelines to follow in considering Bernard's life, work, and doctrine—three realities that are really inseparable. There are several possible ways to introduce a writer like

St. Bernard. One is to present the events of his life, and then to speak
of his character, and finally of his writings. This method, however,
might very well break the unity that existed between his interior contemplative activity and his equally intense exterior action. St. Bernard's
personal development is expressed in his writings. It is only in the light
of that development that we can realize the significance he attached to
his works and understand their content. I will not recall here all the
events in which St. Bernard was involved, but will place his writings
within the framework of his development, indicating the precise merit
of various works from which representative excerpts have been selected
for this volume.

His Life Reflected in His Written Works

We have very little historical information about Bernard's early years,
normally such an important period in anyone's life. There is a hagio-
graphical account attributed to the eminent theologian William of St.-
Thierry, who knew Bernard after he had become Abbot of Clairvaux.
During Bernard's own lifetime, William was given the task of writing
his biography, with a view to keeping it for posterity, but he was a good
distance from Clairvaux, where Bernard lived, and wrote without the
latter's knowledge. He never consulted Bernard or questioned any of
his brothers, although several were monks at Clairvaux. Book One of
William's *First Life* of Bernard is a theological masterpiece but hardly a
model of objective biography. He employed the standard themes of traditional hagiography, whether pre-Christian, Christian, or monastic:
dreams, heavenly visions, and victory over temptations against chastity. Then, too, he may have projected his personal problems on St. Bernard. Above all, he presented a theological interpretation for the
phenomenon of the newly founded (1098) Cistercian Order, of which
Bernard was the most famous member. He was primarily concerned to
show the Abbey of Clairvaux as a model of monastic life; this he accomplished with some idealization.

    We do know something of the family into which Bernard was born
in 1090. His family belonged to the minor nobility of Burgundy, his
father being a knight and his brothers destined to become the same.
Bernard, however, had been sent by his parents to a small school kept
by the Canons Regular at St.-Vorles, near Dijon. While we know nothing of his schoolmasters, we can presume that at least some of them

were excellent, for Bernard emerged from their care a remarkable thinker and a well-trained Latinist. Since thousands of children studied at St.-Vorles and similar schools, and there was not another St. Bernard among them, his uniqueness cannot be explained by schooling alone; account must be taken of his truly extraordinary natural gifts and the exceptional graces he received. At best, we can say that the teaching method followed at St.-Vorles and elsewhere, which we know from many sources, could transform an extremely gifted child into a stylist of renown.

Bernard himself said nothing about his childhood and made only a few veiled references to his teenage years. After finishing his studies, he probably returned to the family estate at Fontaine-les-Dijon, where the fortified castle still stands, evoking the twelfth century and its way of life. There were many young noblemen, like Bernard's brothers, with little to do except hunt, or take part in tournaments and other violent pastimes. They also engaged in the frequent wars between various châteaux.

Bernard did mention "literary matches" in which many participated. During the long evenings in the courts of the low and high nobility, people liked to listen while troubadours and minstrels recounted stories, told tales, and sang songs of little substance; sometimes the courtiers tried to outdo them by composing verses in the troubadours' style. It is possible that Bernard, too, may have tried his hand, but we do not know.

He must have had his share of the various temptations that are the lot of the young in any age. It is likely that they were accompanied by that special intensity which marked his every experience, for later on he would speak of temptations with astonishing realism—for example, in his fifth Sermon on Psalm 90. When, as an adult, he began to express his ideas on human existence, there was no indication of any particular obsession. His strong aggressiveness was certainly apparent; it was God's gift and a mark of natural energy that was capable of transformation through grace. Aware of this side of his personality, he spoke of it as a vital force to be controlled, not repressed. He never claimed complete success at keeping his aggressiveness in check, and historians bear this out. But he seems to have achieved, perhaps at great cost, a psychological equilibrium resulting in a joyful disposition that drew others to him.

In the year 1111, at the age of twenty-one, he decided to become a monk at Cîteaux, the Cistercian proto-monastery, then in its first fervor, and located only a few miles from the château where he was born. His great enthusiasm made him unwilling to keep his ideal to himself and he managed to bring his uncle, his brothers, and a group of young noblemen round to the same vocation. He even persuaded his sister, Humbeline, to leave her husband and become a nun. In 1112, he and his companions entered Cîteaux. His undisputed leadership of the group is an example of the kind of drawing power he always had over others; such a gift can be problematical and easily abused. He was by no means the eldest but he had authority over them all, not so much because he became their abbot as because they recognized the sincerity of his religious convictions.

In 1115, just three years following his arrival at Cîteaux, Bernard was sent to found a monastery at Clairvaux in Champagne, to which he led his brothers and companions, and attracted other young men as well. Soon he was in a position to make other foundations, in 1118, 1119, 1121, and almost every year after that. He made 68 foundations in thirty-five years and was the principal promoter of his Order, which, at the time of his death, comprised some 350 houses, of which 164 were answerable more or less directly to his authority. They extended across the whole of Europe, from Scandinavia to southern Portugal, from northern England to central Europe. A spiritual motivation had to be ensured in each monastery, beginning with the motherhouse. It has been estimated that between 800 and 900 monks had been part of the community of Clairvaux before Bernard's death. Some of them were sent to daughterhouses that, in turn, made other foundations. Thus, there were thousands of men, generally young, who left society and often a military career to take up the cloistered life. If to this number one adds the members of some 290 other Cistercian monasteries founded during Bernard's lifetime, one has some idea of the tremendous peace corps, with tens of thousands of members, that Bernard helped to establish. What architect of peace has played such a role in his century or in any other?

At first, Bernard taught only his monks, but before 1124 the prior of his monastery, in the name of the community, asked him to set down in writing his doctrine on humility. He thus obtained Bernard's first work, which is also his first masterpiece: his treatise *The Steps of Humility and Pride*. Bernard's message was, however, destined to go beyond the confines of Clairvaux and in fact he was consulted from all sides. About the same time, he drew up the *Letter on Love* at the request of the monks of the Grande Chartreuse. It contains the heart of his message on the love of God and is the first and most detailed explanation of monastic love in the twelfth century. It became the eleventh text in his collection of letters, and he considered it important enough to reproduce at the end of the treatise he wrote shortly after: *On Loving God*.

He took advantage of some leisure time while convalescing from an illness to compose a series of three (later four) long homilies on the Gospel of the Annunciation: *In Praise of the Virgin Mother*. In the preface, he confesses that he felt compelled to write for he could not keep to himself all that he felt. The more he enjoyed contemplative solitude with God, the more responsible he felt for sharing with others the interior light he had received.

During his first period of literary activity, he also produced the *Apology to William of St.-Thierry*, which he dedicated to the Benedictine abbot. William had urged him to take part in a controversy involving some Cistercians and the monks of Cluny: The former accused the latter of lacking in fervor, while the Cluniacs maintained that the new Order broke with tradition. The polemic was heated. Since Bernard had no part in originating the dispute and intervened only because he was asked to, he assumed the role of mediator. Once involved in the conflict, he wrote spiritedly and, in the second part of the *Apology*, composed a satire on the Cluniacs that is a model of its kind. He gives an amusing description of the supposed abuses at Cluny, not all of which can be verified in historical or archeological documents. However, he also expressed himself with such conviction and warmth of feeling that he achieved his purpose. The abbot of Cluny, Peter the Venerable, was defensive about certain points in the *Apology* that he felt needed modification, but he also profited from the lesson and legislated reforms along the lines suggested by the abbot of Clairvaux. It would seem from the manuscript tradition that most traditional monks, making allowances for exaggeration, welcomed the author in their libraries. He had given them proof of his fairness by devoting the first part of his treatise to humbling the Cistercians, who boasted of their new observance; continuing with this theme, he composed some of the finest pages ever written on the legitimate diversity that contributes to the richness of the Church and is perfectly consistent with its unity.

From that point on, Bernard of Clairvaux was no longer simply a monastic teacher, but was asked to extend his teaching office to those engaged in pastoral care and to other areas of Church life. In 1127 or 1128, Henri Le Sanglier, Archbishop of Sens, asked Bernard for the discourse that became *On the Conduct and Duties of Bishops*. This would be a formidable undertaking presenting certain difficulties. The request for such a tract suggested to Bernard that there were, in fact, abuses to condemn. Moreover, writing such a work might place him on the wrong side of the archbishop, a high-ranking prelate whose ecclesiastical province included the diocese of Langres, in which Clairvaux was located. Bernard did, however, take up the challenge and spoke out with courage and earnestness. His love for the poor and concern for the virtue and holiness of Church leaders were an evident part of his message, which was well received and became one of his most frequently copied works.

The Council of Troyes (1128) was the first public Church business outside the monastic realm to receive Bernard's attention. This council set up the first regulations concerning the Knights Templar, a new religious institute that had been established at Jerusalem by Bernard's cousin, Hugh of Payns. At the latter's request he wrote *Book in Praise of the New Militia* between 1128 and 1136. The new religious community, similar to Third Order members and attached to a community of Canons Regular, presented two problems. First of all, how to justify the fact that their role, which was to protect pilgrims and other Christians in the Holy Land, led them on occasion to fight and even kill their enemies? Making use of arguments that were perhaps more valid in his own day than in ours, Bernard tried to persuade them that everything depended on their motives. He reminded them that they, too, might become combat victims. Death is, for all of us, the great encounter with God, who will then judge our hearts and intentions. If the knights used their arms not out of hatred, but to defend a just cause with the least amount of violence, they had nothing to fear. In his warnings to the Knights Templar, Bernard also expanded on a theme he had treated elsewhere: his satirical criticism of secular knighthood as empty and violent. He was not satisfied with condemning its evils or placing it in opposition to a religious knighthood. His monasteries, which he was fond of comparing to spiritual fortresses, became the training ground for an enormous army of what he called "warriors for peace."

The Knights Templar posed a second problem—whether it might not be better for them to lead a contemplative life like the Canons who guaranteed the service of prayer in the Temple, rather than waging war in the street. Since they were performing their military service on holy ground, St. Bernard told them, they should at least profit from the location to meditate on the mysteries that had unfolded there. To help them follow his advice, Bernard wrote a series of excellent meditations

on all the great events connected with human salvation that took place
in the Temple of Jerusalem, at Bethlehem, in Nazareth, and on Cal-
vary. He spoke of all the places where Jesus gave proof of his love, and
of the Holy Sepulchre where his resurrection revealed that the Father
had accepted his sacrifice by having him enter into glory. Thus, even
the interior crisis of the first military Order gave St. Bernard opportunity to bring himself and others to the contemplation of God.

Shortly after the council, a schism broke out in the Roman
Church; the legitimate Pope, Innocent II, found himself faced with a
rival, Anacletus. Princes took sides in the division of the papacy and in
1130 a meeting was held at Etampes, in France, where Bernard rallied
the weight of French opinion round Pope Innocent. For eight years he
was involved in reestablishing unity in several ways. He accompanied
the Pope in his travels through France in 1130 and 1131. In 1132, he
defended the papal cause in the south of France. The following year,
the Pope, having taken refuge at Pisa, summoned Bernard, who intervened in the Pope's favor in Genoa, Milan, and other Italian cities, after
which he returned with the Pope to Rome. In 1135, he took part in the
Diet of Bamberg and the Council of Pisa, and traveled again through
northern Italy, still working to achieve Church unity. Bernard returned
to Clairvaux but, in 1137, was recalled to Rome by the Pope and cardinals; again, he labored to bring the schism to an end, which was finally accomplished in the following year.

In the midst of all his moving about, he managed to write a long,
subtle work, again dedicated to William of St.-Thierry, which he called
On Grace and Free Will, borrowing one of St. Augustine's titles. The
interesting Prologue informs us how Bernard snatched opportunities
for writing, and reveals the principal source of his teaching, namely,
his experience. During the same period, students and teachers in city
schools were having spirited discussions on problems affecting the
Christian life of the faithful and the pastoral responsibility of the clergy.
But the brightest monks and abbots were no longer remaining silent
either, nor were they content to solve administrative problems at their
meetings. Bernard began at this point by recounting one of these group
conversations. One day, he had publicly praised "the work accomplished in him by God's grace"; "on the one hand, I recognized (*agnos-
cerem*) that grace had placed goodness within my reach; on the other
hand, I perceived (*sentirem*) that it was responsible for my progress; and
finally I hoped that it would help me to advance even further." Someone near Bernard had put to him a series of questions which he quotes,

then answers and uses as a point of departure for his exposition. At the outset, he quotes a New Testament passage, frequently cited thereafter: the Epistle to the Romans. He is especially concerned with chapters five to eight, in which St. Paul describes, analyzes, and resolves the conflict he himself experienced between the inclination toward sin and the life of the Spirit. Centuries later, this was the decisive text in the genesis of Martin Luther's doctrine. The last sentence of Bernard's treatise is a gloss on Romans 8:30: "Those whom God has justified, and not those whom he found justified, he has also glorified." It was Bernard's wish to rewrite a commentary on this basic text in the style of his own time, for it is the key to interpreting all Christian experience.

In 1135, just when he was most taken up with finding a solution to the schism of the Roman Church, Bernard was invited by a Carthusian friend, Bernard of Portes, to undertake a commentary on the Song of Songs. The sole object of the biblical poem is to exalt the love that once had united two young spouses, and that had become the symbol of God's Covenant with Israel and later with the Church. It is also a figurative representation of the intimate relationship between Christ and those who live according to the Spirit. Bernard of Portes was perhaps not the only one to realize that the time had come for the Abbot of Clairvaux to undertake a comprehensive literary work. No doubt he envisaged a masterpiece that would display the full range of the Cistercian's talent and contain the richness of his experience, both of the interior life and of Church affairs, which he had acquired in the course of twenty years' work in the service of God and men. At first, Bernard hesitated; then he agreed to do the work. He was too open-minded to limit himself to a literal explanation of each verse of the text from beginning to end. Instead, he used the biblical poem as a pretext to speak of all the things he held dearest concerning the spiritual life, the mysteries of the faith, and the mission of the Church. Toward the end of 1136, he was interrupted when called to Rome for the third time, owing to the schism. He had already drawn up twenty-four sermons.

On his return from Rome he resumed work in the summer of 1138 and began by making a new draft of the twenty-fourth sermon. He also wrote an introduction to the revised sermon in which he explained the significance of his recent journey. Not one to be distracted or overtaken by events, Bernard kept control over his own plans despite outside occurrences. Thus, he easily took up his writing again at the verse where he had left off and was hard at it for eighteen years, until the moment when death prevented the completion of a sermon. For the rest of his life his great opus was the underlying task of this busiest of men. His eighty-six sermons on the Song of Songs are actually a series of treatises based much more on his own experience than on the text of the poem; in fact, he does not go beyond the first verse of the second of the eight chapters of the biblical book. But he discovered a way to expound at length on a number of issues: his Christian reaction to the death of his brother Gerard, his views on clergy reform, and a rebuttal of the errors of the heretics of the Rhineland, as well as an error attributed to Gilbert de la Porrée, Bishop of Poitiers. Despite digressions, the connecting thread running throughout the work is the relationship of love, which unites the three divine Persons to the Church, and in and through the Church to all its members. It is in light of this relationship of love that he analyzes facts pertaining to himself and to the Church.

Because of the success of his various interventions, Bernard became publicly known and was increasingly caught up in conflicts of doctrine, politics, and monastic life. While passing through Paris in 1140, he addressed a group of student clerics urging them to put an end to the vices in which some of them indulged. While we do not have the actual text of his appeal, we know that it had the desired effect. Many students turned to monastic life and followed Bernard to Clairvaux. This was notably true of Geoffrey of Auxerre, who had been a disciple of Peter Abélard. He was to become Bernard's secretary, later his biographer and successor, and continued his sermons on the Song of Songs. A short time later, Bernard put together a sermon entitled *On the Conversion of Clerics*, which is undoubtedly the substance of his Paris discourse. In it he gives a most penetrating psychological analysis of all the forms of selfishness that worm their way into the hidden corners of the heart. He then goes on to describe the joy of those who turn away from selfishness and live according to the Beatitudes.

The year 1140 marks the first, brief digression in Bernard's ordinary activities. Until that time, he had refrained from intervening in theological disputes but now yielded to the insistences of William of St.-Thierry. The latter, who had become a Cistercian at Signy, one of Clairvaux's daughterhouses, urged Bernard to oppose the teachings of Master Abélard, which were considered dangerous by some of his contemporaries. Bernard hesitated, resisting the demand. But William sent him an entire dossier summing up the incriminating errors and assembling ideas and passages from the Church Fathers for a rebuttal. Once again convinced that he could be of service to the Church, Bernard threw himself into the controversy with all his fiery spirit. On both sides the arguments were violent. Between Bernard and Abélard there passed the usual anathemas as each one, invoking the apocalyptic language of the Old Testament, tried to convince the other of the truth of his position. Bernard attended a bishops' meeting at Sens in 1140 where Abélard's ideas were not discussed in the presence of the teacher's followers, as Bernard had hoped; they were delated to Rome. Bernard then launched a propaganda campaign in the form of letters to influential members of the Curia. With the help of documentary material received from William of St.-Thierry, he wrote a long epistle, similar to a treatise, intended for the Pope. It was the one hundred nineteenth letter of his collection and entitled "Against the Errors of Abélard." The brilliant master of the Paris schools had developed bold new insights concerning the doctrines of the Trinity, Redemption, and Grace, which were restated and clarified by subsequent scholars and proved beneficial to many. But William, Bernard, and others thought that Abélard's ideas, as then presented, posed a threat to Christian faith. The epistle also served as an opportunity for Bernard to proclaim his own faith and love. The final pages of this letter-treatise contain some of his most beautiful writing on the mystery of Jesus.

At the request of two Benedictines, who were at odds with their abbot over the interpretation of certain points of the Rule of St. Benedict, Bernard wrote, shortly before 1143, a very subtle treatise entitled *On the Precept and Its Application*. It contains a definitive clarification of the delicate relationship between the monastic Rule and the power of those responsible for its application. While setting certain limits on the authority of superiors, he placed no limits on charity and the obedience that it prompts. In 1145, Bernard traveled to the south of France to oppose the errors of two popular preachers, Peter of Bruys and his disciple, Henry; their teachings ran the risk of calling into question the very groundwork of Church and state. A second period of digression for Bernard began in 1146. It came late in his life and lasted only two years. It resulted from the part he played, at the request of Eugene III, the first Cistercian Pope, in launching a Crusade intended to save Christian holdings in the Holy Land.

The Pope and the king of France, Louis VII, had thought of calling for a French Crusade. Securing agreement among the French nobility for such a project was certainly difficult, but not impossible. However, it was not sufficient to decide to wage a holy war. Prospective soldiers, whether nobleman or peasant, had to be stirred to enthusiasm and Bernard seemed the only one who possessed sufficient moral authority to

put over the idea of a sacred campaign. He obeyed the order to enlist
support for the holy cause and was present at Vézelay in 1146 when
the king's herald read the papal document calling for the start of the
Crusade. Bernard's vision, however, went beyond just another holy
war. His monastic idealism—certainly not his knowledge of politics or
military operations—led him to suggest a Crusade in which the Christian rulers and people of East and West would take part. He drew up
several letters explaining his idea; one in particular, of great length, was
adapted to various recipients but the message was essentially the same
for all. Hitherto, volunteers for a Crusade had been motivated by the
promise of indulgences, privileges, and other advantages. Bernard
wished to change all that. He described the Crusade as an exclusively
spiritual undertaking, an opportunity to renounce sin and turn to God,
and to increase one's love for Jesus Christ. In place of the cruel and
senseless wars fought by Christian knights in their own countries, Bernard demanded an act of pure generosity. This moving letter gives us
some idea of Bernard's words as he preached in favor of the Crusade.
The text has been copied, printed, read, and translated down to our
own day by people with no Crusade in mind. Yet it has made them
reflect on themselves, on what God had done for them in Christ, and
on what they could and ought to do for him in return, whatever the
circumstances of their lives.

     For a year and a half, from autumn 1146 to the spring of 1148,
Bernard traveled through France, Flanders, the Rhineland, and Ba-
varia, to win over the monarchs, nobility, and general population to the
idea of the Crusade. He was not entirely successful. Rivalries sprang
up fairly quickly among those who had gone off to fight; hostility was
also reported between the Crusaders and the governments of the countries through which they passed. Toward the end of 1149, the enter-
prise fell apart and Bernard was held responsible. Insofar as he was not
well informed on contemporary political conflicts and the difficulties of
such an undertaking, he could be considered responsible for the deba-
cle. But the principal cause of the Crusade's failure was the dissension
between sovereigns and knights. Bernard saw the defeat as an insult to
God. He accepted the personal humiliation that followed and the en-
suing unpopularity of his monasteries. But he did not become discour-
aged.

     Continuing his promotion of clergy reform, he began to write the
Life of St. Malachy, an archbishop of Armagh who, while traveling on
the Continent, had recently died at Clairvaux. Bernard had scarcely

known him personally and was not at all acquainted with Ireland. But he obtained some information from that country, which he used to sketch a portrait of Malachy as a reforming bishop, for such he conceived him to be. His life of the Irish bishop served to illustrate a pastoral treatise concerning Church prelates that had been composed some time previously for the Archbishop of Sens.

Following a council at Rheims in April 1148, Bernard grew alarmed at the dangers posed by the teaching of Gilbert de la Porrée on the Trinity. His concern is revealed in the five-volume work that occupied his final years. Eugene III, his former disciple, requested a work on papal spirituality, which gave Bernard an opportunity to outline a synthesis of all his concepts. The treatise, entitled *Consideration*, is concerned with self-knowledge and the contemplation of God. This term, which is found in the Bible, had appeared in the *Pastoral Rule*, which St. Gregory the Great intended for the clergy of his day and which, for centuries after him, served as a manual of the spiritual life for bishops and priests. Bernard thought it should be rewritten for his own time. The role of the Pope had evolved since the sixth century when the *Pastoral Rule* appeared. The Roman Curia had developed in a manner that Bernard judged excessive and that gave rise to certain abuses. Once again he spoke his mind as he had done in the treatise *On the Conduct and Duties of Bishops*. He knew that not everyone in the papal entourage approved of this French abbot who interfered so effectively in numerous conflicts. The tension between him and the Italians in the Curia surfaced at the time of the schism of Anacletus and later during the controversy over Abelard. Bernard maintained the friendships he had formed with Italian cities where he was once warmly received; he did not favor the Roman cardinals' tendency toward centralization. As devoted as he was to the cause of unity between Pope and Christians, he refused to be an absolute instrument of centralization; he was more the Pope's man than a Curial agent. So much is evident in the third book of *Consideration*, surely the most virulent attack ever written on the Roman Curia. His position of strength enabled Bernard to avoid flattering or seeking the favor of any of the influential members of Church government; yet his condemnation of abuses was accepted, stated as it was with authority and within the lofty context of the spiritual life. He was, in fact, as successful as he had been with the *Apology* on the subject of Cluny, and the treatise *On the Conduct and Duties of Bishops*. The number of manuscript editions of *Consideration* still preserved in the Vatican Library proves that many Popes, cardinals, and other prelates had their own copy of this work, which was a forceful reminder of their duties as Churchmen. Even in our own day a certain Curial cardinal revealed that each year he reread *Consideration* during his annual retreat.

What might in effect have been a critical work, serving only "to tear down," to use a Pauline phrase, became at Bernard's hands a constructive work, useful for "building up." Rather than beginning with an attack on practical and immediate problems, he started with what is most essential in any spirituality: the difficulty of remaining centered in God while greatly involved in the service of one's neighbor. This is a vital question confronting Christians in every age; the response he gave in this treatise, therefore, is of permanent and universal value. Writing in a confident, pedagogical style, Bernard left aside the concrete, existential situation of the Pope and anyone else engaged in active service. Then he took the reader by the hand, so to speak, and led him from a consideration of himself to an examination of the reality that is below him, then to that which is around him, finally coming to that which is above him. Book Five of *Consideration*, in which he discusses these realities, is his final literary endeavor and represents the summit of his doctrine: quiet contemplation of the mysteries of the Trinity and the incarnation.

By the spring of 1153, Bernard was 63 years old and worn out, but still had enormous spiritual energy. He was in the process of carefully revising his most important works, word by word, so as to leave behind a corrected, definitive edition. However, his physical strength began to ebb and he fell ill, just as serious political problems broke out in Lorraine. The Archbishop of Trèves came to Clairvaux asking him to go to Metz and act once again as mediator. Bernard got up, went off to Metz where he fulfilled his mission, and returned to his monastery, where he died on August 20, 1153.

There were many ecclesiastical issues in which Bernard was involved that have not been touched on here. Nothing has been said, for example, of his activities on behalf of Church reform or of his efforts to renew and expand communities of monks and Canons Regular, including foundations made by Clairvaux, which were one of his most constant concerns. His occasional partiality toward Cistercians gave rise to problems, notably in the case of episcopal appointments to Langres and York, when his judgment was less than objective. At other times as well—during conflicts between rulers and nobility, on the occasion of marriages with their juridical, political, and canonical consequences— Bernard was so convinced of the rightness of his course that he exaggerated in a way that rhetoric alone cannot explain. He omitted or played down certain facts while emphasizing others, and too willingly listened to hearsay, which was sometimes untrue.

Contradictions also occur in his writings. At times he caught himself in inconsistencies for which he expressed regret and asked forgiveness, and suppressed those passages in his letters before sending them out. But this was not always the case. When considering Bernard's motives, then, it is very difficult to unravel what is purely human from what is faithful to the Gospel. Surely God alone is the judge. But historians have the right to get to the bottom of such inconsistencies, which although infrequent are nonetheless regrettable. However, in most cases he acted as peacemaker, trying, often with success, to reconcile enemies. He also kept close watch on the spiritual progress of his community and was responsible for the economic development and administration of Clairvaux. All of this gives us some idea of the tremendous activity he carried on, while maintaining the contemplative life without which he could not have written so well on contemplation.

Bernard's action and contemplation are two sides of his character, which come across clearly in his letters and sermons. It has been estimated that he sent a thousand letters or so, more than five hundred of which have been preserved. They vary greatly in length—from a few lines to long treatises—although most are a few pages long, and they are equally diverse in subject matter. They form a literary unit, however, because Bernard did not, as a rule, send a simple business letter giving concrete instructions about specific problems. His epistles, elevated in tone with scriptural allusions, spoke of the spiritual life, stressed motivation and intention, and recalled fundamental truths. His correspondence is thus somewhat disappointing to the historian who finds in it more in the way of ideas and feelings than detailed information. The latter was confided to the messenger, who passed it along orally to the recipient. The written text itself was concerned with placing every situation within the entire context of Church reform. Bernard was fully aware of the doctrinal nature of his letters and spent the last years of his life, aided by his secretary, Geoffrey of Auxerre, putting together an official collection intended for publication. He selected 225 letters, and revised the text and arranged it in a most systematic manner. An early selection indicates the tone of the letters: It consists of texts describing the principal aspects of the monastic vocation and life. Next, following the chronological order of the Popes, he organized letters in hierarchical order to Popes, cardinals, bishops, abbots, laymen, and women. It is clear from the choice of his texts and their presentation that Bernard wanted to create a true "mirror of the Church," holding out to each member a program for his or her life. He wished also to indicate the principles to be followed in resolving various cases as they arose. Thus this corpus of documents written on different occasions has become a summary of applied spirituality.

The other set of writings that reflect Bernard's lifelong teaching is his liturgical sermons, which are the longest and most contemplative of his works. Bernard gave many sermons, especially to his monks, but never wrote any of them down. Fortunately we can reconstruct his sermons and capture his oral style, thanks to the hundreds of sentences his listeners jotted down, giving either a summary or the development of his actual preaching. These remnants are important source material that were forgotten until our own time and discovered during preparation of the recent critical edition of the complete works of St. Bernard. They indicate the extent to which Bernard's doctrine influenced the daily life of his monks, and reveal much about their psychology as well as his own.

Like the Church Fathers, Bernard wrote in various literary categories—treatises, sermons on the Song of Songs, letters, saints' lives, and sermons for the liturgical year. He drafted hundreds of liturgical sermons, none of which were actually preached in the form that has come down to us. His extant sermons are those that were dictated to a secretary, who marked them up by way of editing, and then made them public. Depending on circumstances, the secretary sometimes had a considerable part to play in the work of copying both the sermons and the letters. Certain texts underwent several different editions, and among these there are varying degrees of authenticity. St. Bernard never wrote on anything but wax tablets, naturally a perishable record. He has left nothing written in his own hand, not even a signature. The problems that arise with homiletic works can be solved only with the help of the manuscript tradition, which, happily, is abundant, even unique in history. When he had decided to deliver a message in the form of a sermon, Bernard conformed to the rules of that genre: He pretended to have an audience in front of him and imagined their reactions to what he said, although, of course, he was speaking only in the presence of a scribe. But the tone of the sermon was always one of a "contemplative discourse," teaching the truths of the faith and their effects in the Christian life.

Bernard's sermons are concerned for the most part with the mysteries and scriptural texts celebrated and proclaimed in the liturgy. A percentage of them are devoted to "various topics": virtues or vices, and monastic observances. Early on, these texts circulated as a fairly long and rather organized series of sermons. Little by little, however, they came to be grouped in categories, reflecting the development of the liturgical cycle. Toward the end of his life, Bernard himself put together a vast collection of his sermons, which forms a genuine commentary on the liturgical year. Beginning with Advent and going through to the mysteries celebrated at the end of the Church year in November, Bernard discusses the liturgical seasons and the feasts of Our Lord, Our Lady, and the saints. He wrote an actual treatise for each of the major Church feasts. He began with the Old Testament development of the particular event, then explained its dogmatic content and significance in terms of the New Testament, coming at last to its moral and psychological application. His sermons, which recently have become the object of methodical study by scholars, reveal a vast amount of dogmatic and practical theology and are yielding ever new riches.

So far we have seen St. Bernard's development and the evolution of his work. There is a certain internal logic to the growth pattern that gives it a unity in spite of the vicissitudes of his life, which spans an age in which the Church underwent extraordinary contention. His life consisted of a series of experiences that stemmed from his dedication to the Church. They often involved conflicting situations and his writings show how he reacted to these circumstances, and to personal and general problems. In each case, he reflected on the human condition and on God's activity in transforming it, and found meaning in the confusion of chance events. St. Bernard should be read in the same manner as he wrote: His writings should be seen as a reflection of his experiences as he interacted with people and events. His spirituality derived from a particular period of history but he was able to draw lessons from it that are of permanent and universal value. Although his writings were often occasioned by circumstances, they give us an insight into his profound beliefs, which are those of classical Christianity and, as such, will continue to be shared by a great many readers.

Significance and Sources of His Message

Problems with St. Bernard

St. Bernard's written works run to some 3,500 pages. It is far from easy to select passages that form only 10 percent of the whole and yet give an idea of the totality. Nor is it any less difficult to put his compositions in order. It must be said at the start that St. Bernard is not an easy author; one of the problems is that he says so much about everything. His is the logic of love that is without measure, drawing all things to itself, as to its center. It would not be entirely satisfactory to follow a strictly chronological order in presenting the chosen texts. The dates of some of the works are not known with certainty; at times, he wrote very different works in the same period. To adopt a systematic order would imply a subjective element and constitute an interpretation. This last method, however, cannot be completely avoided since Bernard himself has not put together any system or left a summary. We are dealing here with a poet, rather than a professor, who freely casts his ideas in every direction, leaving his readers to organize them according to their needs and inclination. A compromise, then, would seem to be necessary in presenting his works. In the beginning we will give two of the early treatises that briefly set out the motivating doctrinal principles of Bernard's life. At the end, I will offer selections from two of the great works of his mature period to demonstrate how the whole of this doctrine influenced his personal life and activity. In between, various other texts will show how his course of action proceeded from his doctrine.

There are problems when trying to present extracts from so large and varied a body of work. Bernard was a contemplative who realized the value of time and wrote at leisure. Speaking of a precept in the Book of Wisdom, he said: "The writer achieves wisdom only with time." Modern man is in a hurry; he likes to discover ideas quickly without much reading and even his prayer is often hasty. The aim of the ancient and medieval spiritual authors was not to provide food for reflection; rather, they sought to encourage an experience through recollections of a poetical nature. They gave free rein to their imagination in a way that, to us, seems more like fantasy than thought. They wrote playfully of symbols and were given to variations on biblical themes that appear more rhapsodic than strictly theological. The medieval style often seems obscure but is, in fact, mysterious: The deliberate lack of clarity hides inexhaustible treasures. Each reading of St. Bernard brings to light unsuspected riches, whether the reader is influenced by the ancient thought of Plato or more modern thinkers like C. Jung or P. Ricoeur. The exegesis of St. Bernard's works is in its early stages; as human knowledge advances, it will suggest certain clues, as yet unknown, for the interpretation of his writings.

The purpose of an introduction is not to give in advance a summation of the texts chosen or of the works selected; nor should it explain the entire content of the writer's thought. Instead, it should indicate the problems that may arise when reading the works; additionally, it should offer guidelines to the reader by placing excerpts within the context of the entire work and drawing attention to certain aspects that may not be immediately apparent. The introduction should, however, allow the reader the joy of personal discovery. It may discuss certain things that are not in the selected texts but are necessary to an understanding of them. Without going into detail, it ought to propose a few basic ideas that will encourage some readers, at least, to proceed to a reading of the entire work.

It can be said that for Bernard everything begins and ends with experience and, in between, experience is the object of reflection. God is the source of all things, including experience, but the first object of man's thought is himself and the experience of his unique personal history. He tries to understand that history with the help of God's grace and in light of his word. This experience of himself and his pitiable condition sends him back to God and causes him to experience his love; it also leads him to put that love into practice according to the circumstances in which he is called to serve his brothers in the Church. None of these aspects of St. Bernard should be neglected; to treat only the theory or only the asceticism would be to break the unity of his thought. Bernard's theology is practical and authentic; although it involves a measure of speculative thinking, it is rooted in and intended for everyday life.

History and Experience

The first point to be clarified in any introduction to the writings of St. Bernard is his use of Sacred Scripture, for it can present a serious obstacle to the modern mind, which is so accustomed to critical and scientific exegesis. His biblical sense is not unique but is shared with the Church Fathers and other medieval spiritual writers. Some have pushed the method even farther than he but Bernard's use of Scripture is so free and constant—and marked by seeming imagination—that it risks losing the modern reader and requires, therefore, some clarification.

His idea of Scripture can be summarized by saying that it is, for him, a pretext, in both senses of the word. First, it is a text that predates his own experience and thinking and in that sense is a "pre-text." He was able to interpret his experience only because it had its continual source in the Church. He could thus similarly understand the solution that the Spirit of God brought to his problems, or more exactly, to the problem that he had with himself. Once his understanding and relationship to God had improved, he could freely use Scripture to speak of himself to God, and of God to others. Everything in the Bible then served as a "pretext" for his liberal proclamations.

Love is the sole object of the sacred texts that recount the history both of salvation and of personal experience. Everything comes from and must lead to love. Salvation history is a love story between God and his people, between God and his Church, between God and each person. God is the source, origin, and inspiration of the Bible—a belief that determines how it is read and utilized. God's love is self-revealing; it is expressed through the inspired authors and later through his Incarnate Son. God continues to speak in the words he has left us and through his Spirit, who continues in us the work he began with the biblical writers. The sacred author—and to the greatest degree, Jesus Christ—speaks and writes because of love, under the influence and control of that love which he has experienced.

Out of love God seeks us and wants us to seek him. He longs for us, draws us to himself, and is present to us through his powerful words and in his Word. Through grace, he does everything to ensure that we will go to him to experience an encounter of loving union. God's presence in the Bible is actual and effective. Scripture, which provides the attractive wrapping on divine love, is written for all men collectively as well as each person individually. We are asked to remove the cover and find the hidden contents within; in this way, sacred history, which is universal, objective, impersonal, and external, becomes *our* history. The Bible does more than recount history, even holy history, or present a collection of truths. Its facts and ideas serve as both pre-text and pretext for this encounter between two loves: that of God for man and man for God.

Since we are creatures of the flesh who, with all animals, are receptive to sensations and thereby form images, God has adapted himself to our nature to explain his mysteries. From every level of human experience he has used symbols that we must now decipher. The symbolic meaning must be understood with the help of the same Spirit who inspired the biblical texts. Thus we are to take part in the experience of the sacred authors and help one another to understand, through analogy, the meaning of God's mysteries.

Bernard saw his teaching role as essentially that of a biblical exegete. He was fully aware that he could exercise that function only with the help of God's grace; accordingly, he often asked, at the beginning and end of his sermons, for prayers for enlightenment. Tradition has regarded him chiefly as an exegete and the earliest artists depicted him holding the Book, opening it and explaining it. His very title "Doctor Mellifluous" was bestowed because of his interpretation of Scripture and has nothing to do with the characteristic sweetness of honey. Instead, the epithet is in keeping with a traditional explanation, derived from Origen and developed by Bernard himself. According to the theory, one draws the hidden meaning from the literal sense of the biblical text, just as honey is made to flow from the honeycomb or as Moses drew water from the rock.

We could illustrate these considerations with several quotations that have been put together in specialized studies, but the texts given in this volume will provide enough examples. Whenever necessary Bernard explained each word of the text as strictly and precisely as twelfth-century methods allowed, and it may be inferred that he invites the modern reader to make use of the scientific exegesis of our time. But customarily he used a text that was considered familiar—a pre-text—as a pretext to speak of God, as God had spoken through the inspired poets and as the Church speaks in her liturgy—with the freedom born of love. This poetic language may not be the only one possible but it is certainly best suited for bringing the history of salvation within the experience of each person and for referring indirectly to the mystery within that history and experience. Scripture verses filled his mind and memory to overflowing; they were always on the tip of his tongue, but he did not use them indiscriminately. Generally his intuition suggested a basic text that capsulized his thought exactly but he prepared himself and his reader with all sorts of references and recollections. Then the experience was expressed and the key quotation given, often preceded by a lemma such as "And finally . . . *Denique,*" which was an indication that the reasoning was concluded.

In Bernard's method there is an authentic reasoning process that is quite different from that of logic and abstract speculation. In his treatise *On Grace and Free Will*, he demonstrated his ability to make use of abstract ideas and speculative reasoning. But he always endeavored to have his reader share in his own thinking. He assimilated the Bible so completely that it became part of himself and he had no need to refer to the text before quoting it to verify his statements. He cited Scripture from memory and often as it was given in the antiphons and responsaries sung in the liturgy, where text and melody were adapted to one another. Through Scripture he received his faith, in the Church and through its tradition. Then he used Scripture to give expression to that faith, sharing its "taste" and "savor," as he said. The content of the message must first be known or perceived, as it were, through the exterior senses; it must next be assented to. The condition for arriving at that kind of spiritual perception is love, without which the Bible becomes a dead letter. And the result is wisdom—in Latin *sapientia*, which indicates taste and flavor—with its blessings of joy, love, thanksgiving, and song.

We can read St. Bernard with a grasp of his theology and without annoyance at his poetry if we are open to his charm, if we let him "enchant" us, literally; for his style, which includes a biblical reference in nearly every line, is what he himself has termed a spiritual canticle: *carmen spiritus*. Ideally, he should be read in Latin and out loud so as to appreciate the music of his words. Much of his prose is actually poetry in verse, with rhyme, assonance, and a refined sense of rhythm. Any translation, however careful, must necessarily lose something of this harmony and part of the biblical flavor. In reading Bernard, we must sing with him; as he said of his sermons on the Song of Songs: "Only the voice that sings can understand, *Sola quae cantat audit*."

Scripture is so important in Bernard's works that there is a temptation to neglect his other sources. He quoted from authors before his time but it is extremely rare for him to give credit, even to a Father of the Church. This was undoubtedly part of the living tradition he had received from the readings at the Divine Office or in community, or from those he did privately, or from conversations he had with William of St.-Thierry or other spiritual and learned men. At times too much effort has been made to put references after some of his sentences, as though he had borrowed them from others. He depended especially on a general atmosphere and a rich tradition. He had certainly read the texts of St. Anthony, St. Augustine, and St. Gregory the Great, and

Origen's commentary on the Song of Songs; from these Fathers he retained certain germinal ideas, which he later developed with constructive freedom.

The only theologian from whom he definitely borrowed some ideas was another monk and abbot, a contemporary of his youth and a spiritual author as well as a metaphysician: St. Anselm of Canterbury. Bernard was not always his match when it came to the power of dialectic. But on at least one important point he extended St. Anselm's thought, explaining it by means of a subtle yet clear distinction, which has to do with the relationship of freedom and grace, and is found in his treatise on that subject. Elsewhere in his work, Bernard admits the contributions of his predecessors; however, he goes beyond them and makes them applicable first to himself and then to his readers, whom he invites to do the same.

THE WAY OF LOVE: FROM HUMILITY TO ECSTASY

On the path leading back to God, the point of departure is humility and the point of destination is love. Both are a question of experience, then a matter of reflection, and at length become motivating principles put into practice.

Interior Struggle

St. Bernard's religious experience has sometimes been described almost exclusively in terms of what we usually call the mystical experience, that is, those rare occasions when a handful of Christians may enjoy sublime states of prayer and union with God. It is true that in his work references to his experience can sometimes be construed in that way; however, we must elaborate on his meaning, which extends to man's awareness of himself and his wretchedness and takes into account his distance from God. It is this fundamental understanding that awakens the call to God and prepares the individual to discern God's response and receive his "visit." From this point of view, there can be no "mystical" experience without a prior "ascetic" experience. All of Bernard's teaching has this experiential quality, as we say today, and I will explain this statement with certain examples.

The point of departure for Bernard's entire doctrine is an intense, personal experience of the interior struggle. All of his theology is merely a reflection on this primary fact in light of the Gospels and St. Paul. He reflected on it daily, recognizing that it was also the experience of every man. Man had lost the perfect spiritual freedom that permitted continual union with God through an unwavering adherence to the divine will, but he can still regain that freedom. He does not despair for he knows that God became man and saved us in Jesus Christ, and that hereafter his salutary grace is at work in us. Thus, there are always two sides to the question: a deep realism that causes humility, and a sure hope that gives rise to courage and optimism. These are the two traditional aspects of what has been described as compunction by St. Gregory the Great and the monastic tradition. Etienne Gilson has written to the effect that the philosophy of St. Augustine is essentially a metaphysics of conversion, because it is dominated by the one fact of the religious experience of his own conversion. Even so, it could be argued that St. Bernard's doctrine is a theology of compunction, fostered by the basic monastic experience as tradition described it and as he knew it—he and a great many monks with whom he was so close, in whose name and for whom he spoke and wrote. This comes through clearly in the thousands of references scattered throughout his work.

In realistic, often moving, and sometimes exaggerated terms, Bernard frequently declares the limits of the human condition, what today's philosophers call man's finiteness. Depending on the case, he gives more or less attention to the states of mind that, according to today's philosophy, characterize existence: anxiety, loneliness, failure, absurdity, reason's inability to explain everything, the tendency toward discouragement, and anguish in the face of death. Still, if Bernard had remained at that point, he would have added nothing to what the pessimistic moralists of ancient times and the latter-day preachers had said all along. His description of the interior struggle serves as the starting point for a reflection that shows Christian hope as the remedy for human need. "Misery," as he says in connection with Scripture, calls upon "mercy," using a word play that also has its origin in the Bible. (*Note:* In Latin, mercy is *misericordia;* in French, *miséricorde.* Thus, the pun is lost in English.) In contrast to the sinner-self there is God, who is all-holy, whose power is as great as his love, who can and will come to man's aid, and who has already done so in Jesus Christ. Using scriptural concepts and allusions, Bernard describes a kind of alchemy that transforms weakness into a capacity for grace through which man may act according to God's will and proceed toward his encounter and ultimate union with the Lord.

"Weakness" and "temptation" are at first experienced matter-of-factly. They next become the object of "thought," "meditation," "self-knowledge," and then of "discernment." "Conscience" grasps their positive value and meaning as an opportunity for conversion and a return to God. The battlefield of the human heart and the victory to be won there provide the theme for his sermons on Lent and on Psalm 90; the latter is a psalm in time of temptation, which Jesus cited when he was tempted in the desert. The psalm and especially the words *oculis tuis considerabis* are the occasion for a development of contemplative knowledge, which is an inward-looking glance of self-judgment, as clear and searching as possible. Since this is a glance of faith, it sees within our true self already altered, transformed, and on the path to glorification through the working of grace. Contemplative knowledge has two inseparable objects: self-truth and self-judgment on the one hand, faith in God's kindness on the other; this explains the profound optimism of the Christian who, having taken the measure of his condition, does not yield to despair. Bernard describes man's internal contradiction—the difficulty of so many discordant elements in us—and then shows that grace is already bringing them into harmony. This is a true cause for wonder. He refers to the path by which we travel from misery to glory and thereby gives an indication of the last four books of *De Consideratione*. His declaration that harmony is possible among so many contrasting elements in man causes great admiration for God's work throughout the world and in all of creation. Bernard attributes this attitude especially to contemplatives.

Hi vero qui cum Maria soli Deo vacant, considerantes quid sit Deus in mundo, quid in hominibus, quid in angelis, quid in seipso, quid in reprobis, contemplantur quia Deus est mundi rector et gubernator, hominum liberator et adiutor, angelorum sapor et decor, in seipso principium et finis, reproborum terror et horror. In creaturis mirabilis, in hominibus amabilis, in angelis desiderabilis, in seipso incomprehensibilis, in reprobis intolerabilis.

[There are those who, along with Mary, are concerned with God alone. They dwell on what God is in the world, in human beings, in angels, in himself, and in the condemned. They dwell on the reality of God as the ruler and lord of the world, as the liberator and helper of men, as the delight and beauty of the angels, as beginning and end within himself, as the terror and fright of wrongdoers. He is marvelous in his creatures, lovable in men, desirable in angels, beyond comprehension in himself, and intolerable in the reprobate.]

All of Bernard's teaching is concerned with this passage from "flesh" to "spirit," in the Pauline sense, and from self-centeredness to an openness to the whole of creation as the result of going beyond oneself, of surpassing that instinctive self, as yet unliberated by grace. In its most elevated forms, this going beyond will be the *excessus* or going out of self that is ecstasy. But apart from these exceptional cases, those rare, brief moments, the monk, who performs the duties incumbent on every Christian with total dedication, must try throughout each day to surpass himself, to raise himself to the level of the grace that is already present and active in him. This he attempts by ascetic practices: by contemplating Christ in Scripture and by prayer and mortification in all its forms. In this way, he will succeed in rediscovering his true self on its true level, namely, on the level of the spiritual life, or that of the Spirit. He will also find the true self of others, and of God; these three discoveries constitute the three degrees of charity.

It has not always been sufficiently noticed that the entire Bernardine theory of the restoration of the image of God in man is a "monastic" doctrine. It includes a concept of grace and freedom that is of remarkable accuracy as a theory; the doctrine also involves the practice of asceticism, or the daily use of concrete means by which man strives to make himself anew, according to Christ's example. St. Bernard's treatises on "theology" are inseparable from the text of his letters and sermons in which he gives details on how the monk can live up to his ideal. From this point of view, books such as the *Apology* and *The Rule and Dispensation*, as well as other writings on obedience, provide the necessary complement to works of a more dogmatic character. Those who study the history of doctrine are especially given to lingering over the latter.

Man's end is to recognize truth, which is God. To do this he must be aware that his relationship with God is based on need. The obstacle to the relationship is pride; the remedy is humility. Grace is the condition for meeting God in Christ. The result is the esteem man places on his dignity, rediscovered in God's image. While self-ignorance and pride lessen man's worth, humility, which recognizes man's need as well as his capacity for God, reveals man to himself. In this way, he emerges from himself and ascends; he grows and reaches new dimensions of love, both for God and for neighbor. In this context, Bernard uses the expressions *sese excedere* and *extendere*. The humble man becomes gentle and merciful: *miser, mitis, misericors*. Thus, faith and asceticism—or, more exactly, living faith transformed in humility and charity—cause the real self to emerge from the ego, to use current expressions. Faith and asceticism awaken the ego to the freedom enjoyed by the real self and enable it to become a person in the sight of God, who delights it with communion and fellowship.

Bernard always conveys this message of glory, but tempered by his message of humility; it is a doctrine of extreme realism that considers man's wretched condition and, at the same time, displays perfect confidence in the glory that is already within him and simply awaits the moment to show forth its effects. Literary expression will reveal a little of that hidden light which can be perceived with the eye of faith. With St. Bernard and other great spiritual writers, the intensity of experience can explain the strong character and impassioned speech and, consequently, accounts for a degree of exaggeration in his writing. Whether speaking of the depths of man's vileness or the heights he may reach during visits from the Word of God, Bernard seems at times to go too far, to go beyond the limits of what is reasonable, or at least what is normal and customary. Actually, he simply reveals about himself what is true of all of us. His writings are an indication of his thinking, which is contemplative and, at the same time, concerned with the well-being of others. Each of his works began with a particular purpose in mind, but in each one Bernard achieved universal application. The more a person understands himself, the more he can enlighten others about themselves.

Knowledge and Love

The treatises on humility and love must be read in the light of this knowledge about oneself and others. The two works are parallel and complement one another. One is concerned with the degrees of knowledge and the other with those of love. Humility is the knowledge or, more exactly, the active recognition, the acknowledgement, of the truth about three realities: first, about ourselves and our finiteness; second, about others: Since the misfortune of the human condition is common to all people, we have no right to judge or feel superior to anyone else; third, about God, who, in his Son Jesus Christ, has shown us the way to return to the truth and the fullness of life, which is beyond our limitations. Through this "contempt for self," which is a true appreciation of self taking into account our tendency toward evil as well as our ability to accept God, we come to the profound truth that is at the very heart of our existence, without which our existence would have no meaning and, in that sense, no existential truth.

All of this would not be possible except for God's grace, which reconciles us to what Christ has revealed, taught, and lived. He was and is the Image of God and the model we are to imitate and conform to. He submitted to the "law" of suffering and death in order to free us from the law and from the slavery of sin. "If we believe in Him and therefore imitate his humility, we are admitting the truth about ourselves. The weight of our distress no longer oppresses us; the certainty of being able to reach God makes our ascent to Him less difficult." Our charity becomes limitless, embracing even our enemies; it urges us to be visibly compassionate toward everyone and enables us to accept all difficulties. Little by little ardor and fervor replace misery and pain.

Now purified, the "heart" experiences peace. It can contemplate God; that is, it can behold him without seeing him, for it is already united to God as a wife is joined to her husband. Here many quotations spring to mind from the Song of Songs, which Bernard expounded at length in the great work that occupied his final years. The essence of his message is already germinally present in this treatise on humility, an achievement of his youthful period. This discourse also stresses the role of the Holy Spirit, whose liberating work enables us to go beyond our finiteness, to be open to everyone, and to be united to the One who is All. Thus, as a result of humility, which is a true realization of himself and his relationship to every other being, man is able to give meaning and direction to his existence. He is made for union with God: Such is his reason for being, and he has the assurance of being able to fulfill his calling.

In the treatise on love, the degrees of love correspond to those of knowledge. They are also three in number, the fourth being an exceptionally rare foretaste of the absolutely perfect love to come in heavenly glory. We must love ourselves, love others, and love God.

Love of self begins with acceptance of our carnal condition, namely, that we exist in a body and with a body; not simply that we "have" a body but that we are a body. We must ensure all its basic needs: food, clothing, and proper care. But we must love it in moderation, unlike the love we owe to God, which ought to be wholehearted.

Here we see the reason for Bernard's profound optimism concerning the body and his insistence on ascetic practices to keep it under control. For if we give in to all its impulses, we cannot master the succeeding degrees of love. Our body may make us carnal, but we are also endowed with a mind, which allows us to be open to others.

We should note at first that our human condition, a combination of finiteness and possible greatness, is undeniably the common lot of all human beings. Our love, therefore, must become "social," and this implies recognition of the following truth: We exist in a society from which we receive and to which we must contribute, and this entails many practical consequences of which Bernard often spoke to his monks. He greatly insisted on "social grace" as a requirement for any communal life; this is a trait equally necessary for any Christian. Everything that Bernard said about fraternal love in the rest of his work, and everything he did throughout his life in the service of his neighbor, was simply the practical application of the social character of love.

This love must, however, lead to God. Loving God with all one's being means, at first, with one's entire body. Being master of one's body and refusing to give in to all its instinctive urges does not destroy it. Even the martyr does not lose his body forever; it will be restored to him in glory and will share in infinite, eternal love, with the human being completely united to the Risen Christ. He in whom the fullness of divinity dwelt bodily has now entered into the light of the Father, the Word, and the Spirit. Anyone united to him will also enter that light. The body, then, during earthly life and for all eternity, is a "companion" that God gives to the soul, and as such it must be loved. *"Nec sane dixerim ut vel ipsam odio habeas carnem tuam. Dilige eam tamquam tibi datam in adiutorium."* [Nor would I say that you should hate your own body. Love it as something that has been given to you to help you.]

This supposes that the body is a good thing, even if it bears the mark and consequences of sin like the rest of man. It must be recalled, too, that for Bernard the "concupiscence of the flesh" that is discussed in the New Testament is not a reality of the body, but of the "flesh," in the sense that St. Paul uses that word: Concupiscence involves the whole being in its sinful condition. This is what Bernard expresses when he says at times that concupiscence is found not in the body, but in the "heart." When the heart has been healed, purified, and redirected, it takes the body with it in its flight to God. Bernard firmly believed that man could control his appetites. His realistic acceptance of the libido and his belief in its possible sublimation, with the help of grace, strike a modern note. Once we grasp the meaning of Bernard's medieval language—itself a legacy of the Bible—we see how he casts a Christian light on what psychology confirms but cannot resolve from a theological point of view.

Another feature of St. Bernard that brings him close to modern psychology is the importance he places on desire. In it he sees a form of love, pointing to the possession of and union with God that will be completely realized only in our future life beyond time. St. Bernard gives a very strong meaning to the word "desire"; it is not simply a feeling of discontent or an emotional tendency toward what would fill the present emptiness. It is a vital and positive fact: Desire is *the* form that love takes in our earthly existence. God is present in this desire, which he has placed in the depth of our being to enable us to overcome the disappointments caused by every other desire. The desire for God is already a genuine manner of possessing him; it is the certainty that God is present to us, through faith, in spite of his apparent absence; it is the sure hope that this absence will be transformed into total presence, this darkness into light.

Placing ourselves in Bernard's perspective, we grasp the dynamic of the ascending degrees of love, from its most ordinary forms, accessible to everyone, to its most sublime manifestations. The heights of love are granted rarely, briefly, and only to a few, but they have been promised to everyone, forever, and in a definitive manner; then desire will give way to possession because faith will be transformed into vision. Here Bernard presents a very realistic, practical, and progressive program; it begins with meditation on the examples Christ has left us from his earthly life and ends in "ecstasy," that state in which a person is transported outside himself and is, for a moment, united with his life in glory, thus experiencing a foretaste of his existence for all eternity. Bernard is in complete conformity on this point with the traditional doctrine of the Church Fathers, according to which the experiences of the mystics are a prophetic anticipation of the blessed gifts proper to the Risen Christ and to those who have been raised with him.

OPENING OURSELVES TO THE MYSTERY OF GOD

All of Bernard's teaching on the topics already mentioned presupposes a dogmatic theology of God, Christ, and the Holy Spirit. Not only does he assume faith in these mysteries but he often refers to it in a rather developed manner. Many of his texts speak explicitly of faith in God's mysteries. I will quote from some of them, also draw attention to the major theses that make up his thought.

God is the origin of all things; he is the absolute being discussed in Book V of the *Consideration;* he is the Trinity spoken of in the eighth sermon on the Song of Songs. In the latter, Bernard tries to give an idea of the triune God by comparing him to what is similar and dissimilar, and by describing the interchange between the one who kisses, the one who is kissed, and the kiss that unites them.

Not only has this ineffable mystery been revealed to us, but it has also been communicated and shared in the mysteries of the Incarnate Word. In order to speak to men, God made an image of himself, since men, as corporal beings, cannot understand or express things without images. The Bible, which is a book of mental pictures, places within our reach all the symbols, characters, and parables by which God prepared the coming of his Image and his Word. Moreover, the New Testament makes us witnesses of the parable of Christ's entire earthly life, from the time he was born of the Virgin Mary to the moment he ascended to the Father. Bernard's Christology is so elaborate, coherent, and complete that any attempt to summarize it would risk impoverishment and distortion. Here I shall cite just two important facts necessary for understanding the significance of the texts presented in this volume.

The first is the effective and exemplary importance attached to the human experience of Christ, of which Bernard often spoke, especially with reference to the passage in the Epistle to the Hebrews that tells of Jesus learning obedience and suffering through what he experienced. In his Son, God wished to share man's experience of finiteness. This is illustrated in a text taken from one of the sermons on St. Andrew (1.6) devoted to the theme of the Cross—the Cross of Christ, the Cross of the Apostle and martyr, the Cross of the Christian:

> *Quid magnum fuerat, Domine Iesu, si, accedente hora propter quam veneras, intrepidus stares, tamquam qui potestatem habebas ponendi animam tuam, et nemo tollebat eam a te? Aut non longe gloriosius fuit, quando quidem totum propter nos agebatur, ut non modo passio corporis, sed etiam cordis affectio pro nobis faciat, et quos vivificabat mors tua, tua nibilominus et trepidatio robustos, et maestitia laetos, et taedium alacres, et turbatio quietos faciar, et desolatio consolatos? Lego quidem in Lazari resurrectione, quia infremuit spiritu et turbavit seipsum. Sed esto interim quia se ipse turbavit, non conditionis*

necessitate, sed suae beneplacito voluntatis. Nunc autem aliquid iam
amplius audio. Usque adeo siquidem praevaluit ea quae fortis est ut
mors dilectio, ut Christum Dei angelus confortaverit. Quis, quem?
Evangelistam audi: Apparuit, inquit, angelus confortans eum. [How
great it was, Lord Jesus, as the hour for which you had come ap-
proached, that you stood intrepid as one holding the power to lay down
your own life and not have someone take it from you. Yet only a little
more glorious was it that you did all of this for our sake. You com-
mitted to us not only your body's suffering but also your heart's af-
fection. Your death gave us life, your fear made us brave, your sadness
made us joyful, your loathing made us eager, your trouble made us
tranquil, and your desolation consoled us. I read that at the resur-
rection of Lazarus, your spirit groaned and writhed in distress. Yet
this happened not because it was forced on you, but because you con-
sented to it out of kindness. Now I hear something else more clearly:
For all this time love, which is as strong as death, has prevailed, so
that the angel of God could comfort Christ. Who comforted whom?
Listen to the Evangelist: The angel appeared and comforted him.]

Yet nothing is brought to completion in the Passion alone. Like the whole of his human existence from the moment of the incarnation, the suffering of Christ on the Cross was directed toward his glorification, which is made manifest in the brilliance of the ascension. Bernard had great devotion to the mystery of the ascension and initiated a solemn procession at Clairvaux to mark the feast; this was contrary to the usages of Cîteaux but came, in time, to be adopted by the whole Order. He has left more sermons on the ascension than on almost any other mystery, including the Passion. He saw the ascension as the fulfillment of the mystery of love in which the Incarnate Word returned to the glory of the Father. Formerly hidden in the humility of the flesh, the Son now sends the Holy Spirit to men to unite them to the Father in love. The ascension symbolizes Christ passing from the life of the flesh to glory in the life of the Spirit. This transition from flesh to Spirit can be accomplished in us because it has first taken place in Christ. The Spirit comes to us by means of the flesh of the Lord, which is united to his divinity; by the flesh of the Son of man, we are raised to the Spirit of the Son of God.

Bernard's Christology is made complete by a theology of the Holy Spirit—a pneumatology—the elements of which are scattered through-out his works. He discusses the Holy Spirit in relation to the Father and the Son, in relation to Christ, and to each of us. He is fond of expanding on the biblical theme of the "gifts" of the Spirit, which today we call charisms. Among the variety of the gifts, he distinguishes those we receive for ourselves from those we receive for the sake of others. The former are infused; the latter are poured out upon us. We must know how to "discern" between the two categories of gifts and this insight is itself an effect of the Spirit within us. Then, we must learn to help others to see clearly within themselves; this endeavor is the correct object of counseling (*consilium*), which is intended to encourage the freedom of the other person, not to stifle it. Bernard credits "the Spirit of freedom" with our ability to choose and decide in a manner consistent with God's plan for us. If we are submissive to the workings of the Holy Spirit in us and attentive to his promptings, he blesses us with fervor and joy. When we are open to the Spirit, we can receive him and listen to him: "Which of you, in the secrecy of his heart, has sometimes heard the Spirit cry out: Abba, Father? It is the one who felt moved by the same Spirit as the Son who takes for certain the Father's love. Be confident, whoever you are, be confident and doubt nothing. In the Spirit of the Son, recognize yourself as the Father's daughter, as the spouse of the Son or His sister."

Such is the goal of what we traditionally call the "interior life": to instill in us the very life of the Trinity; to allow Christ to live and act in us. Christ, the mediator between the Father and mankind, having received the fullness of the Spirit, sent him to us and continues that action. In his Letter 113, written to the nun Sophie, Bernard contrasts what is exterior and seems outside (*foris*) with what is interior (*intres*); then, in a sentence applicable to everyone, he sums up the personalized character of Christian spirituality: It is, he says, simply the actual presence of Christ in us, which St. Paul speaks of in the Epistle to the Ephesians (3:17): "*Intres est quod delectat, quia intres est quem delectat, nisi forte tu dubitas habitare Christum per fidem in corde tuo.*" [What you love is within you, since he whom you love is within you, unless perhaps you doubt that Christ dwells by faith in your heart.] Finally, as it says in Psalm 44:14, all the glory of the King's daughter comes from within.

THE SPIRITUAL CANTICLE

Having established the truly objective foundation of the life of every Christian, we turn to individual psychological differences, which Bernard frequently explained in his sermons on the Song of Songs. The sermons treat many subjects, as noted above; here we will confine our discussion to topics relating to the experience of union with God. As we refer to these themes, following the author's order of presentation, the continuity and harmony of the work will emerge from its seeming disorder. The themes will also call to mind and sum up everything discussed so far.

Key ideas that will determine subsequent developments are set out at the beginning of the work. The Song of Songs is a poem in praise of Christ and the Church, sung to the King of Kings and Lord of Lords. It also expresses the longings of the sanctified soul. The union with God, which is extolled by the symbol of the kiss, indicates the presence of the grace of the Incarnate Word in the soul. "His living and effective word is a kiss," St. Bernard says, "not a meeting of lips, which can sometimes be deceptive about the state of the heart, but a full infusion of joys, a revelation of secrets, a wonderful and inseparable mingling of the light from above and the mind on which it is shed" (2,2). The soul contemplates the mystery of God and experiences the effects of his presence. Through the Incarnation, Christ the Mediator brings God's mercy to man in his distress. Filled with God's presence, the soul, while remaining fully human, is no longer in distress; rather, like Mary Magdalene, the sinner who renounced her faults and adopted a life of holiness, the soul can say: "I am black, but beautiful."

Here, Bernard sees man's redemption more in terms of the incarnation than of Christ's death and resurrection. The incarnation is the fundamental Christian mystery from which the other mysteries unfold; it also marks the completion of all the divine preparations. It was fitting for God to assume flesh but this favor was delayed until our own time. At long last, "God took flesh for the sake of people who delight in flesh, so that through it they might learn to delight in the spirit as well" (6,3). The gift of union with Christ is that much greater because we waited for it so long.

Bernard always places himself in a historical perspective; in the light of history we can better understand and appreciate God's gift of himself to men. The incarnation derives its meaning from the Old Covenant, which it prolongs, and from eschatology, for all its effects will be accomplished at the end of the world. The just people of the Old Testament awaited the incarnation but it did not come in their time. We in the Church possess Christ but look toward heaven where we will see him face to face.

The kiss of the Father and the Son is the Holy Spirit. Christ gives the kiss to his spouse, or bride, whom he fills with his Spirit. The Spirit, in turn, unites the bride to the Father through the Son. Mystical union is the extension of the relationship of love that exists among and unites the three divine Persons. The bride, who is actually the Church and the soul, hopes that this mystery of charity will be fulfilled in her. The fulfillment can take place only through the working of the Holy Spirit, who enables the bride to experience mystical knowledge in which love becomes understanding.

Man can know God without loving him. Beginning with creation, he can proceed rationally to the idea of the first cause, but this will tell him only of the divine essence, not of the relationship within the Holy Trinity. Mystical knowledge, however, having love as its source and object, pleases and gratifies the soul. It is a share in the loving knowledge of the divine Persons, a share Christ granted to the Apostles and, through them and the Church, to all sanctified souls. Bernard's only intention is to communicate that knowledge or, more exactly, to prepare us for it in mind and heart. He is fully aware that it is God, not man, who brings about the mystical experience and inclines the soul to receive his gift.

Bernard frequently uses the word "experience." In the first sermon, he writes: "Only the touch of the Holy Spirit teaches, and it is learned by experience alone. Let those who have experienced it enjoy it; let those who have not, burn with desire, not so much to know it as to experience it." (1,11). The experience is the culminating point in the Christian life to which all the soul's progress must tend. As we grow in grace and learn to trust in the Lord, our experience of love increases until we come to feel God's kiss on the mouth. In the early stages of conversion, we approach the feet of the Lord; later we reach his hands; the kiss on the mouth is an experience reserved for those who have achieved perfection.

This experience, however, occurs but rarely and we may ask: What does it involve? The kiss is an event complete and absolute in itself; its unity would be lost were its elements separated. Thus Bernard does not analyze the experience, but simply describes it. He tries to summarize the richness of the experience in a subtle statement that speaks of a pleasant contemplation, of peace and ecstasy (4,4). Each word in the definition is significant and is necessary to the meaning of the other words. Ecstasy, peace, contemplation, and pleasure: each corresponds to one of the effects of grace that elevates the soul and enables it to enjoy the sustained presence of God. The soul feels a certain relation with the Bridegroom. At the beginning of conversion, it smelled the fragrance of God but remained far from him. Now the soul comes close to him and the two meet.

From time to time—"rarely," says St. Bernard—God takes the soul to himself and delights it in loving ecstasy. This communion with God is always a brief experience and the soul is filled with an understanding of God's mercy. The cleaving of the mind to God brings about an intoxicating joy that quiets and stills the mind's activity.

Expertus potest credere (he who has been tested can believe): This axiom inspired by the writings of St. Bernard sums up the expressions he is fond of using. "We speak of divine things known only to those who have experienced them" (41.3). "It is my duty to speak and I may not be silent; my words stem from my own experience or from that of others" (57.5). Thus, St. Bernard explicitly, if not clearly, testifies to God's visiting the soul. What, then, are these visits?

There are many ways to see God. In heaven we shall see him face to face, as he is, *sicuti est*. On earth we know him in different ways, most commonly in creation. God's works show *that* he is, not what he is. He sometimes revealed himself to the patriarchs and prophets through visions and voices in a manner that appealed to the senses and imagination. Yet, these were only exterior manifestations. God still remained outside the souls he enlightened. But he sometimes deigns to enter the soul that, purified by desire and consecrated to love, prepares him a place. The soul then experiences God's presence from within. This is known as the "visit."

The visit must be preceded by constant prayer and longing. God comes infrequently but one must always be filled with desire for him. Love is constantly on the watch. Suddenly its flame grows and, with the sudden burst of unaccustomed ardor, the presence of God is recognized. "It burns with sweetness" (57,7). The love that springs from desire gives way to the love that comes from God's presence. The latter is more ardent and intense. Normally after quite some time has passed, God's grace enables men of prayer to think less of their sins and take greater delight in meditating on his Word. From time to time, the Bridegroom shows them his face and permits them to gaze on him in unspeakable joy. They advance from light to light under the guidance of the Holy Spirit.

Previously, such men had felt the need for a physician because temptations of the flesh still had a hold on them. They were sorry for their faults, which had to be corrected; for this, God gave them his remedies, not his kisses. But the same Jesus who is physician of the soul is also its Spouse. He takes away all the bitterness that the soul found in itself and fills it with his sweetness. After healing the soul, he gives himself to it completely, raising it above apathy and weakness, and speaking to it of himself. Listening to him, the soul must realize that this is not its own voice, nor are these its own thoughts. They are the words of the Bridegroom, *verba Verbi*, the words of the Word (32,4).

The soul must receive a special charism, that gift of the Holy Spirit which St. Paul refers to as "the discerning of spirits" (1 Cor 12:10), in order to recognize the voice of the Word (32.6). By itself the soul is not sufficiently discerning, even after testing and purification. For the thoughts inspired by the Bridegroom are similar to our own, since they call into play the same powers of the mind. Their source, however, is different: They come from God, not from us. Our thoughts are evil and carnal, while his are good and spiritual. God does not come to us in bodily form because he is a Spirit, nor does he act in the soul any longer through the exterior senses as he did with the Old Testament prophets. Now he reveals himself through the intimacy of love. He is received into the innermost heart, which he fills with his loving presence. He does not appear; he enters the soul. He touches and excites the heart, communicating his love without saying much, for his effects speak of his presence (31.6).

Bernard tells us that God is not above using the service of angels to reveal himself. Does his household not include angels who see the Father's face? They bring about the soul's encounter with God, either by taking the soul up to God or by bringing the Bridegroom to the soul. They help man to contemplate and then to speak of his experience. The necessary conditions for the "visit" include the help of the angels, as well as the work of God and the purifying of heart and memory. Learning is of little use in all this for it cannot obtain or explain the visit. In these matters, the essential thing is to be "sensible and balanced," *sapere ad sobrietatem* (36,2). In his thirty-sixth Sermon, Bernard affirms both the benefits and the limits of Christian knowledge. He may have written that sermon during the time of his quarrel with Abélard, whose method of understanding was so profoundly different from everything Bernard preached. How far apart is the mystic from the teacher! In explaining his concept of learning in the Church, Bernard undoubtedly justifies his conduct toward the innovators who jeopardize the faith of the uneducated. But he also goes on to declare that his mystical understanding owes nothing to human knowledge. The limits of rational knowledge first come to light through humility, which is simply true self-knowledge, and then through the experience of God's sweetness. Although legitimate and useful to the Church, rational knowledge is not enough to bring about the mystical experience.

The soul must be roused to mystical experience by the Holy Spirit (*incitamenta spiritus*). St. Bernard speaks of the soul as "being of one mind with God, wed to the Lord of angels" (40,4); these actions are clearly beyond its capacity. For the mystical experience, the soul must be alone, free even of intelligent thoughts; everything, even neighborly concern, is put aside and the soul and its spouse are alone. The joyful pleasures that the soul experiences vary according to its dispositions. Like the children of Israel who ate manna in the desert, each one is satisfied according to his capacity and relish for God. The sweetness of God's presence delights the palate of each soul in a different way, and to each one God reveals different aspects of himself, varying the joys he bestows. The rapture, transport, and ecstasy of the soul do not constitute the beatific vision, but the man who seeks God lives at times in the shadow of Christ, and the darkness of faith prepares him for the vision. In a certain sense, the mystical experience is already "a vision" (45,6), although inferior to what will be seen in heaven, and a unique and inexpressible dialogue. The soul no longer sees the Bridegroom as King, but as Beloved. It gazes on him but cannot see him; it holds silent conversation with him, yet does not speak. The soul welcomes the Bridegroom in wonder and thanksgiving that grow stronger as he gives himself to the spouse even more. This mutual praise produces a kind of intoxication in the soul.

God's visit does not last long but its effects remain. During mystical union, the individual is dead to concupiscence and, subsequently, is much less inclined to do evil. The ecstasy is beneficial to the creative powers, the memory, and other mental faculties, while the lower appetites no longer dull the soul and impede contemplation. Despite the continuing effects of the visit, however, the withdrawal of the Bridegroom's presence causes the soul much suffering, which lasts until he comes again. Alternating throughout life between union with and separation from its Spouse, the soul knows both the joy of his coming and the sadness of his going away. The suffering is that much greater for having tasted such sweetness.

"Whoever drinks of this water will thirst again" (Jn 4:13). The Bride pines away with love and is in cruel torment; having enjoyed union with the Beloved, she now finds it more painful to be separated from him. The Bridegroom's slowness to return is a bitter affliction to the Bride and his absence only heightens both her desire and her sorrow. However he may hurry to ease her impatience, she is consumed with longing until he returns. Between visits, the Bride bears up under her suffering and even finds a measure of peace by "gathering the fruits of good works and enjoying the sweet scent of faith" (51.3). She delights in a feast of heavenly goods during holy meditation and probes the secrets of God's will, moving heaven by her devoutness. In spirit, she passes through the dwellings of paradise, where she is awed by the band of apostles and prophets, the victorious martyrs, and the choirs of angels. In fasting and prayer, she recalls the kindness of the Lord, and is sustained by the loftiest thoughts until the Beloved returns.

These personal, intimate visits are simply the extension of the coming of the Word to mankind through the incarnation. The union of the soul and the Bridegroom is the fulfillment, the realization of the union of Christ and the Church. "Together we make up the Church and each one participates in its blessings" (57.3). Each of us receives the graces and benefits that are bestowed on the entire Church. The Church is one with Christ; "the Church is not one soul; it is the unity or, better yet, the unanimity of many souls" (61.2), each of whom is indebted to all the others. Graces that the individual soul receives must be placed at the service of all, if the needs of the Church so require. In the following passages, Bernard gives us the key to the amazing continuity that he was able to maintain between contemplation and activity. During his long years of service he came to be called the "pillar of the Church."

> After the Bridegroom has gazed on the soul with kindness and mercy, his voice softly whispers the divine will. His voice is love itself, and love never rests but is continually urging the heart to do God's bidding. The spouse also hears the call to rise up in haste and take up the work of saving souls. The nature of true, pure contemplation is such that, while kindling the heart with divine love, it sometimes fills it with great zeal to win other souls for God. The heart gladly gives up the quiet of contemplation for the work of preaching. Once its desires are fulfilled, the heart quickly returns to contemplation, as to the source of good works. In the same way, once it has tasted anew the delights of contemplation, it joyfully dedicates itself

to new works. Nevertheless, the soul fears the changing affections and fluctuating movements between contemplation
and action. It is likewise wary of becoming overly attached to
anything, lest it turn away, even slightly, from the divine
will. (57,9)

Thus, the Bride is ever-watchful and listens for the steps
of the Bridegroom, so as not to be taken unawares by the time
or swiftness of his visits. She knows when he is near and when
he is far away; he does not surprise her even if he comes in
haste. In recompense, not only does he regard her with
mercy, but he delights her with loving words and his voice
fills her with joy. (57.10)

"Come back, my beloved," Bernard exclaims after each visit of the
Bridegroom. Jesus comes so that the soul will cling to him; he goes away
so that the soul will call him back. He wants us to love him and takes
certain steps to win our love: He gives himself so that we will enjoy his
presence; he then leaves us so that we will long for it even more. "It
may be rash to say so, but I confess that the Word of God has come to
me several times. He has often entered my soul and sometimes I have
been unaware of his coming. But I sensed that he was there and I remember his presence. At other times I was able to anticipate his coming, but I could not discern the moment he arrived or left. . . . Did he
enter my soul? Did he come from without, or was he not already within
me? I realize there is nothing good in me. I was raised far above myself. . . . No sight or sound revealed the Bridegroom, but a single
movement of my heart told me he was there" (64,1–6).

What, then, is taking place here? The mystical experience eludes
analysis but to understand what is involved, we must weigh St. Bernard's own words. The dialogue of love becomes increasingly urgent,
as the Bride and her beloved exchange their impassioned declarations.
The Bride can no longer remain silent; yet she is at a loss to express
what she is experiencing. Unable to contain the intense love of her
heart, she no longer minds what she says. She sighs and pours out the
ardor that consumes her. The words on her tongue are left unuttered;
the dialogue of love between spouse and beloved gives way to a burst
of love.

The canticle is a nuptial song that lends itself admirably to expressing the language of love. "Run through this wedding song and you
will see that the Bride, filled to overflowing and enraptured with love,

does not speak but shouts for joy." From that point on, the nuptial theme dominates Bernard's thinking and provides the poetry for its subsequent development. "My beloved is mine and I am His." These words from the Song of Songs (2:16) represent a mutual assent, an embrace. There is an outpouring of love. Everything takes place in the heart and reason is powerless either to effect or express this mutual love.

The marriage between the soul and the Bridegroom is the continuation of the union between the Word of God and mankind. The Father has sent his Son, who in turn has sent his Spirit to the Church. Those who humble themselves in imitation of Christ and serve his Church with perfect detachment will attain intimate union with him. The "infused love" with which God fills their hearts makes them grow in humility. The more they realize their sinfulness, the more they understand God's bountiful kindness toward them, for he establishes a measure of equality between his creature and himself. "Oh, the sweetness, the mercy, and the strength of his love! The ruler of all has become one of us. What has brought this about? Love has accomplished this; love which is unconcerned with its dignity, rich in graciousness, strong in attachment, effective in persuasion. Is there anything stronger than love? It triumphs over God. And yet, is there anything gentler? He is love" (67,4).

Love, then, is the last word, and the key word, of this message, and it is the reason that the message remains partly a mystery. Bernard chose to present his doctrine in poetic imagery taken from the Song of Songs, for he wanted the subject of union with God to remain shrouded in mystery. This aspect of his teaching deserves greater attention even though all the studies on St. Bernard try to make his message explicit. It is certainly of interest to know how his doctrine is interpreted, but in these pages it is important to set forth the doctrine itself. Its theological richness and the lyricism of its expression do not rule out a keen psychological insight. These qualities alone explain why so many Christian men and women have recognized in the writings of St. Bernard a description of their own state of mind.

COMING BACK TO THE WORLD OF MEN

Toward the end of the last sermon on the Song of Songs that his duties may have allowed him to finish (85,13), Bernard clearly states that the joy of union with God must not prevent the individual from responding to the needs of his fellow-man. The whole of his life was marked by a movement from action to contemplation. His writings have shown us what filled his heart; we must now consider how he shared his gifts with others. At the end of this Introduction and of the selection of texts that follow, we too must leave the heights of contemplation to see how Bernard placed his knowledge, talent, and generosity at the service of others. There can be no question of recalling all his activities; a few symbolic examples will be enough to give a glimpse of the motives of his actions.

First, there is the circle of relatives and friends—those nearest to him. In his twenty-sixth sermon on the Song of Songs, he expressed at length what he felt on the death of his brother, Gerard. Gerard was one of his natural brothers, but he had others; he was also one of his monks, but they too were numerous. Why did he speak of this brother with such warmth and grant him such favor? Because Gerard was more than brother and monk; he was a friend. What Bernard set out to write in the form of a sermon is a treatise on spiritual friendship and it is from that point of view that he approaches different aspects of the Christian life: companionship, mutual help, the mystery of death, and the practice of counselling. Because he was filled with the Holy Spirit, Gerard could help Bernard and others to discern what the Spirit was asking of them in the various circumstances of death. Bernard especially wanted to show, using a personal example, what he always taught: that love for God, far from excluding love for human beings, transformed it instead and made it a precious form of charity. The affections of the heart present no obstacle to the experience of God, once they have been freed from all egotism and every trace of self-interest, and directed toward the living Christ at the center of one's being. On the contrary, affection demonstrates an altruistic dimension that grows to include everyone. And so, beyond the rhetorical element obviously present in this text, there appears an intense human quality. The literary devices used in the sermon do not prevent it from being a masterpiece of Christian humanism; it is a sincere, open, and intense work that has consoled generations of Christians affected by the separation of death.

In the first part of this Introduction, we have already discussed the role that St. Bernard played in the second Crusade. There is no need to go over that ground again, but there is good reason to reproduce in this volume the two key texts that confirm Bernard's emphasis on discerning the reasons that motivate human actions. Before the Crusade, the reason was the desire to act nobly out of love for Christ. After the

Crusade and its failure, the reason was the humility to accept the defeat of one's plans, especially when purely human interests and egotistical designs corrupted intentions that should have been pure. These two texts, rare among the writings of St. Bernard on the Crusade—the encyclical-letter 363 and the beginning of Book II of the *Consideration*—also allow this affair, which was a chance event, to be restored to its properly limited place in the life of St. Bernard. Those who have not read Bernard's works present him as warlike and violent; reading him is sufficient to show him as he truly was. He is certainly not to be held responsible for belonging to an age whose culture was different from our own, but he wished to remove himself from that culture in order to place himself on the spiritual plane.

Finally, we come to Bernard's letters—a third category of evidence that reveals him in an unmistakable light—particularly those that communicate his humanity. People came from all over to consult him about various problems: doctrine, Church policy, monastic reform, and especially questions having to do with the spiritual life or simply with human relations. He once wrote to Pope Eugene III, "People say that I am the Pope, and not you. They come to me from all sides weighted down with their cares. It would be scandalous and sinful to refuse my help to so many friends" (Letter 239). Sometimes he even took the initiative in writing, often in order to defend the weak. Historians continue to examine and comment on his long letters, which tell us something of his era, or of his position on political, doctrinal, or Church affairs.

There is another category of letters in his writings, less important in the history of ideas and facts than in the history of the human heart. These are the letters that have been chosen for inclusion here, for they give us a glimpse of a side of Bernard that should not go unnoticed. Gone for the moment is the man involved in politics and the Church, and in his place we see simply Bernard the man—as he is—the man of God and the saint; the man with all his deepest reactions and the saint whose entire psychology is imbued with grace, despite its persistent weakness. The saint is always a man of heart and, as such, is deserving of our meditation. The letters that tell us little or nothing of the public, official life of the abbot of Clairvaux have a great deal to say about his interior life and everyday existence. They could be called his private letters, for they reveal much in the way of his personal feelings. We have selected some of them for this volume.

Bernard's letters contain certain forms of expression, inevitably taken from the literature of his day, that reveal him to be large of heart, the father of his monks, the friend, the saint consumed with kindness, and the noble Christian who feels for the poor and who loves the little ones. How close to us he was in his thinking, and how wrong we have been in the past to give almost all our attention to the official documents that have sometimes hardened our attitudes! As a result, we have perpetuated a picture of an austere man and leader, whose authority led at times to injustice. It is certainly true that tendencies in Bernard's character and temperament may warrant this harsh judgment. It would be less than truthful to retain only a negative assessment of St. Bernard or to stress it overmuch, just as our portrait would be incomplete if we looked only at his sublime virtues and extraordinary graces. He himself never gave in to that temptation and spoke more often of his weakness than of the divine favors he received. At the end of Letter 70, he recalled an incident when he became angry for no good reason; he then accuses himself of his fault and urges others not to follow his example of rashness. On other occasions he protests against the praise he has received; he uses irony when speaking of himself. His firm charity prompted him to write with much tenderness and affection in his two letters to Countess Ermengarde; but as he once said of Gerard, "He is a man," and he cannot conceal the workings of his mind when addressing a woman. Some of his letters are for the purpose of counseling, in which he put his teaching into practice.

Leaving aside the question of the voluntary embrace of religious life in Bernard's time, he extends an invitation in his vocational letters to friends to come and share the joys of monastic life. During his many absences, he wrote letters to his monks assuring them that he is with them in spirit; he sends them his spiritual direction, tells them that the separation is painful to him and that he hopes to see them again soon. There are requests for forgiveness in which he gives proof of great tenderness. He intervenes with merciless superiors, urging them to have pity on a delinquent monk and welcome back one who has left the monastery and is now repentant. There are letters of consolation to those who are suffering either because of a death in the family or because a son has entered the cloister. Bernard composed letters of reconciliation attempting to smooth over a difference of opinion or make enemies forget their quarrel. Finally, there are letters of pure friendship, whose sole end is to give pleasure and express the affection and gratitude he feels for his correspondent.

In all these writings, St. Bernard speaks openly of his soul and even of his body. He loves with a heart of flesh and wishes others to understand that fact. Christ for him is not a remote God with whom we are united in ecstasy when we are taken out of ourselves; he is present in every man whose salvation he wills and it is in our fellow-men that we begin to serve the Lord. And when we cannot act effectively for our neighbor, we can at least tell him that we wish him well and desire his happiness. This is why we have chosen some of Bernard's compassionate letters that bring to light his concern for the poor; for if any attitude conforms to the Gospel, it is the latter. It is also the reason that we conclude with long excerpts from his portrait on the charity, humility, and compassion that ought to activate Christians. What he wrote for a bishop in Letter 42 has value for everyone and always.

These, then, are examples of Bernard's practical mysticism; they are also demonstrations of his accurate knowledge and his proper love for self, for others, and for God. In the concrete situations instanced in his letters, he showed that what he taught elsewhere in a theoretical manner was truly feasible.

In conclusion, it is not necessary to stress the importance of such a message for our time. It has been recognized and handed down through the centuries since St. Bernard's time, for the abundance of manuscripts and editions of his writings is rare in literary history. His message has been welcomed by different traditions: There is a whole series of studies on St. Bernard and translations of his works in Lutheranism. Luther himself read, quoted, and praised Bernard; he was attracted to the medieval saint whose writings gave attention to the conflict in man between the law of sin and that of the Spirit. Calvin, too, appreciated him, and today the explanation of his work continues. The experiential, existential—even phenomenological—nature of his teaching makes St. Bernard close to many modern thinkers and those who come under their influence. At the same time, since his is grounded in the Scriptures, he brings us back to the sources, and to the Source itself, of all Christian spirituality.

ABBREVIATIONS: WORKS OF BERNARD OF CLAIRVAUX

Abael	Epistola de erroribus Petri Abaelardi
Adv	Sermo in Adventu Domini
Ann	Sermo in Annuntiatione Dominica
Asc	Sermo in Ascensione Domini
Conv	Sermo de Conversione ad Clericos
Csi	De Consideratione
Dil	Liber de Diligendo Deo
Ep	Epistola
Gra	Liber de Gratia et Libero Arbitrio
Hum	Liber de Gradibus Humilitatis et Superbiae
Miss	Homiliae super Missus est in Laudibus Virginis Matris
Mor	Epistola de Moribus et Officibus Episcoporum
I Nov	Sermo in Dominica I Novembris
O Asspt	Sermo in Dominica infra Octavam Assumptionis Beatae Mariae Virginis
OS	Sermo in Festivitate Omnium Sanctorum
Pent	Sermo in Die Sancto Pentecostes
Pre	Liber de Precepto et Dispensatione
QH	Sermo super Psalmum Qui Habitat
Quad	Sermo in Quadragesima
SC	Sermo super Cantica Canticorum
Tpl	De laude Novae Militiae
V Mal	Vita Sancti Malachiae
CCCM	*Corpus Christianorum Continuatio Medievalis*
CCSL	*Corpus Christianorum Series Latina*
Coll OCR	*Collectanea Ordinis Cisterciensis Reformatorum*
CSEL	*Corpus Scriptorum Ecclesiasticorum Latinorum*

LTR   *Sancti Bernardi Opera Omnia*, ed. J. Leclercq, C. H. Talbot, and H. M. Rochais, 8 vols. (Rome, 1957–1980)

PL   *Patrologia Latina*

RB   Regula Benedicti, ed. R. Hanslik, CCSL 75 (Turnholt, 1960)

VP   *Vita Prima Sancti Bernardi*, PL 185

Zinn   *Richard of St. Victor*, ed. G. A. Zinn, Classics of Western Spirituality (New York, 1979)

TRANSLATOR'S NOTE

The numbering of sections and sub-sections follows the Latin text and represents standard practice in the conflation of two long-standing traditions of numbering.

TREATISES

ON CONVERSION

Bernard's sermon On Conversion was given in 1140 in Paris, as a public discourse. It is unique among his sermons in the audience to which it is addressed, and also in its point of departure. Bernard is not for once preaching to the converted, to those who are trying with all their might to make progress on the road to the presence of God. He is speaking to those who have not yet set out, or at least not purposefully. The term conversio at this date had, most commonly, the sense of "deciding to enter a religious order"; but for Bernard it is also conversion of the heart.[1]

He spoke perhaps in the cloister of Notre Dame, to an audience of scholars and students from the schools of Paris: Notre Dame, St. Geneviève, and perhaps St. Victor. His biographer Geoffrey and Peter Lombard were in the audience (both were at one time pupils of Hugh of St. Victor). More than twenty of those who heard him were converted. They declared their intention of following him to Clairvaux. He took them to the abbey of St. Denis for the night, and when the next morning they returned to Paris three more joined them. Their conversions were to prove lasting. They were all professed at Clairvaux a year later.[2]

---

1. See my article "A Change of Mind in Some Scholars of the Eleventh and Twelfth Centuries," *Studies in Church History* 15 (1978):27–39.
2. VP III, Preface, IV.ii.10.

I. That No One Can Be Converted to the Lord
unless the Lord Wills It First,
and Calls Him with an Inner Voice

1. You have come, I believe, to hear the Word of God (Acts 3:44,
19:10). I can see no other reason why you should rush here like this!
I approve of this desire with all my heart, and I rejoice with you in
your praiseworthy zeal. For blessed are those who hear the Word of
God—if, that is, they keep it (Lk 11:28). Blessed are those who are
mindful of his laws, provided that they obey them (Ps 102:18). Such
a one has the words of eternal life indeed (Jn 6:69), and the hour
comes—would it were here now!—when the dead shall hear his
voice and they who hear it shall live (Jn 5:25). For, "To do his will
is to live" (Ps 29:6).

And if you would like to know what his will is: It is that we should
be converted. Hear what he himself says, "It is not my will that the
wicked should perish" (Ez 18:23), says the Lord, "but rather that they
should turn from their wickedness and live" (Mt. 11:14).

From these words we see clearly that our true life is to be found
only through conversion, and there is no other way to enter upon it (1
Tm 6:19). As the same Lord says, "Unless you are converted and become like little children, you will not enter the kingdom of heaven" (Mt
18:3). Truly, only little children will enter, for it is a little child who
leads them (Is 9:6), he who was born and given to us for this very end.
I seek then the voice the dead will hear and when they hear it, live (Jn
5:25). Perhaps it is even necessary to preach the Gospel to the dead (1
Pt 4:6).

And meanwhile a word comes to mind, brief,[1] but full of meaning,
which the mouth of the Lord has spoken, as the prophet bears witness.
"You have said," he cries undoubtedly speaking to the Lord his God,
"be converted, sons of men" (Is 1:20, 40:5; Ps 89:3).

It seems wholly fitting that it is conversion that is required of the
sons of men; it is absolutely necessary for sinners. The heavenly spirits
are told to give praise, as the same prophet says in the Psalm, "Praise
your God, O Sion" (Ps 147:12); that is more appropriate for the righteous (Ps 32:1).

---

1. *Verbum Abbreviatum;* this pun is also used by Peter the Chanter later in the century
as the title of his manual for preachers, PL 205.

2. As to the remainder of what he says: "You have said" (Ps 89:3), I do not think that is to be passed over carelessly or heard unreflectively. For who dare compare the sayings of men with what God is said to have said? The Word of God is living and effective (Heb 4:12). His voice is a voice of magnificence and power (Ps 28:4). "He spoke and they were made" (Ps 148:5). He said, "Let there be light, and there was light" (Gn 1:3). He said, "Be converted" (Ps 89:3), and the sons of men have been converted. So the conversion of souls is clearly the work of the divine voice, not of any human voice. Even Simon son of John (Jn 21:15), called and appointed by the Lord to be a fisher of men, will toil in vain all night and catch nothing until he casts his net at the Lord's word. Then he can catch a vast multitude (Jn 21:15ff; Mt 4:19).

Would that we, too, might cast our net at this word today and experience what is written, "Behold he will give his voice the sound of power" (Ps 67:34). If I lie (Jn 8:44), that is my own fault. It will perhaps be judged to be my own voice and not the voice of the Lord if I seek what is my own and not what is Jesus Christ's (Phil 2:21). For the rest, even if I speak of the righteousness of God (Ps 57:2) and seek God's glory (Jn 8:50, 5:44), I can hope that what I say will be effective only if he makes it so. I must ask him to make this voice of mine a voice of power.

I admonish you, therefore, to lift up the ears of your heart to hear this inner voice, so that you may strive to hear inwardly what is said to the outward man. For this is the voice of magnificence and power (Ps 28:4), rolling through the desert (Ps 28:8), revealing secrets, shaking souls free of sluggishness.

II.   THAT THE VOICE OF THE LORD SPEAKS AND
MAKES ITSELF HEARD TO ALL,
AND PRESENTS ITSELF EVEN TO THE SOUL
WHICH DOES NOT WANT TO HEAR

35.   There is no need to make an effort to hear this voice. The difficulty is to shut your ears to it (Is 33:15). The voice speaks up; it makes itself heard; it does not cease to knock on everyone's door (Rv 3:20). "Forty years long," he says, "I was with this generation, and I said, 'They err constantly in their hearts' " (Ps 94:10). He is still with us. He still

speaks, even if no one listens. He still says, "They err in their hearts"; Wisdom still cries in the streets (Prv 1:20–21). "Come to your senses, evildoers"² (Is 46:8).

This is the beginning of God's speaking (Hos 1:2). And this word which is addressed to all those who are converted in heart (Ps 84:9) seems to have run on ahead; it is a word which not only calls them back but leads them back, and brings them face to face with themselves³ (Ps 49:21). For it is not so much a voice of power (Ps 67:34) as a ray of light, telling men about their sins (Is 58:1) and at the same time revealing the things hidden in darkness (1 Cor 4:5). There is no difference between this inner voice and light, for they are one and the same Son of God and Word of the Father and brightness of glory (Heb 1:3).

So, too, the substance of the soul would seem to be spiritual and simple in its way, without any distinction of senses; the whole soul seems to see and hear at once, if we can speak of it in that way. For what is the purpose of the ray of light or the Word but to bring man to know himself? Indeed, the book of conscience⁴ is opened, the wretched passage of life up to now recalled to mind; the sad story is told again; reason is enlightened and what is in the memory is unfolded as though set out before each man's eyes. But reason and memory are not so much "of" the soul, as themselves the soul,⁵ so that it is both gazer and that which is gazed upon, brought face to face with itself (Ps 49:21) and overcome by the force of its realization of what it is seeing (Rom 2:15). It judges itself in its own court. Who can bear this judgment without pain? "My soul is troubled within me" (Ps 41:7), says the prophet of the Lord, and do you wonder that you cannot be brought to face yourself without being aware of sin, without disturbance, without confusion?

---

2. Literally "return to the heart." In Vulgate and early Christian Latin usage the heart (*cor*) is the seat of thought.

3. Cf. Augustine, *Confessions*, VIII.7.16–18, ed. M. Skutella and L. Verheijen, CCSL 27 (Turnholt, 1981).

4. The *topos* of the book of conscience is used by Alan of Lille in his manual on preaching later in the century, and widely elsewhere.

5. On these powers of the soul, see Augustine, *De Trinitate*, X, ed. W. J. Mountain and Fr. Glorie, CCSL 50 (Turnholt, 1968).

III. How by This Means the Soul's Reason Can Judge and Discern How to Point to All Its Own Evils and Criticize Them, as if They Were Written in a Book

4. Do not hope to hear from me what reason seizes on in your memory to blame, what it judges, what it discerns. Listen to the inner voice; use the eyes of your heart, and you will learn by experience. "For no one knows what is in a man except the spirit which is within him" (1 Cor 2:11). If pride or envy or greed or ambition or any other vice is hidden, it can scarcely escape (Tb 2:8) this examination. If there is fornication, rape, cruelty, deception, or any fault at all, it will not be hidden from this judge who is himself the guilty party; nor will it be denied in his presence.

For however quickly all the prurience of delighting in iniquity passed, and however briefly the enticements of pleasure were attractive, the memory is left with a bitter impression, and dirty footprints remain.[6] Into that repository as if into some cesspit runs all abomination and uncleanness. It is a big book in which everything is written with the pen of truth (Jb 19:23). The stomach endures that bitterness now (Rv 10:9–10). Although as it was swallowed it gave a passing pleasure to the taste, that was soon forgotten. I grieve for my stomach; I grieve for it (Jer 4:19). Why should I not grieve for the stomach of my memory which is congested with such foulness?

My brothers, which of us, if he suddenly noticed that the clothing which covers him was spattered all over with filth and the foulest mud, would not be violently disgusted and quickly take it off and cast it from him indignantly? But the soul which finds itself contaminated in this way cannot cast itself away as a man can cast away his clothes (Sg 5:3). Which of us is so patient and so brave that if he were to see his own flesh suddenly shining white with leprosy (as we read happened to Moses' sister Mary), he could stand calmly and thank his Creator (Nm 12:10)? But what is that flesh but the corruptible garment in which we are clothed?

And how should we think of this leprosy of the body in all the elect but as a rod of fatherly correction (Prv 29:15) and a purgation of the heart (Ps 44:7)? It is a great tribulation and a most just cause of sorrow

---

6. Virgil, *Aeneid*, III.244, ed. J. Mackail (Oxford, 1930).

when a man who has been woken from the sleep (Jn 11:11) of wretched pleasure begins to perceive his inward leprosy, which he has brought upon himself with much zeal and effort. No one hates his own flesh (Eph 5:29). Much less can the soul hate itself (Jn 12:25).

IV. THAT HE WHO LOVES WICKEDNESS IS SHOWN TO HATE NOT ONLY HIS SOUL BUT ALSO HIS FLESH

5. Perhaps this text in the Psalm strikes one of you, "He who loves wickedness hates his own soul" (Ps 10:6). But I say he hates his body, too (Eph 5:29). Surely he hates what he is saving up day by day for hell, what by his hardness and impenitence of heart (Rom 2:5) he is treasuring up for the day of wrath? For this hatred of body and soul is not so much found in the form of a feeling; rather it is revealed by its effects. Thus the madman hates his body when he lays hands on himself when his powers of rational thought are asleep. But is any madness worse than impenitence of heart and an obstinate will to sin? If a man lays wicked hands on himself it is not his flesh but his mind that he tears and damages (Jb 13:14). If you have seen a man tearing at his hands and rubbing them together until they bleed, you have a clear image in him of the sinner's soul. Pleasure turns to pain and agony follows itching. While the man was scratching he ignored the consequences although he knew what would happen. In the same way we have lacerated ourselves and given ourselves ulcers on our unhappy souls with our own hands— except that in a spiritual creature it is more serious because its nature is finer and so more difficult to mend. We have not done it in a spirit of enmity, but in a stupor of inner insensibility. The absent mind does not notice the internal damage, for it is not looking inward, but perhaps concentrating on its stomach—or beneath the stomach. The minds of some men are on their plates,[7] of others in their pockets. "Where your treasure is," he says, "there is your heart" (Mt 6:21). Is it surprising if a soul does not feel its wound when it is not noticing what is happening to it, and is somewhere else far away (Lk 15:13, 17)? The time will come when it will return to itself and realize how cruelly it has eviscerated itself in its wretched pursuit. For it could not feel that while it was like a filthy spider weaving a web out of its own body with insatiable greed to catch its vile booty of flies.

---

7. Terence, *Eunuch*, IV.vii.46, ed. J. Sargeaunt (London, 1953).

V. OF THE PUNISHMENT OF SOUL AND BODY AFTER DEATH AND OF THE FRUITLESSNESS OF REPENTANCE

6. But this return will undoubtedly be after death, when all the gates (Dn 13:17) of the body by which the soul has been used to wandering off to busy itself in useless pursuits and to go out to seek the passing things of this world (1 Cor 7:31) will be shut (Ez 44:2), and it will be forced to remain within itself; for it will have no means of escaping from itself.

Truly that will be a most dreadful return and eternal wretchedness, when it can no longer repent or do penance. For where there is no body there is no possibility of action (Mt 24:28). Where there is no action, no satisfaction can be made. Thus to repent is to grieve; to do penance is a remedy for sorrow. He who has no hands cannot lift his heart in his hands to heaven (Lam 3:41). He who has not come to himself before the death of the flesh must remain trapped in himself for eternity.

But in what a self? Whatever he has made himself in this life, such he will be found when he leaves this life, or perhaps even worse, for he will never be better.[8] For he has himself. Now he lays down his body; now he receives it back again, yet not to penance but to punishment, where the state of sin and flesh will be seen to be so much alike that however our body is punished its sin can never be expiated and the body's torment can never be ended nor the body killed by torture. Truly indeed vengeance rages forever, for it can never wipe out sin. Nor can the body's substance be worn away, for then the affliction of the flesh (Eccl 12:12) would come to an end. He who fears this, let him beware, brothers; for he who does not take care will fall into it.

In the present we must feel and throttle the worm of conscience, rather than nurturing it and thus nourishing it for eternity.

7. To come back to that voice we were speaking of. It is good that we should come to our senses (Is 46:8) while "the way is open by which he shows us his salvation" (Ps 49:23), he who with such zealous love calls back those who have strayed.

Let us not meanwhile resent the gnawing of that worm within. Nor let a dangerous tenderness of mind or pernicious softness persuade

---

8. The doctrine of purgatory was not fully developed until the late twelfth century.

us that we want to hide our present trouble. It is far better for it to gnaw
now, when it can be destroyed by gnawing itself to death. For now, let
it gnaw at the putrid stuff, so that it may consume it by its gnawing,
and be itself consumed, and in that way it will not begin to be cherished
into immortality. "Their worm," it says, "does not die and its fire is not
extinguished" (Is 66:24). Who will endure the gnawing (Ps 147:17)?

For now a manifold consolation eases the torture of the accusing
conscience. God is kind and does not allow us to be tempted beyond
what we can bear (1 Cor 10:13), or let the worm do us too much harm.
Especially at the beginning of our conversion, he anoints our ulcers
with the oil of mercy, so that we may not be too much aware of the
seriousness of our illness or the difficulty of curing it. In fact the ease
of his healing seems to smile on the penitent. But after a time, that vanishes, when his senses have been trained and the battle is given into his
own hands (Heb 5:14), for him to win and learn that Wisdom is stronger
than all things (Wis 10:12). In the meanwhile, he who has heard the
voice of the Lord, "Come to your senses, evildoers" (Is 46:8), and who
has discovered the wickednesses in the depth of his heart, is eager to
root them out one by one, and curious to find out how each of them got
there. The entrance—or, rather, the entrances—are not hard to find if
you look. But no little grief comes from his examination for he finds
that death came in through his own windows (Jer 9:21).[9] It becomes
clear that the roving eyes, the itching ears, the pleasures of smelling,
tasting, and touching, have let in many of them. For the spiritual vices
we were speaking of are still difficult for the fleshly man to see (1 Cor
2:13–14). That is why he perceives less clearly or not at all those which
are the more serious, and his conscience is not troubled as much by the
memory of pride or envy as by the recollection of shameful or wicked
deeds.

VI.   How It Seems to Some That the Human Will Can Easily Obey the Divine Word

8. And behold, a voice from heaven saying (Mt 17:5), "Be still, you
have sinned." And this is what it says. An overflowing sewer now con-

---

9. Anselm of Canterbury was fond of this image of windows. See *Memorials of St.
Anselm*, ed. R. W. Southern and F. S. Schmitt (London, 1969).

taminates the whole house with intolerable filth. It is vain for you (Ps 126:2) to empty it when the filth is still flooding in, to repent while you do not cease to sin. For who approves of the fasting of those who fast for strife and contention (Is 58:4), and smite with the fist of wickedness, but indulge themselves and do as they please (Is 58:3). "This is not the fast that I have chosen," says the Lord (Is 58:6). Close the windows, fasten the doors, block all entry carefully, and when at last you are not contending with the entry of fresh filth you will be able to clean up what is already there (1 Cor 5:7). If a man thinks (Jas 1:7) that what he is asked to do is easy, it is as though he did not know about spiritual warfare. For who can say that I do not know how to govern my own members? So fasting puts an end to gluttony, and forbids drunkenness; the ears are stopped up to prevent them hearing of blood, the eyes turned from vanity (Is 33:15); the hand is directed not to acquisitiveness but to almsgiving, and put to work to stop it thieving (Ps 118:36–37), as it is written, "He who was a thief is a thief no more; instead he works with his hands to do good, so that he may have something to give to the needy" (Eph 4:28). If you do not know, it is she to whom at first you told us to be obedient, and to give in fully to her wishes" (Rom 6:12).

At this speech the wretch grows pale and is struck dumb with confusion. For his spirit is troubled within him (Ps 142:4).

But the members come to their unhappy mistress without delay to complain bitterly against their master and bewail his hard commands. The greedy sense of taste complains at the meanness of the limit set to it, and the forbidding of the pleasure of gluttony. The eye complains that it is told to weep and not wander. While these complaints are going on, the will, stirred up and fiercely angry, says, "Are you telling me a dream (Gn 37:9) or a story?" Now the tongue, which has discovered its own cause for complaint, says, "It is all as you have heard. For I, too, have been ordered not to tell stories (1 Tm 1:4, Ti 1:14) or lies and speak from henceforth nothing but what is serious and necessary."

9. While he promulgates laws and makes decrees in this way for his own members, they suddenly interrupt the voice that is giving them orders and cry with a single impulse, "Where does this new religion come from (Acts 17:19)? It is easy for you to give orders as you like. But someone will be found who will oppose them, who will make new laws to contradict them." "Who is she?" he asks. They answer, "It is someone who is lying at home paralyzed (Mt 8:6) and deeply tormented."

VI.   HOW THE WILL OF MAN RESISTS THE DIVINE VOICE BY GLUTTONY, CURIOSITY, AND PRIDE, AND BY ALL THE FLESHLY SENSES

10. Then the little old woman jumps up furiously, forgetting all her weariness. With hair standing on end, her clothes torn, her breast bared, scratching at her ulcers, grinding her teeth, dry-mouthed, infecting the air with her foul breath (Ps 34:16; Mk 9:17), she asks why reason (if any reason remains) is not ashamed to attack and invade the wretched will. "Is this your conjugal faithfulness?" she demands. "Is this the way you feel compassion for me in my suffering? Up to now you have spared me, and not added to the pain of my wounds (Ps 68:27). Perhaps it seemed to you that something ought to be subtracted from my large dowry? But when you have taken this away, what is left? You have merely added to the wretchedness of this weary creature; and you know how once you respected all my wishes.

"But now, would that the threefold malignity of this dreadful sickness under which I labor had fallen on you not me. I am voluptuous. I am curious. I am ambitious. There is no part of me which is free from this threefold ulcer, from the soles of my feet to the top of my head (Is 1:6). My gullet and the shameful parts of my body are given up to pleasure; we must name them afresh, one by one. The wandering foot and the undisciplined eye are slaves to curiosity. Ear and tongue serve vanity, while the sinner's oil pours in to make my head greasy (Ps 140:5). With my tongue I myself supply whatever others seem to have omitted in my praise. I am greatly pleased both to receive praise from others and, when I conveniently can, to praise myself to others, for I always like to be talked about, whether by myself or by others.

"To this sickness your great skill is also in the habit of applying many dressings. Then my very hands, straying everywhere, have no particular task, but now they show themselves to be wholly enslaved to vanity, now to curiosity, now to pleasure. Even so, not all, nor even one of these has ever been able to satisfy me, for the eye is not satisfied by what it sees, nor the ear by what it hears (Eccl 1:8). But would that sometimes the body were all eye or the members all turned into a gullet to eat with (1 Cor 12:17). Then indeed I might have that little consolation which, despite my begging, you are trying to take away from me." So she spoke, and backing away in indignation and fury, she said, "I shall hang on; I shall hang on for a long time."[10]

VI.   Reason, Now at Last Stirred to Anger, Answers Back and Is Not Easily Confounded

11. Now the reason understands its vexation. Now it realizes something of the difficulty of what it has undertaken, and the ease with which it thought to proceed seems an illusion. It sees that the memory is full of filth. It sees more and more filth freely pouring into it. It sees the windows open to death and cannot close them (Jer 9:21), because the will is still weak, although she is yet in command; and from her ulcers a mass of bloody pus is flowing everywhere. Worst of all, the soul sees itself contaminated, not by someone else, but by its own body, which is no other than itself. For the soul is so constituted that just as it is the memory which is befouled so it is the will which destroys. For the soul itself is nothing but reason, memory, and will.[11] But now reason is found to be blind, for it did not see all this until now; weak, for it cannot repair what it recognizes; and the memory is found to be foul and fetid; and the will weak and covered in itching sores (2 Mc 9:9). And, to omit nothing which belongs to the man, his very body rebels and every single member is a window (Jer 9:21) through which death enters the soul and ceaselessly makes the confusion worse.

VII.   The Breath of Consolation When the Soul Hears of the Promised Happiness of the Kingdom of Heaven

12. When it is in this state, let the soul hear the divine voice; in wonder and amazement let it hear him saying, "Blessed are the poor in spirit, for theirs is the kingdom of heaven" (Mt 5:3). Who is poorer in spirit than he who in the whole of his own spirit finds no rest (Lk 11:24), nowhere to lay his head (Mt 8:20)? Here, too, is holy advice, that he who displeases himself pleases God (1 Cor 7:32; 1 Thes 2:4), and he who

---

10. Cf. Statius, *Thebaid*, II.429, ed. H. J. Mozley (London, 1928).
11. See note 5.

hates his own house, a house full of filth and unhappiness, is invited into the house of glory, a house not made with hands, which will be everlasting in the heavens (2 Cor 5:1). It is not surprising if he trembles (Gn 27:33) at the greatness of his condescension, if he finds it hard to believe what he has heard (Rom 10:16), if, struck with astonishment, he cries, "Does wretchedness then make a man happy?"

If you are in that state, have faith. It is not wretchedness but mercy which makes a man happy, so that humiliation turns to humility and need to strength. "You shall set aside for your inheritance a generous rain, O God; it was failing, but you have made it perfect" (Ps 67:10). That weakness is a benefit which seeks the help of a physician and he who faints does so to his salvation when God perfects him.

That He in Whose Flesh Sin Still Reigns Cannot Hope for This Kingdom, And so We Must Note What Follows: "Blessed Are the Meek," and so on.

But because there is no way to the kingdom of God without the firstfruits of the kingdom, and he to whom it is not given to rule his own members cannot hope for the kingdom of heaven, there follows, "Blessed are the meek, for they will inherit the earth" (Mt 5:4). To put it more plainly, "Check the wild motions of the will and take care to tame the wild beast. You are in bonds. Strive to untie what you can never break. The will is your Eve. You will not prevail against her by using force."

VIII. 13. There is no delay. The man, breathing again at these words, and thinking again that his task is not impossible, shamefacedly approaches the angry viper and tries to quell it. He speaks of the temptations of the flesh and denounces worldly consolations as vanities, trivial and worthless, short-lived and most dangerous to all who love them.

How to Make an End of the Goings In and Out of Lust and Gluttony, and the Vanity of Curiosity And the Love of Riches

"For this reason," he says, "call yourself a wicked and unprofitable servant" (Mt 25:30; Lk 19:22). You cannot deny that you have never been able to satisfy all these demands, even moderately. The pleasures of the throat, which are so highly regarded today, take up scarcely two fingers' breadth; and the small enjoyment of that little fragment is prepared with such trouble and gives rise to such anxiety! By this the upper and lower parts of the body are enlarged, and the swelling stomach is not so much fattened as made pregnant with destruction; and when the bones cannot bear the weight of the flesh, various diseases follow.

With what labor and expense (sometimes of good reputation and honor), even at what danger to life, is the seductive whirlpool of lust stirred, so that the sulfurous vapor, though it glows very little, may drive its maddened victims with goads, and treat their intoxicated hearts like bees which first pour out honey and then sting.[12] This is the man whose heart is torn, whose desires full of anxiety and regret, whose acts of abomination and ignominy, whose fate of remorse and shame, are fully recognized at last for what they are.

14. What do these vain spectacles benefit the body or seem to confer on the soul? For you will find no third part of man which might benefit from curiosity. Frivolous and vain and empty is that consolation, and I do not know what harder lot I could solicit for him than that he should always have what he wants; he who when fleeing sweet peace delights in restless curiosity. It is quite clear that only the passing of all these "delights" is a joy. Besides, it is obvious from its very name that the "vanity of vanities" is nothing (Sir 1:2). Vain indeed is the labor which is carried out from zeal for vanity (Ps 126:1). "O glory, glory," says the wise man, "among the thousands of mortals, you are nothing but a vain puffing up of the ears!"[13] And yet how much unhappiness do you think this (which is not so much happy vanity as vain happiness) produces? For it causes blindness of heart (Mc 3:5; Eph 4:18), as it is written, "My people, those who call you blessed deceive you" (Is 3:12). It produces the stiff-necked fury of animosity, the anxious labor of suspicion, the cruel torment of frustration, and the wretchedness of envy, which receives more misery than pity. Thus the insatiable love of riches is a desire which brings far more torment to the soul than their enjoyment brings refreshment. For the acquisition of riches is found to be all labor, their possession

---

12. Boethius, *Consolation of Philosophy*, III, metr.7, ed. Bieler, CCSL 94 (1957), p.47.
13. *Ibid.*, III, pr.6, p. 45.

all fear, and their loss all sorrow. Then, "Where there are many riches, there are many who consume them" (Eccl 5:10), and indeed other people's use of their riches leaves the rich only the reputation for wealth and the cares of wealth. And in all this for so slight a thing, or not even that—for nothing. To think nothing of that glory which the eye has not seen nor the ear heard, nor has it entered the heart of man, that glory which God has prepared for those who love him (1 Cor 2:9), seems to be not so much lack of sense as lack of faith.

On Unworthy Slavery to the Vices, The Uncertainty When Death Will Come, And the Unhappiness of Amassing Riches

15. Surely it is their own fault that this world which lies in the Evil One's grip (1 Jn 5:19) deludes with vain promises souls which forget their creation and their dignity, souls who are not ashamed to feed swine, to keep company with swine in their desires, and not even then to be satisfied with their disgusting food (Lk 15:15–16)? From this comes such infirmity of purpose and wretched abjection that this noble creature is not ashamed to live in slavery to this foulness of the body's senses, although he is capable of enjoying eternal blessedness and the glory of God's greatness (Ti 2:13). God created him by his own breath, distinguished him by making him in his own likeness, redeemed him by his blood, gave him faith, adopted him by the Spirit (Rom 8:15; Gal 4:5). When the soul deserts such a Bridegroom and pursues such lovers (Hos 2:7), it is not surprising that it cannot grasp the glory that is prepared for it. It is fitting that it should hunger for husks and not be given them, when it preferred to feed pigs rather than feast at the Father's table (Lk 15:16). It is the work of madness to feed what is barren and brings forth nothing, and to be unwilling to give anything to the widow (Jb 24:21), to care nothing for the heart and to give the flesh everything it wants (Rom 13:14), to fatten and caress a putrid body which is destined before long to be the food of worms (Is 14:1). For who is unaware that to worship mammon (Mt 6:24) and to serve avarice (which means serving idols) (Eph 5:5; Col. 3:5), or to chase eagerly after vanity, is clear evidence of a degenerate soul?

THAT WORKS DONE IN THIS LIFE ARE LIKE THE
SEEDS OF EVERLASTING REWARD

16. Granted that the world seems for now to give those who love it great and honorable things; everyone knows that it is faithless. Certainly these things do not last and it is uncertain even when they will end.[14] Often they are lost to a man while he is still alive. He is sure to lose them when he dies.

And what in human life is more certain than death and more uncertain than the hour of death? Death is not merciful to poverty. It is no respecter of riches. It spares no one for the sake of his noble birth, his behavior, even his age; it waits at the door for the old and ambushes the young. Unhappy is he who in the dark and slippery places (Ps 34:6) of this life gives his energies to work which cannot last and does not recognize that it is vapor which appears for a moment (Jas 4:15) and vanity of vanities (Eccl 1:2). Ambitious man, have you obtained some dignity you have long desired? Hold on to what you have. Miser, have you filled your coffers? Be careful not to lose it all. Has your land been very fruitful? Pull down your barns and build greater (Lk 12:16). Make square buildings round.[15] Say to your soul, "You must have goods laid up for many years." There will be someone to say, "Fool, this night your soul will be required of you. To whom will all that you have stored up belong?" (Lk 12:18 ff).

17. And would that only this collection perished and not their collector too! He will perish more terribly. It would be better to sweat over work which has no purpose than at work which has a deadly result. But here the wages of sin is death (Rom 6:23) and he who sows in the flesh will reap corruption from the flesh (Gal 6:8). For our deeds do not pass away as they seem to. On the contrary, every deed done in this life is the seed of a harvest to be reaped in eternity. The fool will be amazed when he sees the huge yield of the few seeds he has sown; good or bad, according to the quality of the seed. He who bears this in mind will never think sin a trifle, because he will look to the future harvest rather than that which he sows. Men sow unknowingly; they sow, hiding the mysteries of iniquity (2 Thes 2:7), and disguise the notes of vanity (Ps 25:4); the business of darkness is done in the dark (Ps 90:6).

---

14. Cicero, *De Senectute*, XX.74, ed. W. A. Falconer (London, 1923).
15. Horace, *Ep.*, I.i.100, ed. H. Rushton Fairclough (London, 1923).

IX.   That It Is Impossible for the Sinner to Hide

18. "I am surrounded by walls," says the man. "Who can see me" (Sir 23:25)? Even if no man sees you, you are seen. The wicked angel sees you. The good angel sees you. God who is greater than good or wicked angels sees you. The accuser (Rv 12:10) sees you. The multitude of witnesses (Heb 12:1) see you. The Judge himself sees you, before whom you must stand trial (Rm 14:10), on whose gaze it is madness to turn your back (Sir 38:15). It is terrible to fall into the hands of the living God (Heb 10:31).

Do not be in a hurry to think yourself safe. Ambushes are concealed from you, but you cannot hide from them. Ambushes are concealed, I say, and just as you cannot find them, so you cannot fail to fall into them. He who made the ear hears and he who put the eyes in your head sees (Ps 93:9). No wall of stones cuts off the Sun's rays. Not even the wall of the body is impenetrable to the gaze of truth. He sees those he has made. All things lie bare to his eyes, which penetrate more easily than a two-edged sword (Heb 4:12). He not only sees; he distinguishes the paths of our thoughts and the sources of our feelings. If he did not see into the uttermost depths of the human heart (Sir 42:18) and perceive what lies in it better than it does itself, man would not fear the sentence of the Lord his judge so much, even when he is not aware of anything which can be held against him. The apostle says, "I know of nothing against myself. But I am not therefore justified. It is the Lord who judges me" (1 Cor 4:3ff.).

19. If you boast that you can frustrate human judgment by pretense, be sure that he whose eye is on men even for sins they have not committed will not overlook the sins they do commit. If you stand in such fear of your neighbor's knowledge of what you are, how much less should you shrug off the opinion of those to whom iniquity is the more hateful and corruption far more execrable? If you do not fear God but only the eyes of men (Lk 18:2, 4), remember what you cannot fail to know, that the man Christ knows all the deeds of men (1 Tm 2:5). So, then, what you would scarcely dare before men, you should be the more reluctant to dare before him. What you would not, I do not say, be allowed to do, but like to do, while your fellow-servant is watching, you should be horrified even to think of doing in the presence of your Lord. Otherwise, if you live in fear of the eye of the flesh rather than the sword which has power to destroy the flesh (Dt 32:42), that fear you fear will come upon you, and what you dread will happen (Jb 3:25).

There is nothing hidden which is not to be revealed; nothing secret which will not be known (Lk 12:2; Mt 10:26). When the works of darkness (Rom 13:12) are brought to light they will be accused by the light (Jn 3:20), and not only abominable hidden obscenities, but also the wicked business of men who sell mysteries for money, and the fraudulent whisperings of men who invent deceits and pervert judgment (Jb 34:12; Eccl 5:7). All these will he who knows everything, who sees into the heart and bowels (Ps 7:10; Rv 2:23), reveal, when he begins to bring lamps to Jerusalem (Wis 1:12).

X.20. What therefore will they do, or rather, what will they suffer, those who have committed sins, when they hear, "Go into everlasting fire," you who have not done good works (Mt 7:23, 25:41, 45; Lk 13:27). When will he be admitted to the wedding-feast, he who has neither girded his loins to abstain from evil, nor kept his light burning to do good (Lk 12:35)? Then neither the integrity of virginity nor the brightness of the lamp will be able to excuse the lack of one thing: the oil (Mt 25:1). Or what tortures must be believed to lie in wait for those who in this life have done not merely wrong, but perhaps the worst of evils (Eccl 8:11), if those who have received good things here are to be so tormented that in the midst of the flames their burning tongues are not cooled by even one tiny drop of water (Lk 16:24)?

Let us therefore beware of wrongdoing and let us not commit sins freely within the Church, trusting that it casts a wide net, knowing that fishermen do not keep everything the net brings in, but when the boat comes to shore they choose the good fish and throw away the bad (Mt 13:47). Let us not be content to gird our loins. Let us also light our lamps (Mt 5:15) and be conscientious in doing good works (Gal 6:10), bearing it in mind that every tree, not only that which bears bad fruit but also that which does not bear good fruit, will be cut down and thrown into the fire (Mt 3:10, 7:19; Lk 3:9), that "eternal fire which has been prepared for the devil and his angels" (Mt 25:41).

21. For the rest, let us so turn our backs on evil and do good (Ps 36:27; Ps 33:15) that we may seek peace (1 Pt 3:11) and not glory. For glory is God's and he will not yield it to anyone else. "My glory," he says, "I will not give to another" (Is 42:8, 48:11). And it was a man after God's heart who said, "Not unto us, O Lord, not unto us, but to thy name give glory" (Ps 113:9). Let us remember, too, what Scripture says, "If you offer aright and do not divide rightly, you have sinned" (Gn 4:7). This "division" of ours is right, brothers; let no man question it. If there is anyone who is displeased by it, let him know that it is not

we who make it but the angels. It was the angels who first sang, "Glory to God in the highest and peace on earth to men of goodwill" (Lk 2:14).

Let us therefore keep oil in our vessels (Mt 25:4), lest (perish the thought) we beat in vain on the doors of the wedding-feast when they are already closed, and hear the dread word of the Bridegroom answering us from within, "I do not know you" (Mt 25:12). Death stands beside the entrance still, not only of unrighteousness, unfruitfulness, vanity, but also of pleasure itself.[16] That is why we need fortitude against the temptation to sin, so that, strong in the faith, we may resist the roaring lion (1 Pt 5:8ff.), and with this shield (Prv 30:5; Neh 2:3) manfully repel his fiery arrows (Eph 6:16). We need justice to do good. We need prudence, so that we may not be reproved with the foolish virgins. Lastly, we need temperance, so that we do not, in the midst of our pleasures, one day hear what that wretched man heard, when, feasts and fine garments set aside, he prayed for mercy and heard, "Remember, son, that you have received good things in your life and Lazarus bad things; now he is comforted and you are tormented" (Lk 16:25). How terrible is God in his counsels concerning the sons of men (Ps 65:5)! But if he is terrible, he is also merciful, when he does not hide the nature of the judgment which is to come. "The soul which has sinned will die" (Ez 18:4). The branch which has not borne fruit will be cut off (Jn 15:2; Mt 3:10). The virgin who has no oil shall be shut out of the wedding-feast (Mt 25:12); and he who has received good things in this life will be tormented in the life to come (Lk 16:25). If perhaps all these four are to be found in anyone, his state is clearly very desperate.

That the Flesh Resists the Spirit Which Is Beginning to Fear God and Try to Do Good

22. The reason suggests these things inwardly to the will, the more abundantly as it is taught the more fully by the illumination of the Spirit. Happy indeed is he whose will has given itself up and taken the advice of reason, so that although at first it is fearful, afterwards it is cherished by heavenly promises and brings forth the spirit of salvation.

---

16. RB 7.24.

But perchance the will is found rebellious and obstinate, and not merely impatient, but, worse, after warnings, impervious to threats and prickly when flattered. Perhaps it will be found that the will is not moved at all by the suggestions of reason, and replies with a flash of anger, "How long am I to endure you (Mt 17:16; Lk 4:41)? Your preaching does not move me (Jn 8:37). I know that you are clever, but your cleverness does not fool me." Perhaps, then, the will, calling upon the members of the body one by one, urges them harder than ever to give in to their desires (Rom 6:12) and act wickedly (Rom 6:19). That is an only too familiar daily experience to all of us, that those who are giving their minds to conversion are tempted the more strongly by the desires of the flesh (1 Jn 2:16), and those who seek to leave Egypt and escape from Pharaoh are driven harder to make bricks out of clay (Ex 1:14, 5:19–21).

23. Would that such a one might turn aside from ungodliness and be careful not to fall into that terrible abyss of which it is written, "The ungodly man thinks nothing of it when he comes to the depths of wickedness" (Prv 18:3). He can be cured only by the most powerful remedy, and he will easily fail, unless he takes care to follow the physician's advice and do what he tells him. The temptation is fierce. It brings a man close to desperation (Heb 6:8) unless he gathers all his forces to take pity on his soul which he sees to be so wretched and pitiable, changes his attitude, and listens to the voice of him (Rv 10:4, 10:8) who says, "Blessed are they who mourn, for they shall be comforted" (Mt 5:5). Let him mourn abundantly, for the time for mourning has come and his state is greatly to be wept over. Let him mourn, but not without holy love and in hope of consolation. Let him bear in in mind that he can find no rest in himself, but all is full of misery and desolation. Let him bear it in mind that there is no good in his own flesh (Rom 7:18), and that this wicked world offers nothing but vanity and affliction of spirit (Eccl 1:14, 2:11, 17, 4:16). Let him consider, I say, that neither within nor beneath nor around him is any consolation to be found, so that at last he may learn to seek what is to be sought above (Col 3:1) and to hope for what comes from above. Yet let him mourn meanwhile, bewailing his sorrow (Jb 10:20). Let his eyes pour out water (Ps 118:136). Let his eyelids not close in sleep (Prv 6:4). Truly, the eye which was in darkness before is cleansed by tears and its sight sharpened, so that it is able to gaze into the brightness of that most serene light (Acts 22:11).

XII. After Grief Comes Comfort and the Kindling of the Desire to Contemplate Heavenly Things

24. From now onward, let him gaze upward through the window, look out through the lattice (Sg 2:9), and follow the guiding star (Mt 2:1) with all his attention and, zealously imitating the Magi, let him seek the Light in the light (Ps 35:10). He will find a wonderful place to pitch his tent (Ps 41:5), where a man may eat the bread of angels (Ps 77:25). He will find a paradise of pleasure planted by the Lord (Gn 2:8). He will find a garden of sweet flowers. He will find a cool resting-place, and he will say, "O that that wretched will would listen to my voice, so that it might enter in and see these good things and visit that place! Here indeed will it find further rest, and it will disturb me less when it is itself less disturbed." For he speaks the truth who says, "Take my yoke upon you and you will find rest for your souls" (Mt 11:29).

Trusting in this promise, she addresses the angry will more soothingly and with a cheerful expression, and in the spirit of gentleness (1 Cor 4:21) which befits her, says, "Do not be indignant. I am not able to cause you to stumble. I am your body; your own self. There is nothing to fear or to dread."

Do not be surprised if the will's reply is more bitter than ever. It says, "Too much thinking has made you mad" (Acts 26:24). For the moment, let the reason wait quietly and hide its doings, until, talking of this and that, it can bring the subject up opportunely, saying, "Today I discovered a most beautiful garden, a very pleasant place. It would be good for us to be there (Mt 17:4). For it does you harm to be tossed on this bed of sickness, to be turning over your sorrow on your bed, to be grieving heavy-hearted in your chamber (Ps 4:5). The Lord will be near to him who seeks him, to the soul which hopes in him (Lam 3:25). He will attend to the vows of his suppliants, and he will minister to them in the power of his word" (Heb 4:12). The will's desire will be moved, and not only to see the place (Mt 28:6); it will also long to enter it (Jn 20:4–8), little by little, and make its dwelling there (Jn 14:23).

XIII. How Resting in This Contemplation the Soul Delights in the Taste of Him and Learns from Him

25. Do not think that this inward paradise of pleasure (Gn 2:8) is corporeal. It is not with the feet but with the affections that a man enters

it. Nor is it the plentifulness of earthly trees that makes it desirable to you, but the joyous and lovely (Ps 146:1) plantation of spiritual virtues which grows there. It is an enclosed garden (Sg 4:12), where a sealed fountain gives forth four springs (Sg 4:12) and a fourfold virtue comes from a single source of wisdom. There, too, the whitest lilies spring, and when the flowers appear the voice of the turtle-dove is heard (Sg 2:12). There the perfume of the Bride gives off a most sweet fragrance, and other scents abound. There the north wind is still and the south wind softly blows (Sg 1:11; 4:16). There in the midst is the tree of life (Gn 2:9), the apple tree of the Song of Songs, more precious than all the trees of the wood, in whose shade the Bride finds coolness and whose fruit is sweet to her taste (Sg 2:3).

There continence shines and the vision of pure truth illuminates the eye of the heart (Eph 1:18). The most sweet voice of the inner Comforter brings joy and gladness to the ears (Ps 50:10). There the most lovely odor of a fruitful field which the Lord has blessed (Gn 27:27) is carried to the nostrils of hope (Sg 2:14). There a foretaste of the incomparable delights of love is enjoyed, and the mind, anointed with mercy and freed from the sharp thorns and briars by which it was once pricked (Is 10:17), rests happily with a clear conscience (Acts 23:1; 1 Tm 1:5).

These are not among the rewards of eternal life. They should be thought of as wages of the soldiering of this life (1 Cor 9:7). They do not belong to what is promised to the Church in the future, but rather to what she is promised now (Gal 4:23–25; 1 Tm 4:8). For this is the hundredfold reward which is set before those who despise the world (Mt 19:29).

You do not need any speech of mine to commend this to you, The Spirit reveals it himself (1 Cor 2:10). You do not need to look it up in the pages of a book. Look to experience instead. Man does not know the price of wisdom. It comes from hidden places and it has a sweetness with which no sweetness known to living men (Jb 28:12, 13; Ps 26:13, 51:7) can compare. It is the sweetness of the Lord, and you will not recognize it unless you taste it. "Taste and see," he says, "how sweet the Lord is" (Ps 33:9).

The new name which a man knows only if he receives it is hidden manna (Rv 2:7). Not learning but anointing teaches it; it is not grasped by knowledge but by conscience (1 Jn 2:27). It is holy. It is a pearl (Mt 7:6). He who began both to do and to teach (Acts 1:1) will not himself do what he forbids. For he does not think of those who have renounced their former sins and wickednesses as dogs or swine. They are even comforted by the Apostle, who says, "Some of you were like this, but you have been washed and you are sanctified" (1 Cor 6:11). But let the dog be careful not to return to his vomit and the sow not to go back to wallowing in the mire (2 Pt 2:22).

XIV. HAVING TASTED SUCH FOOD THE SOUL UNDERSTANDS THAT THEY ARE BLESSED WHO HUNGER AND THIRST AFTER RIGHTEOUSNESS

26. Therefore in this gate of paradise the voice of the divine whisper is heard (Gn 3:8), a most holy and secret counsel, which is hidden from the wise and prudent and revealed to little children (Mt 11:25). When it hears this voice reason not only grasps what it says but communicates it readily to the will. "Blessed are they who hunger and thirst after righteousness, for they shall be filled" (Mt 5:6). It is the supreme advice, and a mystery beyond thinking of. It is "a faithful saying and worthy to be received by everyone" (1 Tm 1:15, 4:9), that he who came to us from heaven came from a royal throne (Wis 18:15). For there was a great famine on earth, and we did not only all come to be in need (Lk 15:14); we are brought to an extremity of need. That is, we are compared with brute beasts and become like them (Ps 48:13, 21). We even hunger insatiably for the husks the pigs eat (Lk 15:16). He who loves money is not satisfied (Mt 5:6); he who loves luxury is not satisfied; he who loves glory is not satisfied; in short, he who loves the world is never satisfied. I myself have known men sated with this world, and sickened by every memory of it. I have known men sated with money, sated with honors, sated with the pleasures and curiosities of this world, and more than a little: to the point of nausea. And by the grace of God it is easy for every one of us to be sated in this way! For it is a satiety produced not by abundance but by contempt. So, foolish sons of Adam, devouring the husks intended for the pigs, you are feeding not your hungry souls but the hunger itself. Indeed, we continue to lack food when we sit at this banquet; unnatural food only sustains hunger. And, to take a plainer example, that of one of the many things human vanity desires, I tell you that man's heart is not satisfied with gold any more than his body is satisfied with wind. Let the miser not be indignant. The same thing is true of the ambitious and the luxurious and the criminal. If perhaps there is anyone who does not believe me, let him believe experience: his own or that of many others.

27. Which of you, brothers, desires to be satisfied and to have his desire fulfilled? Let him begin to hunger after righteousness (Mt 5:6) and he cannot fail to be satisfied. Let him desire that bread of which there is plenty in his Father's house (Lk 15:17), and he will find that the husks of the pigs disgust him. Let him try to taste righteousness even a little, for the more he desires it the more will he deserve it; it is written, "He who eats me will hunger for more and he who drinks me will thirst for more" (Eccl 24:29). For this desire is more in keeping with the spirit of man. It takes possession of the human heart with a more natural and more powerful desire, and energetically casts out all other desires. So the strong armed man is driven out by a stronger (Lk 11:21ff.), as a nail can often be driven out by a nail. "Blessed therefore are those who hunger and thirst after righteousness for they shall be satisfied" (Mt 5:6). Not yet indeed with that which a man shall be filled with and live (Ex 33:20), but with all the other things which had been desired insatiably before, so that from now on the will shall cease to sell the body into slavery and its former lusts (Rom 6:12; 1 Pt 1:14), and expose it to the influence of reason. Instead, it will urge it to continue in righteousness so as to grow with no less zeal than it showed before when it served infirmity unto iniquity (Rm 6:19).

XV. That Our Sins, Once Punished, Are Forgiven, And If They Are Not Repeated, Cannot Be a Stumbling-Block, But Rather Work Together for Good

28 And now the will has been changed and the body brought into subjection to it (1 Cor 9:27), as though the fountain of evil had been dried up in part and the opening covered over. The third task remains and that is the hardest: to purify the memory and pump out the cesspit. How can I forget my own life? Take a thin piece of poor-quality parchment which has soaked up the ink with which the scribe has written on it. Can any skill erase it? It is not merely superficially colored; the ink is ingrained. It would be pointless for me to try to clean it. The parchment would tear before the marks of wretchedness were removed. Forgetting would perhaps destroy the memory itself, so that, in a mental convulsion, I should cease to remember what I had done.

We must ask, then, what keen edge can both clean my memory and keep it intact? Only the living and effective Word which is sharper than a two-edged sword (Heb 4:12), which "takes away your sins" (Mk

2:5). The Pharisee may murmur and say, "Who can take away sins except God?" (Mk 2:7; Lk 5:21). He who says this to me is God and no
one else is to be compared with him. He set out the whole way of discipline; he gave it to his servant Jacob and to his beloved Israel; and after
that he was seen on earth and talked with men (Bar 3:36–38). His pardon wipes out sin, not from the memory, but in such a way that what
before was both present in the memory and rendered it unclean is now,
although it is still in the memory, no longer a defilement to it. For now
many sins come to mind which we know to have been committed by
ourselves or by others. But it is our own sins which defile the memory;
those of others do not hurt it. Why is this, if not because it is our own
sins which cause us shame? These are what we fear to have charged
against us. Take away condemnation, take away fear, take away confusion, and there is full remission of sins. Then our sins will not be
against us but will work together for good (Rom 8:28), so that we may
give devout thanks to him who has remitted them.

XVI.   On the Mercy Which Is Promised to the Penitent
                        and Wretched,
"Blessed," He Says, "Are the Merciful," and so on

29. For him who prays for mercy, there is a fitting reply. "Blessed are
the merciful, for they shall obtain mercy" (Mt 5:7). Have mercy on your
own soul (Sir 30:24) if you want God to have mercy on you. Drench
your bed in tears night after night, and remember to water your couch
with weeping (Ps 6:7). If you take compassion on yourself, if you labor
with groans of repentance (Ps 6:7)—for this is your first step in mercy—
you will indeed find mercy. If you are perhaps a great sinner with many
sins, and you ask a great mercy and many acts of pity (Ps 50:3), you,
too, must strive to show great mercy. Be reconciled to yourself, for you
did yourself grave injury (Jb 7:20) in setting yourself up against God.

    Now that peace has been restored in your own house, it is neces-
sary first to extend it to your neighbor, and that he may give you a new
kiss with the kiss of his mouth (Sg 1:1); as it is written, you must be
reconciled and at peace with God (Rom 5:1). Forgive those who have
sinned against you, and your own sins will be forgiven you (Lk 6:37);
and you will pray to the Father with a quiet conscience, and say, "Forgive us our sins as we forgive those who sin against us" (Mt 6:12).

    If perhaps you have cheated anyone, make good what you owe,

and give what is left over to the poor (Lk 19:8, 18:22, 11:41), and you will be shown mercy (Rom 9:25). "If your sins were as scarlet, they shall be as white as snow, and if they were red as vermilion, they shall be white as wool" (Is 1:18). So that you may not be put to shame for all the devices of your wrongdoing (Wis 3:11), for which you blush now (Rom 6:21), give alms, and if you cannot do so from your earthly substance (Jb 4:7; Lk 11:41), do it from your good will, and they will all be clean. Not only will the reason be enlightened and the will put right, but the memory itself will be purged, and henceforth you will cry to the Lord and hear a voice saying, "Blessed are the pure in heart, for they shall see God" (Mt 5:8).

XVII.   That the Heart Must Be Cleansed If the Soul Is to See God, for, "Blessed Are the Pure in Heart," and so on

30. "Blessed are the pure in heart, for they shall see God" (Mt 5:8). This is a great promise, my brothers, and something to be desired with all one's heart. For to see in this way is to be like God, as John the Apostle says, "Now we are all sons of God, but it has not yet been made clear what we shall be. For we know that when it is made clear we shall be like him, for we shall see him as he is" (1 Jn 3:2). This vision is eternal life (Jn 12:50), as Truth himself says in the Gospel, "This is eternal life, that they should know that you alone are the true God, and him whom you have sent, Jesus Christ" (Jn 17:3).

Hateful is the blemish which deprives us of this blessed vision. Detestable is the neglectfulness which causes us to put off the cleansing of the eye. For just as our bodily vision is impeded either by a humor within, or by dust from outside entering the eye, so too is our spiritual vision disturbed by the desires of our own flesh or by wordly curiosity and ambition. Our own experience teaches us this, no less than the Sacred Page, where it is written, "The body which is corruptible weighs down the soul and the earthly habitation oppresses its thoughts" (Wis 9:15). But in both it is sin alone which dulls and confuses the vision; nothing else seems to stand between the eye and the light, between God and man. For while we are in this body we are in exile from the Lord (2 Cor 5:6).

That is not the body's fault, except in that it is yet mortal (Rom 7:24); rather it is the flesh which is a sinful body (Rom 6:6), the flesh in

which is no good thing but rather the law of sin reigns (Rom 7:23, 25).
Meanwhile the bodily eye (Gn 27:1), when the mote is no longer in it
(Mt 7:4) but has been taken or blown away, still seems dark (Mt 7:3ff.),
as he who walks in the spirit and sees deeply often experiences (2 Cor
12:18; Gal 5:16). For you will cure a wounded limb quickly by with-
drawing the sword, but only if you apply poultices to heal it. For no
one should think himself cleansed because he has come out of the cesspit. No, rather let him realize that he stands in need of a thorough
washing first. Nor must he be washed only with water; he needs to be
purged and refined by fire so as to say, "We have passed through fire
and water, and you have brought us to a resting place" (Ps 65:12).
"Blessed are the pure in heart, for they shall see God" (Mt 5:8). "Now
we see through a glass darkly, but hereafter face to face" (1 Cor 13:12).
Then truly our faces will be completely clean, so that he may present
them to himself shining, without stain or wrinkle (Eph 5:27).

XVIII.   Of the Peacemaker at Peace and Making Peace, "Blessed Are the Peacemakers," and so on

31. Here there follows immediately and appropriately, "Blessed are
the peacemakers, for they shall be called the children of God" (Mt 5:9).
A man is in a state of peace when he renders good for good (Rom
12:17ff.; 1 Thes 5:15), as far as it lies in him to do, and wishes harm to
no one. There is another kind of man who is patient; he does not render
evil for evil (Rom 12:17), and he is able to bear injury. Then there is
the peacemaker, who returns good for evil and is ready to do good even
to someone who harms him. The first is a little child and easily tripped
up (Mt 18:6). In this evil world (Gal 1:4) he will not readily be saved.
The second, as it is written, possesses his own soul in patience (Lk
21:19). The third not only possesses his own soul, but also wins the
souls of many others. The first possesses peace, as far as it lies in him
to do so. The second holds fast to peace. The third makes peace. He,
then, is deservedly blessed with the name "son" (1 Jn 3:1), because he
does the work of a son, for, grateful for his own reconciliation, he reconciles others to his Father too (2 Cor 5:18). So he who has served well
gains for himself a good position (1 Tm 3:3); there can be no better place
in the Father's house than that of his son. "For if sons, then heirs, heirs
of God and co-heirs with Christ" (Rom 8:17), so that, as he himself says,
where he is, there may his servant be too (Jn 12:26).

We have wearied you by talking for so long, and we have kept you longer than we should have done. Now time puts an end to our loquacity, as shame has not.

But remember what the Apostle said; we read that he once went on preaching (Ti 1:3) until midnight (Acts 20:7). "Would to God," to use his words, "that you could bear with a little of my folly. For I care jealously for your good as God himself does" (2 Cor 11:1).

XIX. An Attack upon the Ambitious Who Presume to Bring God's Peace to Others Before Their Own Hearts Are Pure

32. Little children, "Who made it clear to you that you should flee from the wrath to come?" (Mt 3:7; Lk 3:7). For no one deserves anger more than the enemy who pretends friendship: "Judas, do you betray the Son of Man with a kiss?" (Lk 22:48). You, a man of one mind with him (Ps 54:14–15), who used to take pleasant meals with him, whose hand dipped into the same dish (Mt 26:23), you have no part in the prayer with which he prays to the Father and says, "Father, forgive them, for they do not know what they are doing" (Lk 23:34). Woe to you who take away the key not only of knowledge but also of authority; you do not enter in yourself and in many ways you prevent those you ought to introduce from entering in (Lk 11:52). You steal the keys rather than receiving them. The Lord asks about such through the prophet. "They have reigned but not by me. They have chosen princes but I did not call them to the thrones they occupy" (Hos 8:4).

Whence comes such zeal for preferment, such shameless ambition, such folly of human presumption? Surely none of us would dare to take over the ministry of any earthly king, even the most minor, without his instructions (especially when he actually prohibits it) or to seize his benefices or conduct his affairs? Do not suppose then that God will approve of what he endures from those in his great house who are vessels fit for destruction (Rom 9:22).

Many come, but consider who is called. Listen to the Lord's words in their order. "Blessed," he says, "are the pure in heart, for they shall see God" and then, "Blessed are the peacemakers, for they shall be called the children of God" (Mt 5:8). The heavenly Father calls the pure in heart (Mt 5:9) who do not seek for themselves but for Christ, and not what will profit them but what will profit many. "Peter," he says, "do you love me?" "Lord, you know that I love you." "Feed my sheep," he replies (Mt 5:48ff.). For when would he commit such beloved sheep to someone who did not love them? This question of who is found to be a faithful servant is much debated among clerks.

Woe to unfaithful stewards who, themselves not yet reconciled, take on themselves the responsibility for recognizing righteousness in others, as if they were themselves righteous men (Is 68:2). Woe to the sons of wrath (Eph 2:3) who profess that they are ministers of grace. Woe to the sons of wrath who are not afraid to usurp to themselves the rank and name of "peacemaker." Woe to the sons of wrath who pretend to be mediators of peace, and who feed on the sins of the people. Woe to those who, walking in the flesh, cannot please God (Rm 8:8) and presume to wish to please him.

THE STARTLING USURPATION OF THE HIGHEST RANK OF PEACEMAKER BY THOSE WHO HAVE NOT REACHED THE LOWER RANKS, NOT EVEN THE FIRST

33. We do not wonder, my brothers, we who take pity on the present state of the Church; we do not wonder at the basilisk which arises from the serpent-root (Is 14:29). We do not wonder if he who wanders from the way the Lord has laid down steals the grapes from the Lord's vineyard (Is 5:7; Ps 79:13). For the man who has not yet heard in his heart the voice of the Lord calling him (Is 46:8), or if perhaps he begins to hear it, he takes flight back into the undergrowth to hide (Gn 3:9–10), impudently appropriates the rank of peacemaker (Mt 5:9) and takes the place which belongs to a son of God. As a result he has not yet stopped sinning, but is still dragging a long rope. He has not yet become a man who perceives his own poverty (Lam 3:1). He says, "I am rich, and in need of nothing," although he is poor and naked and wretched and pitiable (Rv 3:17). He has nothing of the spirit of gentleness (1 Cor 4:21) with which he could instruct those who are caught in sin (Gal 6:1), bearing in mind his own susceptibility to temptation. He knows nothing of tears of compunction. Rather, he rejoices when he has done wrong, and exults in his worst deeds (Prv 2:14). He is one of those to whom the Lord says, "Woe to you who laugh now, for you will weep" (Lk 6:25). He desires money, not justice (Lk 1:78). His eyes are caught by anything which is showy (Jb 41:25). He hungers insatiably for honor and thirsts for human glory. He has no bowels of mercy (Col 3:12). Rather,

he rejoices in his anger and behaves like a tyrant. He seeks to make a profit from piety (1 Tm 6:5). What am I to say about the purity of his heart? Would that he had not given it over to forgetfulness like a dead man who has no thoughts (Ps 30:13). Would that he were not a "dove gone astray and having no heart" (Hos 7:11). The bodily garment is found to be stained; would that even the outside were clean, so that he could obey at least in part him who says, "Be clean, you who bear the vessels of God" (Is 52:1).

XX. That the Incontinent Do Not Fear Boldly to Take Holy Orders

34. While we do not accuse everyone, yet we cannot excuse everyone. The Lord has left himself many thousands (Rom 11:4). Otherwise, if their righteousness did not excuse us and the Lord of Sabaoth had not left us a holy seed (Rom 9:29), we should have been overwhelmed long ago like Sodom and punished like Gomorrah (Jer 50:40).

The Church seems to have grown. Even the most holy order of the clergy is multiplied beyond counting (Ps 39:6). But even if you have multiplied the people, Lord, you have not made joy greater (Is 9:3), and merit seems to have decreased as much as numbers have increased. Everywhere people are rushing to join sacred orders, and they seize with neither reverence nor consideration upon ministries which the angels themselves regard with veneration. For the ungodly do not fear to take up the banner of the heavenly kingdom or to wear the crown of its jurisdiction, men in whom greed rules, ambition gives the orders, pride holds sway, iniquity is enthroned, lust is the principal ruler. If, following the prophecy of Ezekiel, we were to dig under the wall to see something horrible in God's house, in these men the worst abomination would perhaps appear within the walls (Ez 8:8). Truly, having committed fornication and adultery and incest (1 Cor 6:9; 1 Cor 5:1), some do not fail to go on to ignominious passions and nameless deeds (Rom 1:26). Would that these things (which are still the same breach of proper behavior) were not still being committed today. Would that the Apostle did not need to write these things, nor we to speak of them. Would that when we speak of such abominable things ever crossing any man's mind, no one would believe us.

Is it not true that those cities which gave rise to this filth were once foredoomed by divine judgment and destroyed by fire (Gn 19:24

ff.)? Did not the flame of hell, unable to wait (2 Pt 2:3), come to destroy that accursed nation because its sins were an outstanding eye-
sore and went before it to judgment (2 Tm 5:24)? Did not that fire
and sulfur and that stormy wind (Ps 10:7) wipe out the land as if
aware of such confusion? Was it not all reduced to nothing more than
a dreadful lake? The five heads of the hydra were cut off, but alas,
countless more sprang up. Who has rebuilt the cities of vice? Who
has widened their walls of shame? Who has spread their poisonous
offspring over the earth? Woe, woe, the enemy of men has strewn
the wretched remnants of that sulfurous burning all around; with its
disgusting ashes he has sprinkled the body of the Church (Col 1:18),
and even some of her ministers, too, with its most fetid and foul matter! Alas, "a chosen people, a royal priesthood, a holy nation, a people
for possession" (1 Pt 2:9), who at first were flowing with the divine
and spiritual graces of the Christian religion, is it to be believed that
such things could ever be found in you?

36. Marked with this stain they enter the tabernacle (Ex 28:43;
Nm 8:15) of the living God (Dt 5:26). With this mark on them they
dwell in his temple, polluting the Lord's holy place (Lev 19:8); they
will receive a multiple condemnation, because they carry such burdened consciences and nevertheless enter God's sanctuary (Ps 72:17,
82:13). Such not only do not please God; they anger him, when they
seem to be saying in their hearts, "He will require it" (Ps 9:34).
They anger him a good deal, and set him against themselves, and I
fear that they do so in the very acts which ought to bring them closer
to him.

Would that when they were about to begin to build the tower
they would sit down and count the cost in case they do not have
enough to finish it (Lk 14:28). Would that those who cannot contain
themselves stood in fear of rashly professing a state of perfection or
taking the name of celibates. It is a costly tower indeed, and a great
word, which not all can accept (Mt 19:11). But it would undoubtedly
be better to marry than to burn (1 Cor 7:9), and to remain in the
lower rank of the faithful people and be saved than to live a worse
life in the high rank of the clergy and be judged the more severely.
For many—not all, but still many, so many that they certainly cannot be hidden, nor in their impudence do they want to be—many
seem to have bestowed the freedom in which they were called upon
the flesh (Gal 5:13), abstaining from the remedy of marriage and
then wallowing in wickedness.

XXI. EXHORTATION TO REPENTANCE, AND TO SEEK A HUMBLE
PLACE FIRST AND ONLY AFTER BECOMING WORTHY
TO LOOK TO HIGHER HONOR

37. Spare your souls, I beg you brothers, spare them, spare the blood
which was shed for you (Mt 26:28). Beware of the fearful danger; turn
from the fire which is prepared (Mt 25:41). Do not let the profession of
perfection turn out to be a mockery. Let virtue take a straightforward
form in holiness (2 Tm 3:5). Do not let the form of the celibate life be
vain and empty of truth. Does chastity not stand in danger from pleasure, humility from riches, piety from worldly business, truth from
chattering, love from this wicked world (Gal 1:4)? Flee from the midst
of Babylon, flee and save your souls (Jer 48:6; 51:6). Fly to the cities of
refuge[17] (Jos 21:36) where you can do penance for past sins and also
obtain grace in the present and confidently await future glory. Let not
consciousness of sins hold you back, for where sins abound, grace
abounds the more (Rom 5:20). Let not the severity of penance deter
you, for the sufferings of this present time are nothing in comparison
with past sin, which is forgiven, nor with the glory to come which is
promised to us (Rom 8:18). And there is no bitterness that the prophet's
meal cannot sweeten or wisdom, the tree of life (Gn 2:9), make delicious.
38. If you do not believe words, believe deeds (Jn 10:38). Accept
the evidence of many men's example. Sinners rush from all sides to repent and those delicate by habit and nature alike think nothing of outward discomfort if it eases the gnawing of their conscience. Nothing is
impossible to those who believe (Mt 17:19). Nothing is difficult for
those who love. Nothing is harsh to the meek. Nothing is hard to the
humble, who are assisted by grace (Jas 4:6) and whose obedience is under the tender command of devotion.
Why do you walk in great and wonderful things which are beyond
you? It is a great and wonderful thing to be a minister of Christ and a
steward of God's mysteries (1 Cor 4:1). The order of peacemakers is far
above you, unless perhaps you prefer to leap rather than climb, and
leave out the stages which come first. Would that he who enters in that
way could administer as faithfully as he confidently pushed his way in.
But it is difficult, perhaps impossible, for the sweet fruit of love to ripen

---

17. I.e., monasteries.

from the bitter root of ambition. I say to you, yet not I but the Lord (1 Cor 7:10), "When you are called to the wedding-feast sit down in the lowest place, for everyone who exalts himself will be humbled and he who humbles himself will be exalted" (Lk 14:8–10).

XXII.   On the Endurance of Persecution According to the Last Beatitude, "Blessed Are Those Who Suffer Persecution, . . . Blessed Are You . . . " and so on

39. "Blessed," he says, "are the peacemakers, for they shall be called the children of God" (Mt 5:9). Consider carefully that it is not the people who call for peace but those who make peace who are commended. For there are those who talk but do nothing (Mt 23:3). For just as it is not the hearers of the law but the doers who are righteous (Rom 2:13), so it is not those who preach peace but the authors of peace who are blessed. Would that today's Pharisees—for perhaps there are some—would at least say what they ought, even if they do not do it. Would that those who do not wish to preach the Gospel unless they are paid (1 Cor 9:18) might at least preach it for money. Would that they preached the Gospel if only so that they could eat!

"The hireling," the Bible says, "sees the wolf coming and flees" (Jn 10:12). Oh, that those who are not shepherds today would show themselves to be hirelings in charge of the sheep and not wolves. Would that they did not themselves injure the sheep and flee when no one is pursuing (Prv 28:1). Would that they might not expose the flock to danger when they see the wolf coming. They had to be endured when they were found, especially in time of peace, receiving their pay and, if only for the money (Mt 6:2, 6:5), working to guard the sheep: as long as they themselves did not disturb the sheep and drive them away from the pastures of righteousness and truth for nothing. But persecution separates and distinguishes the hirelings from the shepherds beyond question (Mt 25:32). For when did he who seeks worldly reward not fear passing losses? When did he who wants money more than righteousness endure worldly persecution for righteousness' sake? "The blessed," he says, "are those who suffer persecution for righteousness' sake, for theirs is the kingdom of heaven" (Mt 5:10). This happiness belongs to shepherds, not hirelings. Far less is it the reward of robbers or wolves. They do not suffer persecution for righteousness' sake so much as preferring to endure persecution rather than maintain right-eousness. Truly, it is contrary to their way of working; it troubles them even to hear of it (Wis 2:12ff.).

40. For the rest, you can see men ready to stir up trouble, to bear hatred, to pretend to be ashamed, to ignore curses, to undergo all risks for the sake of avarice and ambition; no less ruinous is the animosity of men like that than the feebleness of hirelings. Their own good shepherd who was ready to lay down his life for the sheep says to the shepherds (Jn 10:10–15), "Blessed shall you be when men shall hate you and when they shall separate you and cast out your name as evil, for the Son of Man's sake. Be glad and rejoice when that happens, for your reward is great in heaven" (Lk 6:22).

Those whose treasure is in heaven have no reason to fear (Mt 6:19–20). There is no reason for them to complain about many tribulations when they are confident of a manifold reward. No, let them rather re-joice, as is fitting, that it is not so much persecution which is increased as reward, and let them rejoice the more that they bear many things for Christ, so that with him henceforth a more abundant reward may wait for them (Mt 5:12). "Why are you fearful, O ye of little faith" (Mt 8:26)? The faithful word stands firm on the changeless truth, for no adversity can hurt you if no wickedness has you in its control. But it is a small thing that it will not hurt you; it will even profit you, and abundantly, as long as righteousness is your purpose and Christ is your cause, with whom "the patience of the poor will never perish" (Ps 9:19). To him be glory now and forever, world without end (1 Pt 5:11; 2 Pt 3:18).

ON THE STEPS OF
HUMILITY AND PRIDE

*The treatise on humility was the first of Bernard's published
works, written within ten years of his foundation of Clairvaux.
The subject was one on which he had given talks in the past, and
Godfrey of Langres, abbot of Fontenay,[1] had asked him for a
book which he could use with his own monks. Godfrey had been
Bernard's prior at Clairvaux until he was sent to be abbot of the
new foundation, and he had had opportunities to hear Bernard's
talk for himself.*

*The title is misleading, as Bernard realized. He writes not
about humility but about pride. He explains why at the end of
the treatise in a little jest: He himself knows more about pride
than humility and so he has written of what he knows at first-
hand. Still, the title had been a stumbling-block to some of his
readers, and he added a note about it to the preface in later copies.[2] But he did not alter the title. He continued to see pride and
humility in an intimate relationship. Those who know the downward path of the descending steps of pride also know the way
back. They can retrace their steps and learn humility (see Hum
57 and 27).*

---

1. On the foundation of Fontenay in 1119, see L. Janauschek, *Originum Cisterciensium*
(Vienna, 1877), p. 8, with a brief biography of Godfrey. Godfrey eventually returned to
Clairvaux.

2. Hum 57 and Retractatio.

THE STEPS

Pride	Humility
1. Curiosity about what is not one's proper concern.	12. Containment of one's interests, which shows itself in a humble bearing and lowered eyes.
2. Light-mindeness: chatter and exclamations about things which do not matter.	11. Quiet and restrained speech.
3. Laughing about nothing; foolish merriment.	10. Reluctance to laugh.
4. Boasting and talking too much.	9. Keeping silent unless asked to speak.
5. Trying to be different: claiming special rights.	8. Regarding oneself as having no special rights in the community.
6. Thinking oneself holier than others.	7. Thinking oneself less holy than others.
7. Interfering presumptuously with the affairs of others.	6. Thinking oneself unworthy to take initiative.
8. Self-justification. Defending one's sinful actions.	5. Confessing one's sins.
9. Insincere confession.	4. Patience in the face of accusation.
10. Rebellion against superiors.	3. Submission to superiors.
11. Feeling free to sin.	2. Desiring no freedom to exercise one's will.
12. Habitual sinning.	1. Constant watchfulness against sin.

RETRACTATION

In this little work I mentioned the Lord's saying in the Gospel that he did not know the day of judgment. I cited the text in support of a point I was making. It was rash to do it from memory, because afterwards I could not find it in the Gospel. I was mistaken in thinking the text said, "Nor did the Son know." It was not a deliberate error. Yet although I remembered the words wrongly, I got the sense right. I should have said, "Not even the Son of Man knows" (Mk 13:32).

What I tried to prove in the argument which I developed from this incorrect quotation was true. But because my error was not noticed until much later, when the book was already published and many copies had been made, I could not pursue the error through them all one by one, and I have been obliged to take refuge in confession.[1]

In another place I wrote something about the seraphim which I have never heard anyone say and nowhere read. It occurs, as my reader will see, at a point where I have said, "I think," wishing to indicate that this was only my opinion, because I could not support it from Scripture.[2]

The title is "On the Steps of Humility," yet I have spoken not of the steps of humility but of those of pride. I have been criticized for this (Hos 5:11), but by those who did not understand, or think about the reason for the title, which I took care to explain briefly at the end of the book.[3]

Preface

You asked me, brother Godfrey, to give a fuller account for you in a book of what I said to the brothers about the steps of humility. I wanted to do justice to your request (Mk 15:15), as it deserved, but I feared that it would be beyond me. I was not able to find the boldness to begin until I had remembered the Gospel's advice (Lk 14:28) and then I sat down and counted up to see whether I had enough resources to complete it. Love conquered my fear (1 Jn 4:18) that I should not be able to finish the work (Lk 14:30). Then another fear swept me from the opposite direction, I began to fear that I should stand in a greater danger of pride if I did complete it than of ignominy if I failed. There I was at the cross-roads, hesitating long between fear and love, undecided to which road I might more safely commit myself, fearing either to try to speak profitably of humility when I should myself be found lacking in

---

1. The misquotation occurs in Hum 11. Bernard, like all his contemporaries, habitually quoted from memory and similar slips are not uncommon.

2. The notion that arguments can be "proved" correct by citing authorities in support of them as well as by reasoning is fundamental to classical and medieval rhetorical theory.

3. Hum 57.

it, or to keep silent and be found useless. And since I saw that neither road was safe, but I had to take one or the other, I chose to do what I could to bring you the fruit of my talk rather than to lurk for my own safety in the harbor of silence. At the same time I feel confident that if perhaps I shall have said anything you approve of, I shall be saved from pride by your prayers; but if on the other hand, which I think more likely, you find nothing worth your attention, then I shall have nothing to be proud about.

The Reward to Which the Steps of Humility Lead

I.1. I am going to speak of the steps of humility which the blessed Benedict set before us to climb (although he does not ask us to count them).[4] But first I shall show if I can where we shall arrive at if we reach the top, so that when you have heard what the reward is, the labor of the climb will seem less.

Our Lord shows us both the difficulty of the way and the reward of the labor. "I am the way, the truth and the life" (Jn 14:6). The way, he says, is humility, which leads to truth. The first is labor; the second is the reward for the labor (1 Cor 3:8). But, you ask, how do I know that he is speaking of humility when he says only, "I am the way"? Listen to this clearer statement, "Learn from me, for I am meek and humble of heart" (Mt 11:29). He offers himself as an example of humility, a model of gentleness. If you imitate him you will not walk in darkness; you will have the light of life (Jn 8:12). What is the light of life but truth, which enlightens every man who comes into this world (Jn 1:9), showing him where true life lies (1 Tim 6:19)? That is why when he said, "I am the way, the truth," he added, "and the life," which, he says, "I give." "For this is eternal life," he says, "to know that you are the true God and to know him whom you have sent, Jesus Christ" (Jn 17:3). Or it is as though you were to say, "I reflect on the way; that is humility. I desire the reward, which is truth. But what if the way is so difficult that I cannot reach the desired reward?" He replies, "I am the life," that is, food for the journey (Dt 15:14; Jos 9:5).[5] To those who go astray and do not know the road, he says, "I am

---

    4. RB 7; cf. Gregory the Great, *Moralia*, IX.36, ed. M. Adraiaen, CCSL 143 (Turnholt, 1979).
    5. *Viaticum:* Bernard probably means food for a journey (Dt 15:14; Jos 9:5), rather than communion brought to the dying, although that usage was familiar in his time.

the way." To those who hesitate to believe, he says, "I am the truth." To those who are already climbing, he says, "I am the life."

I think I have shown clearly enough from this chapter of the Gospel that the fruit of the knowledge of truth is humility. But listen to another text. "I praise you, Father of heaven and earth, because you have hidden these things" (which surely means the secrets of truth), "from the knowing and prudent" (that is, the proud), "and revealed them to the little ones" (that is, the humble) (Mt 11:25). And here it is clear that truth, which is hidden from the proud, is revealed to the humble (Jas 4:6; 1 Pt 5:5).

I.2. Here is a definition of humility. "Humility is the virtue by which a man recognizes his own unworthiness because he really knows himself."[6] This description fits those who have resolved to make the climb and who go from strength to strength, that is, from step to step, until they reach the highest peak of humility,[7] on which, standing as though in Sion (Ps 83:6), that is, at a vantage point, they see the truth.

The lawgiver, it says, "will give a blessing" (Ps 83:8), for he who gave the law also gave a blessing. That is, he who told us to be humble leads us to the truth. Who is this lawgiver? It is the sweet and just Lord, who gives the law to those who have gone astray (Ps 24:8). Those who have turned aside from truth have indeed lost their way. But surely our sweet Lord does not abandon them? No! The sweet and just Lord gives them the law of the way of humility, by which they may return to the knowledge of the truth. He gives them a means of regaining safety, for he is gentle; but not without the discipline of the law, for he is just. He is gentle, for he does not let them perish; he is just, for he does not forget that punishment is necessary.[8]

II.3. And so St. Benedict sets out in twelve steps[9] this law by which men are brought back to the truth; so just as a man comes to the ten commandments of the law (Ex 24:28) and the twofold circumcision (Gn 17:26),[10] which add up to twelve, so truth may be grasped by these twelve ascending steps.

The Lord appears, leaning on the top of the ladder, which is the

6. Compare Augustine, *In Johannem*, Tract 25.16, CCSL 36 (Turnholt, 1954).

7. RB 7.5; cf. SC 34.3.

8. Cf. Anselm, *Cur Deus Homo*, I.12, ed. F. S. Schmitt, *Anselmi Opera Omnia* (Rome/Edinburgh, 1938–1968), Vol. II.

9. RB 7. 10–66.

10. Also Dt 30:6; Jos 5:2; Jer 4:4; Col 2:11.

ladder revealed to Jacob as a model of humility (Gn 28:12).[11] What does he show by his presence there but that the knowledge of truth is to be found at the peak of humility?[12] The Lord looks down on the sons of men (Ps 13:2) from the top of the ladder with the eyes of truth. They cannot deceive and they cannot be deceived, and they look to see if there is anyone who knows God and is seeking him. Surely you can hear him crying from above to those who are seeking him (for he knows who are his own [2 Tm 2:19; Jn 10:14]), "Come to me all who desire me, and be filled with my fruits" (Sir 24:26). "Come to me all who labor and are heavy-laden, and I will refresh you" (Mt 11:28).

"Come," he says. Where? "To me (Mt 11:28), the truth." How? By humility. For what reward? "I will refresh you."

What is this refreshment that Truth promises to those who are climbing and which he gives to those who reach the top? Perhaps it is love itself? To this, as the blessed Benedict says, the monk will quickly come when he has climbed all the steps of humility.[13] Truly, love is a sweet and pleasant food, which refreshes the weary, strengthens the weak (Is 35:3), makes the sad joyful, the yoke of Truth sweet and its burden light (Mt 11:30).

II.4. Love is good food, which is placed in the middle of Solomon's plate (Sg 3:9),[14] fragrant with the many scents (Sg 1:2) of the virtues as if with a multitude of spices (Sg 3:6). It nourishes the hungry and makes them joyful as they eat. There peace, patience, kindness, longsuffering (Gal 5:22), joy in the Holy Spirit (Rm 14:17) are added; and if there are any other fruits of truth or wisdom, they are to be seen there.

Humility also has its feast on the same plate. This is the bread of sorrow (Ps 126:2), and the wine of compunction (Ps 59:5). These are offered first to beginners. To them it is said, "Rise up after you have eaten, you who eat the bread of sorrow" (Ps 126:2).

Then contemplation brings the solid food of wisdom (Heb 5:14), made from the finest flour (Ps 147:14), with the wine which makes men's hearts glad (Ps 103:15). To this Truth invites the perfect with the words, "Eat, my friends, and drink; be intoxicated, dearest" (Sg 5:1).

---

11. RB 7.6.
12. RB 7.5.
13. RB 7.67.
14. The word *ferculum* here can also mean a "litter" on which Solomon himself would be carried.

To those who are not yet perfect he says, "Love lies in the middle for the daughters of Jerusalem" (Sg 3:10). While they cannot yet digest that solid food they are nourished in the meantime with the milk of love for bread, and oil instead of wine. This is rightly called "in the middle," because the sweetness would be too much for beginners, who are held back by fear; and the perfect find it unsatisfying in comparison with the richer sweetness of contemplation. While they are still being poisoned by fleshly delights, and have not yet been purged by the bitter drink of fear, beginners do not yet taste the sweetness of milk. The perfect turn from milk and delight to feast on the more glorious food of which they have had a taste. Only those in between who are still on the way are satisfied by the sweet foods of love which are intended for the young and tender.[15]

II.5. The first food, then, is humility. It purges by its bitterness. The second is the food of love, which consoles by its sweetness. The third is the food of contemplation, solid and strengthening.

Lord God of hosts, how long will you be angry with your servant who prays to you? How long will you feed me with the bread of weeping and give me tears to drink (Ps 79:5ff.)? Who will invite me to the middle banquet of the sweet food of love, where the just feast in the sight of God and exult in his joy (Ps 67:4)? Then I shall no longer cry out to God in bitterness of soul, "Do not condemn me" (Jb 10:1); and feasting on the unleavened bread of sincerity and truth (1 Cor 5:8) I shall joyfully sing in the ways of the Lord (Ps 137:5), for great is his glory. The way of humility is good (Ps 118:71), for by it we seek truth, attain love, and share the fruits of wisdom. Then, just as Christ is the fulfillment of the law (Rom 10:4), so the end result of humility is the knowledge of truth. For he makes himself known to the humble. "He gives grace," therefore "to the humble" (1 Pt 5:5).

III.6. I have said as well as I can with what reward the climber will meet at the top of the steps of humility. I shall now say, as far as I am able, in what order the steps lead to the promised reward of truth.

---

15. These three stages of spiritual growth were traditional; they provide William of St. Thierry with a framework for his Golden Epistle. See M. B. Pennington, "Three Stages of Spiritual Growth according to St. Bernard," *Studia Monastica* 11 (1969): 315–326.

In What Order the Steps of Humility
Lead to the Promised Reward

Because the knowledge of truth itself comes in three stages, I shall distinguish them briefly if I can, so as to make it clearer how the twelve steps of humility lead to the three degrees of truth. For we seek truth in ourselves, in our neighbors, and for its own sake.

We seek it in ourselves in judging ourselves (1 Cor 11:31), in our neighbors by suffering with them (1 Cor 12:26), and in itself by contemplating it with a pure heart (Mt 5:8).

Take note of the order of these degrees as well as their number. First, Truth himself teaches you that the nature of truth must first be sought in our neighbors before we seek it in itself. After this you will be shown why you ought to seek it in yourself before you seek it in your neighbor. In the list of beatitudes which he gave in the Sermon on the Mount the Lord put the merciful before the pure in heart (Mt 5:7–8). The merciful are quick to see the truth in their neighbors when they feel for them, and unite themselves with them in love so closely that they feel their goods and ills as their own. When the weak suffer, they suffer. When their neighbors are led into sin they burn for them (2 Cor 11:29). They "rejoice with those who rejoice and weep with those who weep" (Rom 12:15). With hearts purified by this brotherly love they delight in the contemplation of truth in itself, for whose love they bear the troubles of others.

Those who do not share the troubles of others but, on the contrary, spurn those who weep or mock those who are happy, and do not feel in themselves the feelings of others because they are not moved by their emotion, how can they find the truth in their neighbors? That common proverb fits them well, "The healthy man does not know what the sick man feels."[16] The man who is well fed does not know what the hungry man feels. The sick man more readily feels with the sick and the hungry man with the hungry. For just as pure truth is seen only with a pure heart, so he who is wretched at heart feels more truly with the wretchedness of his brother.

But to have a heart which is sad because of someone else's wretchedness you must first recognize your neighbor's mind in your own and understand from your own experience how you can help him.

---

16. Terence, *Andria*, 309, ed. J. Sargeaunt (London, 1953).

We have an example in our Savior. He wanted to suffer so that he should know how to suffer with us (Heb 2:17), to become wretched so that he could learn mercy, as it is written, "He learned obedience from the things he suffered" (Heb 5:8). He learned mercy in the same way. It is not that he did not know how to be merciful before. His mercy is from everlasting to everlasting (Ps 102:17). But what he knew by nature from eternity he learned from experience in time.

III.7. But perhaps you find it hard to accept the idea that Christ, the Wisdom of God (1 Cor 1:24) "learned" mercy, as if he through whom all things were made (Jn 1:3) had ever been ignorant of anything which exists; especially since the text I quoted from Hebrews to support this view can be understood in another sense which does not seem absurd. Thus, "he learned" can be taken to refer not to our Head in his own Person, but to his body, which is the Church (Col 1:24), and then this is the sense: "And he learned obedience from the things he suffered" means that he learned in his body from what he suffered in his Head. For that death, that Cross, the opprobrium, the scorn, the beatings which Christ endured, what else were they but outstanding examples of obedience for his body, that is, ourselves?

Paul says, "Christ was made obedient to the Father unto death" (Phil 2:8).[17] Under what necessity? The apostle Peter answers, "Christ suffered for us, leaving you an example so that you might follow in his footsteps" (1 Pt 2:21), that is, so that we might imitate his obedience. From what he suffered, then, we learn how it behooves us as just men to suffer deeply for the sake of obedience; for he who was not only man but God did not hesitate to die for it. "And in this way," you are saying, "it was not unfitting to say that Christ 'learned' obedience or mercy or anything else, in his body. At the same time we believe that there was nothing he could learn in time in his Person which he did not know before. And so since Head and body (Col 1:18) are one Christ, he who teaches us to be obedient and merciful is the same as he who learns."

III.8. I do not deny that this interpretation is correct. But it seems that the first interpretation is supported by another text in the same letter, where it says, "For he did not help the angels, but he helped the seed of Abraham. Thus it was fitting that he should become like his brothers in all things, so that he might become merciful" (Heb 2:16–7). I think this is so clearly directed to the Head that it is impossible to take

---

17. RB 7.34.

it to refer to the body. It is certainly of the Word of God that it is said that "he did not help the angels," that is, that he did not assume the angel as one Person with him, "but the seed of Abraham." For we do not read, "The Word was made an angel," but "the Word was made flesh" (Jn 1:14), and flesh of the flesh of Abraham, according to the promise which was made to him at the first (Gn 17:7; Gal 3:29). It was fitting that he should become like his brothers in all things, that is, it was fitting and necessary that he should be able to suffer like us (Jas 5:17), and should experience all the kinds of misery we experience, except sin (Heb 4:15). If you ask by what necessity: so that he might become merciful (Heb 2:16).

You say, why cannot this be correctly referred to the body? But hear what comes immediately after, "For because he suffered and was tempted he is able to help those who are tempted" (Heb 2:18). I do not know how these words are to be better understood than in this way. He wanted to suffer and to be tempted and to share all our human miseries "except sin" (Heb 4:15)—for that is what it is to be "like his brothers in all things"—so that he might learn by his own experience to be merciful and to suffer with us in our sufferings and temptations.

III.9. I do not say that he was made wiser by the experience, but he came to seem nearer to us weak sons of Adam,[18] whom he did not disdain to make and to call his brothers (Heb 2:11). He wanted men to have no hesitation in entrusting their weaknesses to him, who was able as God to heal them and who wanted to do so as one close to them who understood because he had suffered the same weakness himself. It is for this reason that Isaiah calls him "A man of sorrows and acquainted with weakness" (Is 53:3). And the Apostle says, "We do not have a high priest who is unable to feel for our weaknesses" (Heb 4:15). He adds, to indicate how he is able to do so, "He was tempted at every point like us, but without sin" (Heb 4:15).

Blessed is God, blessed the Son of God, in that form in which he did not think it robbery to be equal with the Father (Phil 2:6). I do not doubt that he was impassible before he emptied himself and took the form of a servant (Phil 2:7), for just as he had not experienced wretchedness and subjection, so he had not known mercy or obedience by experience. He knew by nature, but not by experience.

---

18. *Quoad nos:* the notion that God, who is impassible, does not himself feel mercy in his divine nature, but that we feel the effect of that mercy, is explored by Anselm in *Proslogion*, 8, *Anselmi Opera Omnia*, Vol. I. 106. 11–12.

He became not only lower than himself, but also a little lower than the angels (Heb 2:9; Ps 8:6), for they too are impassible, though by grace not by nature. He lowered himself to that form in which he could suffer and be in subjection, for, as it is said, what he could not suffer in his divine nature he learned by the experience of suffering: mercy, and to be obedient in subjection.

Yet by that experience there grew, as I have said, not his knowledge but our faith, when by this wretched mode of knowledge he who had gone far astray brought himself near to us (Eph 2:13). When should we have dared to approach him if he had remained impassible?

But now, with the Apostle's encouragement, we are urged to come in faith to the throne of his grace (Heb 4:16), for, as it is written elsewhere, we know that he bore our weariness and grief (Is 53:4), and we can be sure he will have compassion on us because he has suffered himself (Heb 2:18, 4:15).

III.10. It ought not then to seem absurd if it is said that Christ did not begin to know something he once did not know, but began to know, by learning of it in the flesh in time, the mercy he had known in another way in his divinity from eternity (Ps 102:19).[19]

See if it is not said in a similar figure of speech that when the disciples asked the Lord when the Last Day would come, he said he did not know (Mk 13:32). But how could he be unaware of that day, for all the treasures of wisdom and knowledge lay in him (Col 2:3)? Why did he deny he knew what it is certain he must have known? Surely he did not want to hide it from them by telling them a lie, because it was not profitable for them to know it? Perish the thought! Just as he could not have been ignorant of anything, since he is wisdom, so he could not lie, because he is truth.

He wanted to discourage the disciples' curiosity about something it was not good for them to know. He replied that he did not know what they asked. He did not say that he was utterly ignorant of it, but in this way he was able truthfully to deny that he knew. In his divinity he knew all things equally. Past, present, and future were clear to him, including that day. But he could not know it by experience in any of his bodily senses. For if he did he would already have slain Antichrist with the breath of his mouth (2 Thes 2:8); he would already have heard in his bodily ears the archangel calling and sounding the trumpet (Jos

---

19. Cf. Miss 2.10; LTR 4.28.

6:20) at whose note the dead are to rise (Mt 10:8). He would already have seen with his eyes the sheep and goats which are to be separated from one another (Mt 25:32).

III.11. More: that you may be sure that he was able to say that he did not know when that day would be, in the knowledge he had in the flesh, notice that he answered carefully. He did not say, "I do not know," but, "Not even the son of man knows" (Mk 13:32).[20] The term "son of man" refers to the flesh he assumed. He used this name because he was saying that he did not know something as man, not as God. When he was speaking of himself according to his deity, he usually said not "the son" or "the son of man" but "I" or "me," as in this passage, "Amen, amen, I say to you; before Abraham was, I am" (Jn 8:58). He is clearly speaking here of that being which was before Abraham and without beginning, not that which came after Abraham and was born from Abraham.

At another time he asked his disciples what men thought of him. "Whom do men say," he asks, not "that I am" but, "that the son of man is"? (Mt 16:13). When he went on to ask them what they themselves thought, he said, "But you," not "whom do you say the son of man is?" but "whom do you say that I am?" (Mt 16:15). When he was asking what a carnal people thought about his flesh, he used the name of the flesh, which is properly "the son of man." When he was asking his spiritual disciples about his deity, he did not say "the son of man" but—significantly—"me."

Peter understood that, as we can see from his saying, "You are," he said, not "Jesus, Son of the Virgin," but "Christ, the Son of God" (Mt 16:16). If he had said the first, he would have spoken the truth. But he perceived the questioner's meaning in the wording of the question, and answered aptly and properly, saying, "You are Christ, the Son of God."

III.12. You see, then, that Christ has two natures in one Person, one which always was and another which began to be. And according to that nature which was eternally his he always knew everything. But according to that which began in time (Rom 1:3), he experienced many things in time. In this way he began to know the miseries of the flesh, by that mode of cognition which the weakness of the flesh instructs.

Our first parents were wiser and happier when they did not know

---

20. See *Retractation*, at the opening of Hum.

that which they came to know only foolishly and in wretchedness. But God their Creator, seeking what was lost, came down in mercy in pursuit of his wretched creatures, to where they had miserably fallen (Ez 34:16). He wanted to experience for himself what they were (rightly) suffering because they had gone against his will. He came not out of a curiosity like theirs, but out of a wonderful charity. He did not intend to remain wretched among them, but to free those who were wretched as one made merciful. "Made merciful" (Heb 2:17), I say, not with that mercy which he who remained happy had had from eternity (Ps 102:17), but with that mercy which he discovered as a mediator who was one of us. The work of his holiness, which began at the prompting of the first mercy, was completed in the second; not because the first mercy was not enough, but because only the second kind could fully satisfy us. Both were needed, but the second kind fitted our condition better. Oh, supreme delicacy of thoughtfulness! Should we have been able to imagine that wonderful mercy if we had not seen it come to us in wretchedness? Should we have been able even to conceive of that unknown compassion toward us if the impassability which is everlasting had not come to us in the Passion?

Yet if he who did not know wretchedness had not first had mercy, he would not have come to that which is the mother of wretchedness. If he had not come, he would not have drawn us to himself. If he had not drawn us, he would not have drawn us out.

From what did he draw us out? From the slough of misery and the mire of sin (Ps 39:3). He did not lose anything of his everlasting mercy. But he added this to it. He did not change it but he multiplied it, as it is written, "You will save man and beast, Lord. How you have multiplied your mercy, O God!" (Ps 35:7–8).

IV.13. But let us return to our subject. If he submitted himself to human misery so that he might not simply know it, but also experience it, how much more ought you, not perhaps to make yourself what you are not, but to be aware of what you are, that you are truly wretched; and so learn to be merciful, for you can learn it in no other way.

If you see your neighbor's failing and not your own you will be moved not to mercy but to indignation, not to help him but to judge him, not to instruct him in a spirit of gentleness but to destroy him in a spirit of anger. "You who are spiritual," says the Apostle, "teach in a spirit of gentleness" (Gal 6:1). His advice, or rather his precept, is to be gentle, that is, to help your brother as if he were sick—as you would wish to be helped yourself in sickness. And so that you may know how gentle you may be toward a wrongdoer, "Consider yourself," he says, "lest you too are tempted" (Gal 6:1).

IV.14. Notice how well Truth's pupil follows the sequence of his master's thoughts. In the beatitudes which I mentioned above, just as the merciful came before the pure in heart, so the meek are placed before the merciful (Mt 5:4–8). When the Apostle tells the spiritual man to teach the carnal-minded, he adds, "In a spirit of gentleness." The teaching of brothers belongs to the merciful, and the spirit of gentleness to the meek. It is as though he said that he who is not meek in himself cannot be counted among the merciful. See how the Apostle clearly shows what I promised above that I would show, that truth is first to be sought in yourself and then in your neighbor. "Think of yourself," he says, that is, how easily you are tempted, how prone you are to sin, how easily you let yourself off, and so hasten to help others in a spirit of gentleness (Gal 6:1).

If you do not listen to the disciple's warning, fear that of the Master, "Hypocrite, first cast out the beam from your own eye, and then you will see clearly to cast out the mote from your brother's eye" (Mt 7:5). Pride in the mind is a great beam which is bloated rather than heavy, swollen rather than solid, and it blocks the mind's eye and blots out the light of truth, so that if your mind is full of it you cannot see yourself as you really are.

Nor can you see what you might be. You see what you would like to be and think yourself to be, or hope that you will be. For what else is pride but, as one of the saints defines it, love of one's own excellence? That is why we can say the opposite, that humility is contempt of one's own worth.[21]

Neither love nor hatred can give a judgment of truth. Do you want to hear the judgment of truth? "As I hear, so I judge" (Jn 5:30), not, "As I hate," "As I love," "As I fear."

This is the judgment of hatred, "We have a law, and according to the law he ought to die" (Jn 19:7). There is a judgment of fear, "If we leave him alone, the Romans will come and destroy our place and nation" (Jn 11:48). This is the judgment of love, as David said to his son who wanted to kill him, "Spare the boy Absalom" (2 Sm 18:5). I know that it is decreed in human laws, and in both secular and ecclesiastical

---

21. Augustine, *Ennarrationes in Psalmos*, Psalm 188, *Sermo* 22.5–6, ed. O. Faller, CCSL, 38 (Turnholt, 1956); *De Genesi ad Litteram* XI.xiv.18, PL 34.436. Cf. Bernard in Mor 19, PL 182.821; Div 47; LTR 6ʹ, 267.

causes, that special friends of the litigants may not try their cases, in case they are misled, or mislead others by their love.[22] If love can make you diminish, or even hide, your friend's fault, how much more will your judgment deceive you when you think of your own faults?

IV.15. He who wants to know the whole truth about himself must, when he has removed the beam of pride (Mt 7:5) which is cutting off his eye from the light, cut steps in his heart (Ps 83:6) by which he can find himself in himself, and thus he will come after the twelve steps of humility to the first step of pride. For when he has discovered the truth about himself, or better, when he has seen himself in truth, he can say, "I have believed, and therefore I have spoken. I have been profoundly humbled" (Ps 115:10).

Such a man has come to the depths of his heart (Ps 63:7), and truth is exalted. When he arrives at the second step he will say, in ecstasy, "Every man is a liar" (Ps 115:11). Do you think that David was not here? Do you think this prophet did not feel what the Lord, the Apostle, and we ourselves feel after them and through them? "I have believed," he says, speaking to the Truth. "He who follows me will not walk in darkness" (Jn 8:12).

"I have believed," he continues, "and therefore I have spoken," in faith. In what faith? Believing the truth I have known. Afterward we have, "I have believed," to righteousness, and "I have spoken," for salvation, and "I have been profoundly," that is, completely, "humbled" (Jas 2:23).

It is as though he said, "Because I have not been ashamed to confess the truth against myself which I have come to know in myself, I have progressed to utter humility." "Profound" can be understood as "utter," as in, "He takes profound delight in his commandments" (Ps 111:1). If anyone argues that here the word does not mean "utterly" but merely "very much,"[23] as some expositors say, that is not out of keeping with the prophet's meaning. We can interpret him as saying, "I, when I was still in ignorance of the truth, thought myself something when I was nothing (Gal 6:3). But after I had come to believe in Christ, that is, to imitate his humility, I learned the truth and that truth is raised up in me by my confession. But 'I am profoundly humbled,' that is, I have been greatly lowered in my own estimation" (Ps 115:10).

---

22. Bernard would have known of this rule of litigation as a matter of normal contemporary practice.

23. Bede, *De Orthographia*, PL 90.139.

V.16. The prophet has been humbled then in this first step of humility, as he says in another Psalm, "And in your truth you have humbled me" (Ps 118:75). He has been thinking about himself. Now he looks from his own wretchedness to that of others, and so passes to the second step, saying in his ecstasy (*excessus*), "Every man is a liar" (Ps 115:11).

What is meant by this "ecstasy"? It is that state in which he is carried away from himself and clings to the truth and is able to judge himself (1 Cor 11:31). In that ecstasy of his he says—not angrily or accusingly, but full of mercy and compassion—"Every man is a liar."

What does it mean to say that "Every man is a liar"? Every man is weak, powerless, unable to save himself or others. Just as it is said that "A horse is a deceptive savior" (?Ps 32:17), not because a horse deceives anyone but because he who trusts in his own strength deceives himself, so every man is said to be a "liar," that is, to be frail, mutable. He cannot hope for salvation from himself, nor can anyone else hope for salvation from him. Rather, he who places his hope in man is cursed (Jer 17:5). And so the humble prophet makes progress, led along by truth. What he grieved at in himself, he now grieves at in others. What he sees he grieves at (Eccl 1:18), and he cries, speaking generally but truly, "Every man is a liar" (Ps 115:11).

V.17. This is very different from what the proud Pharisee feels about himself. What does he say in his "ecstasy"? "My God, I thank you that I am not like other men" (Lk 18:11).[24] While he exults in himself alone he arrogantly insults others. David is different. He says, "Every man is a liar." He made no exceptions, in case anyone should deceive himself, for he knew that "all have sinned and everyone needs the glory of God" (Rom 3:23). The Pharisee deceives only himself in making an exception of himself while he condemns others. The prophet does not except himself from the general wretchedness, lest he be left out of the mercy, too. The Pharisee waved mercy away when he denied his wretchedness. The prophet said of everyone, including himself, "Every man is a liar" (Ps 115:11). The Pharisee asserts it of everyone but himself. "I am not," he says, "like other men." He gave thanks not because he was good, but because he was unique. He was not so concerned with his own good as with the wickedness he saw in others. He

---

24. Cf. Ann 3.10; LTR 5.41ff.

had not yet cast out his beam and he was counting the motes in his brothers' eyes (Mt 7:5). For he added, "Unjust, robbers" (Lk 18:11). I think it is not in vain that I have digressed from the subject in hand if I have shown you the difference between the two kinds of "ecstasy."

V.18. Now let us come back to our subject. Those whom truth brings to know themselves it also causes to think little of themselves. It follows inevitably that all that they used to love will now become bitter to them. Brought face to face with themselves, they are forced to see things which fill them with shame. When they are distressed to see what they are, they long to be what they are not, and fear that they will never be by their own efforts. They grieve deeply over themselves, and the only consolation they can find is to judge themselves severely. They hunger and thirst after righteousness (Mt 5:6) and despise themselves utterly out of love for the truth. They demand full satisfaction for themselves, and a better life. But since they see that they cannot do it by themselves—for when they have done all that they were commanded they call themselves unprofitable servants (Lk 17:10)—they fly from justice to mercy. Truth advises them to do so. "Blessed are the merciful for they shall obtain mercy" (Mt 5:7).[25] This is the second step of truth, to look beyond one's own needs to the needs of one's neighbors, and to know how to suffer with them in their troubles (Heb 4:15).

VI.19. By these three things we have mentioned—the grief of repentance, the desire for righteousness, perseverance in works of mercy—the humble purify their hearts of the three impediments of ignorance, weakness, jealousy. And by contemplation they come to the third step of truth. These are ways which seem good to men (Prv 14:12, 16:25), to those who rejoice when they do wrong and exult in wicked things (Prv 2:14). They hide themselves behind their weakness and ignorance (Ps 140:4) so that they can go on having an excuse for their sins. Those who deliberately remain in weakness and ignorance so as to sin more freely smooth over their weakness and ignorance in vain. Do you think it did the first man any good to say that he did not sin of his own free will, but through his wife, that is, as if through weakness of the flesh (Gn 3:12)? What about those who stoned the first martyr? They stopped their ears. Can they be excused on grounds of ignorance (Acts 7:57)? Those who know themselves to be cut off from the truth by a

---

25. Cf. Conv 29, LTR 4.104ff.

strong love of sin and weighed down by weakness and ignorance, let them put that energy into bewailing their sin, and turn their love of sin into sorrow for sin.

Weakness can be overcome by a fervent desire for righteousness. Ignorance can be dispelled by generosity. If now they ignore Truth while he is naked and weak and in need; when he comes, terrifying with power and might and accusation (Lk 21:27; Mt 24:30), and when they recognize him too late, with shame and in vain will they answer trembling, "When did we see you in need and did not minister to you?" (Mt 25:44). They will know the Lord when he comes to judge (Ps 9:17), though now they take no notice of him when he pleads for mercy. The greedy will see him whom they have pierced (Jn 19:37) and spurned.

Let the eye of the mind then be purged of every weakness, ignorance, and jealousy by weeping, by zeal for righteousness (Mt 5:6), and by a continual striving to be merciful. Truth promises the pure in heart that they will see him. "Blessed are the pure in heart for they shall see God" (Mt 5:8).

These are the three steps of truth. We ascend the first by striving to be humble, the second by compassion, the third in the ecstasy of contemplation. In the first, Truth is discovered to be severe; in the second, holy; in the third, pure. Reason leads to the first, in which we think about ourselves. Affection leads to the second, in which we think about others. Purity leads to the third, in which we are lifted up to see what is out of sight.

VII.20. It occurs to me that there is a way in which each of these wonderful works can be thought of as the work of one of the Persons of the undivided Trinity. (If a man such as I, sitting in darkness [Lk 1:79], can distinguish the work of the Persons, who work together as one.) In the first step the Son is seen at work, in the second the Holy Spirit, in the third the Father.

Do you want to hear about the work of the Son? "If your Lord and Master washes your feet," he says, "how much more ought you to wash one another's feet?" (Jn 13:14).[26] The Master of truth set his disciples an example (Jn 13:15) of humility by which he showed them the first step toward truth. Note the work of the Holy Spirit, too. "Love is diffused in our hearts by the Holy Spirit who is given to us" (Rom 5:5). Love is the gift of the Holy Spirit; he gives it so that those who have

---

26. Cf. Ambrose, *De Mysteriis* 6.33, ed. O. Faller, CSEL 73 (Vienna, 1955).

already proceeded to the first step of truth by humility under the discipline of the Son may, through their compassion for their neighbors, come to the second step under the guidance of the Holy Spirit. Lastly, hear what is said of the Father. "Blessed are you, Simon son of Jonah, for flesh and blood have not revealed it to you, but my Father who is in heaven" (Mt 16:17). And this, "The Father will reveal the truth to the sons" (Is 38:19). And, "I confess to you, Father, for you have hidden these things from the wise and revealed them to children" (Mt 11:25).

You see that those whom the Son first humbles by word and example, and upon whom the Spirit afterward pours out love, these the Father receives at length in glory. The Son makes us disciples. The Paraclete comforts us as friends. The Father raises us up as sons. And because not only the Son but also the Father and the Holy Spirit are truly called Truth, it is agreed that one and the same truth, preserving the properties of the Persons, works in these three steps. The first teaches us like a master. The second comforts like a friend or brother. The third embraces us as a father does his sons.

VII.21. The Son of God, the Word and Wisdom of the Father, first mercifully assuming that power of our souls which is called reason, when he found it weighed down by the body (Wis 9:15),[27] a captive to sin, blinded by ignorance, given up to outward things,[28] he mercifully assumed it; he lifted it by his power, instructed it by his wisdom, drew it within himself and employed it in a wonderful way on his behalf as judge. It is truth's task to judge. That is why, out of reverence for the Word to which it is united, human reason becomes its own accuser, witness, and judge (Prv 18:17). From this first union of the Word and reason is born humility.

The Holy Spirit lovingly visited the second power of the soul, the will. He found it infected with the poison of the body, but already judged by reason. He cleansed it with sweetness, making it burn with love and filling it with mercy, so that like a skin which is made pliable with oil it would stretch wide and bring the heavenly oil of love even to its enemies. And so from this second union, of the Spirit of God and the human will, love is born.

The soul is now perfect in two parts, reason and will, the one taught by the word of truth (2 Cor 6:7), the other set on fire by the spirit

---

27. Cf. Pre 59; LTR 3.292; Asc 3.1; LTR 5.131.
28. Cf. Div 45.2; LTR 6–1, 263.

of truth (1 Jn 4:6). It is sprinkled with the hyssop of humility (Ps 50:9), and inflamed by love. It is purged of stains by humility and love smoothes out all its wrinkles (Eph 5:27). The reason never shrinks from truth. The will never strives against reason.

This blessed Bride the Father binds[29] to himself. Now the reason is not thinking of itself; the will does not strive against its neighbor.[30] This blessed soul speaks of this one delight, "The King has led me into his chamber" (Sg 1:3, 3:4).[31]

She has become worthy to enter because of what she has learned in the school of humility where the Son was her teacher. He gave her this warning, "If you do not know yourself, go forth and let your herds graze" (Sg 1:3). She has become worthy, because of what she learned in the school of humility, to be led in love by the Holy Spirit to where charity is stored—to that storehouse which is the care of one's neighbors. There, cushioned by flowers, stayed up by apples (Sg 2:5),[32] that is, by the good deeds and virtues of the saints, she is admitted at last to the King's chamber, for whose love she languishes.

There for a short time, half an hour, while there is silence in heaven (Rv 8:1),[33] she sleeps sweetly and at peace in that longed-for embrace. But her mind is alert (Sg 5:2), and it is filled with the secrets of truth on which she will feed in memory when she comes to herself. There she sees things invisible, hears the ineffable, which no man can utter (2 Cor 12:4). These things exceed that knowledge which night can give to night, for this is the word that day speaks to day (Ps 18:3). Wise men speak wisdom to the wise (Dn 2:21). The spiritual are told spiritual things (1 Cor 2:13).

VIII.22. Do you doubt that Paul passed up these steps when he said that he was carried up to the third heaven (2 Cor 12:2)? But why does he say "carried" and not "led"? If such an Apostle says that he was carried away, to a place of which he had no knowledge by learning about it and could not reach on his own feet even when he was conducted there, let me not presume to think that I, who am so much less

---

29. On the biblical use of this term, *conglutinat*, see Dt 10:15 on the divine bond of love and 1 Sm 18:1 on the human bond of love; also Gn 34:3 on the impure human bond.

30. See Gra 4, LTR 3.148, on the way reason and will are meant to work together.

31. This may be a slip for "cellar." In Div 92.1 he contrasts the "cellar" of Sg 1:3 with the "chamber" of Sg 3:4.

32. Cf. Dil 7; LTR 3:124ff.

33. Cf. Dil 27; LTR 3:142ff.

than he, can get there by any labor of my own. Let me not trust in my own strength or effort.

On the other hand, he who is taught or led follows. He makes an effort. He acts on his own account to reach the place or experience to which he is being drawn, so that he can say, "Not I, but the grace of God in me" (1 Cor 15:10). He who is carried depends not on his own strength but on that of someone else. He is taken where he knows not, and he does not know how. He has nothing to boast about—not the whole, nor even a part—where he acts neither by himself nor with anyone else. And so the Apostle was able to ascend to the first or second heaven "led" or with help. But he had to be carried away in order to reach the third heaven.

For the Son is said to have come down to help those who are ascending to the first (Eph 4:9), and the Holy Spirit is said to have been sent down (Jn 15:26) to lead us to the second. But (although he always works together with the Son and the Holy Spirit) we never read that the Father came down from heaven or was sent to the earth. I read, certainly, that "The earth is full of the mercy of the Lord" (Ps 32:5) and "Heaven and earth are full of your glory"[34] and many things of this sort.

I read, too, of the Son, "When the fullness of time had come, God sent his Son" (Gal 4:4). The Son says of himself: "The Spirit of the Lord sent me" (Lk 4:18; Is 61:1). And by the same prophet he said, "Now the Lord in his Spirit has sent me" (Is 48:16).

I read, too, of the Holy Spirit, "The Holy Spirit, the Paraclete, whom the Father sends in my name" (Jn 14:26) and, "When I am lifted up I will send him to you" (Jn 16:7). Who else is this but the Holy Spirit?

But although the Father is everywhere in his own Person I do not find him anywhere except in heaven, as in the Gospel, "My Father who is in heaven" (Mt 16:17) and in the prayer, "Our Father which art in heaven" (Mt 6:9).

VIII.23. I conclude from this that because the Father did not come down, the Apostle could not climb up to heaven to see him, but he remembers that he was carried there (2 Cor 12:2).[35] "No man has gone up into heaven but he who came down from heaven" (Jn 3:13). In

---

34. Cf. Is 6:3, and *Te Deum*.
35. Cf. Csi 5:3; LTR 3:468ff.

case you think it is the first or second heaven that is spoken of here, David tells you that "His coming is from the highest heaven" (Ps 18:7). He was not suddenly carried away. He was not stolen away. But, "He ascended before the very eyes of the disciples" (Acts 1:9).

Elijah was seen by only one. Enoch was translated (Gn 5:24; Heb 11:5). But our Redeemer "rose," as we read, without help. He ascended by himself, without assistance. He was not carried in a chariot (2 Kgs 2:11). He did not have the help of an angel. By his own power alone, "A cloud received him from their sight" (Acts 1:9).[36] Why the cloud? Did it come to assist him because he was tired? Did it help him rise more rapidly? Did it support him in case he fell back? No. It covered him from the bodily eyes of the Apostles, who, even though they knew Christ according to the flesh, were not to know him further (2 Cor 5:16).

Those whom the Son has called to the first heaven by humility, the Spirit summoned to the second by love, the Father exalts to the third by contemplation. In the first they are humbled in truth and say, "In your truth you have humbled me" (Ps 118:75). In the second they rejoice together in the truth and sing, "How good and how pleasant it is for brothers to dwell together in unity" (Ps 132:1). For we read that "love rejoices in truth" (1 Cor 13:6). Third, they are carried away to the secrets of truth and they cry, "My secret is mine, my secret is mine" (Is 24:16).

IX.24. But why am I, a poor man, running about the two higher heavens with my tongue, talking with more loquacity than spiritual liveliness, when with my hands and feet I am still striving down here? At his bidding and with his help I have put up a ladder for myself (Gn 28:12–13). This is the road which points the way to God's salvation (Ps 49:23). For already I glimpse the Lord leaning on the top of it, and I rejoice already to hear the voice of Truth. He called me and I answered him, "Stretch out your right hand to the work of your hands" (Jb 14:15). You have counted my steps, Lord (Jb 14:15).

But I climb slowly, a weary traveler, and I need somewhere to rest. Woe is me if the darkness surrounds me (Jn 12:35), or if I should flee in the winter or on the Sabbath (Mt 24:20), for now, even at an acceptable time and in a day of salvation (2 Cor 6:2), I can scarcely make my way.

Why am I so slow? Pray for me anyone who is my son, brother,

---

36. Cf. Asc 2:6; LTR 6:130ff.

friend, companion of my journey in the Lord. Pray for me to the Almighty, that he may give my footsteps vigor and that the foot of pride may not come near me (Ps 35:12). For a weary foot is no use in climbing to the truth. The other, the foot of pride, cannot even stand, as you see, "They are cast out. They could not stand" (Ps 35:12).

IX.25. This refers to the proud. But what of their head? What of him who is called "King of the sons of pride" (Jb 41:25)? He, it is said, "did not stand fast in the truth" (Jn 8:44), and elsewhere we read, "I saw Satan falling from heaven" (Lk 10:18). Why did he fall, if not because of his pride? Woe is me (Is 6:5; Jer 4:31) if he who sees from afar (Ps 137:6) beholds me in my pride. He will say to me with a terrible voice, "You were a son of the Most High, but you will die like a man and fall like one of the princes" (Ps 81:6ff.). Who would not shrink at the sound of that voice (Ps 103:7)? It was better for Jacob when the sinew of his thigh shriveled at the touch of the angel (Gn 32:25),[37] than for it to swell, collapse, and fall at the touch of the angel of pride. Would that the angel would touch my sinew and make it shrink, if as a result of this weakness I was able to progress (2 Cor 12:9), for I can make no progress in my own strength. I read further, "The weakness of God is stronger than man's strength" (1 Cor 1:25).

So also the Apostle complained when his sinew was struck not by the angel of the Lord but by the angel of Satan. This was the reply he heard, "My grace is sufficient for you, for strength is made perfect in weakness" (2 Cor 12:7–9).

What strength? Let the Apostle tell us himself. "Gladly will I glory in my weaknesses, so that the strength of Christ may dwell in me" (2 Cor 12:7ff.). But perhaps you do not yet understand of what in particular he was speaking? For Christ had all the virtues. But although he had them all, he especially commended one of them to us in himself (Rm 5:8), that of humility, when he said, "Learn of me, for I am meek and lowly of heart" (Mt 11:29).[38]

IX.26. I, too, Lord will freely glory if I can, in my weakness, in the shriveling of my sinew (Gn 32:25), so that your strength, which is humility, may be perfected in me. For your grace is sufficient for me when my own strength fails me (Ps 70:9). With the foot of grace planted squarely on the ladder of humility, trailing my own weak foot behind,

---

37. Cf. 2 Cor 12:9; SC 29.7; LTR 1.208.
38. *Virtus* can be rendered as "power" or as "virtue"; here Bernard takes it as virtue for the purposes of his argument.

I shall climb safely upward by holding fast to the truth, until I come to the broad reaches of charity. There I shall sing a song of thanksgiving, "You have set my feet on a broad plain" (Ps 30:9).

In this manner I cautiously begin to travel by the narrow way (Mt 7:14), and I come to the truth, even if I come late and with a limp. But I get there safely. "Woe is me that my exile is so long" (Ps 119:5). "Who will give me wings like a dove so that I might fly away" to the truth and "be at rest" in love (Ps 54:7)? But I have no wings. "Lead me then, Lord, in your way, so that I may walk in your truth" (Ps 85:11) and the truth will make me free (Jn 8:32). Woe is me that I ever abandoned it. If I had not climbed down so lightly and carelessly, I should not be striving so long and hard to climb up.

But why do I say "climbed down"? I should rather have said that I "fell." In a way the first expression is more appropriate, because one does not fall to the depths of evil all at once, any more than one leaps to the heights of virtue in a single bound, but only by climbing step by step. So, too, the way down is followed step by step (Sir 19:1). Otherwise, how should we say, "The wicked man is proud all the days of his life" (Jb 15:20)? "There are ways that seem right to a man," but their end leads to evil (Prv 14:12, 16:25).

IX.27. There is a way down, then, as well as a way up. There is a way to good and a way to evil. Avoid the evil way and choose the good. If you cannot do it by yourself, pray with the prophet and say, "Keep me from the way of sin" (Ps 118:29). How? "Show me the mercy of your law" (Ps 118:29). That is, that law which you have given to those who go astray on the way, those who desert the truth, of whom I am one, for I have truly fallen from the truth (Ps 24:8).

But surely if a man falls he will rise again (Jer 8:4; Am 5:1)? Yes. It is in that hope that I have chosen the path of truth (Ps 118:30) by which I shall ascend in humility back whence I fell through being proud. I shall ascend, I say, singing, "Lord, it is good for me that you have humbled me. The law of your mouth is better for me than a thousand pieces of gold or silver" (Ps 118:72).

David seems to offer you the choice of two ways (Ps 1:1, 6). There is only one, as you know; but there is a distinction to be made. We can use different names for the way of sin, by which those who are going down travel, and the way of truth, by which those who are going up journey. It is the same way which goes up to the throne and down from it, the same way to the city and back. One door lets people both into and out of a house (Jn 10:9). The angels appeared to Jacob going up and down by the same ladder (Gn 28:12).

What is the relevance of this? That if you desire to return to the truth you do not need to search for the road. You know it. You came down that way. Retrace your footsteps. Go up by the same steps by which you came down in your pride. Thus he who has sunk to the twelfth step of pride must climb the first step of humility. If it is the eleventh, let him find the second. If the tenth, the third; the ninth, the fourth; the eighth, the fifth; the seventh, the sixth; the sixth, the seventh; the fifth, the eighth; the fourth, the ninth; the third, the tenth; the second, the eleventh; the first, the twelfth. Identify the step of pride you have reached and you will not need to strive to find the way of humility.

The First Step of Pride: Curiosity

X.28. And so the first step of pride is curiosity.[39] You can recognize it by these indications. You see a monk of whom you had thought well up to now. Wherever he stands, walks, sits, his eyes begin to wander. His head is lifted. His ears are alert. You can tell from his outward movements that the inner man has changed. "The worthless man winks with his eye, nudges with his foot, points with his finger" (Prv 6:12 ff.).

These unusual bodily movements show that his soul has fallen sick. He has grown careless about his own behavior. He wastes his curiosity on other people. "He does not know himself, so he must go out and pasture his goats" (Sg 1:7). Goats signify sin. I have rightly called them eyes and ears, for just as death entered the world through sin (Rom 5:12), so it enters the mind through these windows (Jer 9:21). The curious man busies himself pasturing these when he does not care to know in what condition he has left himself within.

And truly, O man, if you concentrate hard on the state you are in it will be surprising if you have time for anything else. Hear what Solomon says, curious man. Hear, foolish man, what Wisdom says. "Guard your heart with all your might" (Prv 4:23), so that all your

---

39. "Curiosity" in Augustine and other Fathers is an inordinate and excessive thing, and it is for that reason that Bernard condemns it. Cf. Div 14.2; LTR 6¹.135; QH 8.5, LTR 4.429.

senses may be alert to protect the source of life.[40] For where will you go when you leave yourself, O curious one? To whom do you entrust yourself while you are away? Do you dare to lift your eyes to heaven,[41] you who have sinned against heaven? Look at the earth and know yourself.[42] It tells you about yourself, because, "Dust you are and to dust you shall return" (Gn 3:19).

X.29 There are two reasons why you might raise your eyes which have no blame attached to them: to ask for help or to give it. David lifted his eyes to the hills to ask for help (Ps 120:1). The Lord lifted his eyes to see the crowds, so that he could help them (Jn 6:5). The one did it in wretchedness, the other in mercy. Both acted blamelessly.

If taking the time, place, and occasion into consideration, you, too, lift up your eyes because of your brother's need, not only do I not blame you; I praise you! Wretchedness is a good excuse. Mercy is a good reason. If you raised your eyes for some other reason I should have to say that you were no imitator of the prophet, or of the Lord, but of Dinah or Eve, or even Satan himself.

For when Dinah went out to pasture her goats she was snatched away from her father, and her virginity was taken from her (Sg 1:7). O Dinah, you wanted to see the foreign women (Gn 34:1)! Was it necessary? Was it profitable? Or did you do it solely out of curiosity? Even if you went idly to see, you were not idly seen. You looked curiously, but you were looked upon more than curiously. Who would believe that idle curiosity or curious idleness of yours would not be idle in the future, but so terrible in its consequences for you and your family and for your enemies too (Gn 34:25)?

IX.30. You, too, Eve. You were placed in paradise to work there and look after it with your husband (Gn 2:15), and if you had done what you were told you were to have passed to a better life in which you would not have to work or be concerned about guarding. Every tree of paradise was given you to eat, except the one which was called the tree of the knowledge of good and evil (Gn 2:16). For if the others were good and tasted good (Gn 2:9), what need was there to eat of the tree which tasted bad? "Do not know more than is appropriate" (Rom 12:3). If you taste what is bad it is not tasty but distasteful. Take care of what is given you as your responsibility. Wait for what you have been promised.

---

40. Bernard, like Augustine, takes the soul to be the life of the body.
41. Bernard is drawing a contrast with the publican of Lk 18:13.
42. Cf. SC 36.7; LTR 2.8.

Avoid what is forbidden, lest you lose what has been given to you. Why do you look so intently on your death? Why are you always glancing at it? What is the good of looking at what you are forbidden to eat?

"I reach out with my eyes, not my hand," you say. "I was not forbidden to look, only to eat. Can I not look where I like with the eyes God gave me?" To this the Apostle says, "I may do anything, but not everything is good for me" (1 Cor 6:12). Even if it is not a sin, it hints at sin. For if the mind had not been failing to keep a check on itself your curiosity would not have been wandering. Even if there is no fault, there is an occasion of sin and a prompter to sin and a cause of sin. For when you are looking intently at something, the serpent slips into your heart and coaxes you. He leads on your reason with flattery; he awakes your fear with lies. "You will not die," he says (Gn 3:4). He increases your interest while he stirs up your greed. He sharpens your curiosity while he prompts your desire. He offers what is forbidden and takes away what is given. He holds out an apple and snatches away paradise. You drink the poison and you will die and be mother to those who must die. Safety is gone before you have even begun to give birth. We are born; we die. We are born to die because we were dying before we were born. This is the heavy burden you have laid on all your children up to this very day (Sir 40:1).

BERNARD'S VIEW OF THE FALL OF THE SERAPHIM

X.31. You too, Satan, were made in the likeness of God, and you had a place not even in the Garden of Eden but in the delights of God's paradise (Ez 28:12). What more ought you to ask? Full of wisdom and perfect in beauty, "Do not seek what is too high and try to look into what is too mighty for you" (Sir 3:22).

Stand in your proper place, lest you fall from it, by walking in the great and wonderful which is beyond you (Ps 130:1). Why are you looking toward the north? I see you now. I do not know what you are thinking, except that it is about something which is beyond your reach. "I will place my throne in the north," you say (Is 14:13).[43]

Everyone else in heaven is standing. You alone affect to sit. You

---

43. In the Bible the north is the place of evil. Bernard uses both the Old Latin and the Vulgate versions. Compare I Nov 2.5; LTR 5.310 and QH 11.4; LTR 4.451.

disrupt the harmony of your brothers, the peace of the whole heavenly realm, and, if it were in your power, you would disturb the tranquility of the Trinity. O wretch, is this what your curiosity has led to, that all by yourself you do not hesitate to offend the citizens of heaven and insult its King? "Thousands of thousands minister to him. Ten times a hundred thousand stand before him" (Dn 7:10). In that court no one has a right to sit, except he who sits above the cherubim (Ps 79:2), and whom the others serve. You want to distinguish yourself from others. You want to pry with your curiosity. You want to push in disrespectfully. You want to set up a throne for yourself in heaven so that you may be like the Most High (Is 14:4).[44]

With what purpose? On what do you rest your confidence? Measure your strength, you fool. Think about the purpose of what you are doing; consider the manner in which you are doing it. Are you presuming to do this with the knowledge of the Most High, or does he not know? Is he willing for you to do it or are you acting against his will? His knowledge extends to everything. His will is for the best. How can you contrive any evil of which he is ignorant or in which he supports you? Do you think he knows and is against what you do, but cannot prevent it? Unless you believe that you are not his creature, (Jb 36:4) I do not think you can be in any doubt about the omnipotence and universal knowledge and goodness of the Creator, for he was able to create you from nothing and he knew how to make you as he willed. How then do you think that God consents to what he does not will to be done and can prevent—unless perhaps I am seeing fulfilled in you (even begun by you) what has been common on earth ever since? As the proverb says, "Familiarity breeds contempt." Is your eye evil because he is good? (Mt 20:15). If you derive your confidence from his goodness you become impudent against knowledge and bold against power.

X.32. This is what you are thinking, O wicked one. This is the wickedness you brood on in your bed (Ps 35:5), and you say, "Do you think the Creator will destroy the work of his hands?" I know that none of my thoughts are hidden from God, for he is God. Nor do such thoughts please him, for he is good (Jn 7:12). I know that I cannot escape his hand if he does not wish me to, for he is mighty (Dn 13:22; 2 Mc 6:26).

---

44. Cf. Gregory the Great, *Moralia in Job*, 29.18, ed. M. Adraien, CCSL 143 (Turnholt, 1979).

But surely there is no reason to be afraid? It is true that my wickedness cannot please him because he is good (Jn 7:12). But would it please him any better to act badly himself? I should say that even if I should act wrongly in going against his will, he would act wrongly in taking revenge. He cannot want to avenge himself for my sin, for he cannot will to lose his good; nor is he able to."

You deceive yourself, wretch, you deceive yourself, not God (Ps 26:12). You deceive yourself, I repeat. Wickedness deceives itself; it does not deceive God. You are trying to deceive him, but he sees everything. You deceive yourself, not God. Despite his great goodness toward you, you are planning to do him wrong, and your wickedness is hateful indeed (Ps 35:3). For what greater sin can there be than to despise your Creator for that which should make you love him more? What greater wickedness is there than, when you have no doubt of God's power to destroy you (for he made you), you rely on his gentleness not to punish you, though he can? You repay evil for good, hatred for love (Ps 108:5).

X.33. This iniquity, I say, deserves not a moment's anger but eternal hatred. You desire and hope to make yourself the equal of your gentlest and most exalted Lord, against his wishes. You want to thrust your hateful self constantly before his eyes, to force him to have you as his unwanted companion, and not to destroy you when he could. You want him to suffer rather than let you perish. He can destroy you if he wishes, but you calculate that he cannot wish to do so because of his gentleness. If indeed he is as you think, your crime is the worse in not loving him. And if he allows himself to suffer rather than take any action against you, is it not wickedness not to spare him who, in sparing you, does not spare himself? But perish the thought that in his perfection justice and mercy should be set in opposition, as though he could not be gentle and just at the same time (Ps 24:8). In fact, mercy is better when it is accompanied by justice, not worse; gentleness without justice would not be a virtue. So then, because you show yourself ungrateful to God's free goodness, by which you were freely created,[45] you do not fear his justice, for in his kindness he has given you no taste of it. And so you boldly go on sinning and mistakenly promise yourself you will not be punished.

Now see yourself, you who regard yourself as just, you who have

---

45. There is a play on words here: *gratis, ingratus, gratuitae.*

known what is good, falling into the trap which you have prepared for your Maker. You plot harm against him which he can avoid if he wishes, but you do not think that he can wish it because he is good. You have not seen him punishing anyone. The just God will turn the harm back on you. God cannot allow his goodness to be insulted with impunity, nor ought he to. But still his goodness tempers the sentence upon you, so that if you repent he will not refuse to pardon you. But your heart is hard and you cannot will to repent (Rom 2:5),[46] and so the punishment will come.

X.34. But now hear the calumny. "Heaven is my throne," says God. "Earth is my footstool" (Is 66:1; Acts 7:49). He does not say "east" or "west" or mention any other region of heaven. He says, "The whole of heaven is my throne." Therefore, Satan, you cannot set up your throne in any part of heaven (Rv 12:8), for he has claimed it all for himself. You cannot set it up on earth, for the earth is his footstool (Mt 5:35). Indeed it is on the solid earth that the Church sits, founded on solid rock (Mt 7:25). What are you going to do? Cast out of heaven, you cannot stay on the earth. Choose for yourself a place in the air (Eph 2:2), not to sit but to hang there, so that you who have tried to shake the stability of eternity may feel the punishment of your own instability. You must wander about between earth and heaven while the Lord sits on a throne high and lifted up, and the whole earth is filled with his glory (Is 6:1ff.). You have no place but the air.

X.35. Some of the seraphim fly on the wings of their contemplation from throne to footstool, from footstool to throne. Others veil the Lord's head and feet with their wings (Is 6:2). I think that this is to teach us that just as the cherubim keeps sinful man out of paradise (Gn 3:24),[47] so a limit is placed on your curiosity by the seraphim, so that you may not be allowed to penetrate the secrets of heaven with impudence and imprudence, and so that you may not know the mystery of the Church on earth. The hearts of the proud have to be content with this. They do not stoop to live on earth like other men (Lk 18:11); but they do not fly to heaven like the angels. Both God's head in heaven and his feet on earth are hidden from them. But they are allowed to see in between so that they may be envious. While they hang in the air they

---

46. Cf. Gra 29.
47. Cf. Csi 5.8; LTR 3.472ff.; and SC 19.2–6; LTR 1.109–12, on the roles of the ranks of the angels.

see the angels going up and down (Gn 28:12), but they do not know what they hear in heaven, nor what they tell on earth.

X.36. O Lucifer, who rose in the morning (Is 14:12),[48] now you are not light-bearer but bringer of darkness, or even of death. Your course was from the east to the south. Why did you alter your course wrongly to the north? The higher you went the more swiftly you came down.

But I am curious, O curious one, about the purpose of your curiosity. You say, "I will place my throne in the north."[49] I know that this is not a bodily north; nor, since you are a spirit, is it a material throne. But I think the north signifies wicked men; the throne, your power over them. For once you were very close to God, and perhaps in his foreknowledge (1 Pt 1:2) you foresaw more clearly than others; you saw these men, not shining with the light of wisdom or burning with spiritual love (Rom 12:11), but empty, and you swaggered as though you were their lord, pouring out on them the brilliance of your cunning and kindling in them the fires of malice, so that just as the Most High reigns in his goodness and wisdom over all the children of obedience (1 Pt 1:14), you want to be king of the sons of pride (Jb 41:25; Ps 2:6) and to rule over them with shrewd malice and malicious shrewdness, and to be like the Most High (Is 14:14). But I wonder, when you foresaw your lordship in the foreknowledge of God, did you not also see your fall? For if you foresaw it, what madness was it that made you desire to rule in such misery that you would prefer to be a wretched lord rather than a happy subject? Would it not have been better to be a companion of those who dwell in light than ruler of those in darkness (Eph 6:12)? It is easier to believe that you did not foresee it. Or perhaps, as I have already suggested, you did not consider God's goodness, but said in your heart, "He will not require me to give account" (Ps 9:34). Or perhaps the vision of your royal rule stuck in your eye like a beam (Mt 7:3) and got in the way, so that you could not see your fall?

X.37. Thus Joseph, when he foresaw the greatness which would be his (Gn 37:5–10), did not foresee that he would be sold into slavery (Gn 37:28), although that was to happen first. It is not that I believe that such a patriarch lapsed into pride, but his example makes it plain

---

48. Patristic sources saw the King of Babylon here as a type of the fallen angel; cf. Lk 10:18.

49. See note 43.

that those who see the future in the spirit of prophecy must be considered to see something, even if they do not see everything. If anyone argues that he was vain to tell his boyhood dream when he did not know its meaning (Gn 37:6, 9), I should answer that that is to be put down rather to the greatness of the mystery or the boy's simplicity than to pride; and if there was any pride in it, he was able to expiate it by what he suffered later. For certain people have delightful things revealed to them at times. The human mind is bound to feel some vanity at knowing such things, especially when they turn out as prophesied. But that vanity which took pride in the greatness of the revelation or the promise it had been granted would not go unpunished perhaps (2 Cor 12:7).

For the physician uses not only ointments but fire and iron, with which he cuts and burns away whatever is superfluous and brings healing by the wound he causes. He removes anything which would prevent the ointment from healing. In the same way, God, the physician of souls, brings temptations upon the soul and sends tribulations. And when it is afflicted and humiliated by these its joy turns to sorrow (Bar 4:34; Jas 4:9). It thinks what has been revealed to it is an illusion. So it comes to be free of vanity and the truth of the revelation endures. Thus was Paul's pride kept in check by the stings of the flesh, though he himself was lifted up by many revelations (2 Cor 12:7). Thus Zachariah's lack of faith was punished by dumbness (Lk 1:20), and the angel's prophecy made to him proved to be true (Lk 1:57ff.). The saints go on in glory or dishonor (2 Cor 6:8). If they fall into common human vanity because of the special gifts they receive, so that they see by grace what is beyond them, they are reminded what they are.

X.38. But what have revelations to do with curiosity? I digressed when I was trying to show how the wicked angel could have foreseen, before his fall, the dominion he was to receive over the wicked, and not have foreseen his own damnation. Many questions are raised about this and by no means all of them have been answered, but this is the point of the discussion: that he fell from the truth as a result of curiosity.[50] He had peered curiously into what was to come and wanted what he was not allowed to have and hoped presumptuous hopes. Rightly is curiosity considered the first step of pride. It was the beginning of all sin (Sir 10:15). Unless it is checked at once it leads swiftly to the second step: levity.

---

50. Cf. Div 14.2; LTR 6^i.135.

The Second Step: Light-mindedness

XI.39. For the monk who instead of concentrating on himself looks curiously at others, trying to judge who is his superior and who is his inferior, will see things to envy in others and things to mock. Thus it is that the light-minded follow their roving eyes and, no longer pinned down by proper responsibility, are now swept up to the heights by pride, now cast down into the depths by envy. Now the man is consumed by foolish envy; now he grows childishly pleased about his own excellence. In one mood he is wicked, in the other vain. In both he shows himself to be proud, because he makes it a matter for self-congratulation both when he grieves to be outdone and when he is pleased to outdo others. He displays these changes of mood in his speech: Now his words are few and grudging; now numerous and trivial; now he is laughing; now he is depressed; but there is never any reason for his mood. Compare if you will these two stages of pride with the last two steps of humility and see whether the last does not quell pride and the last but one light-mindedness.[51] You will find that the same is true for the rest, if you compare one with another.

But now let us come, not descending but teaching,[52] to the third.

The Third Step: Foolish Merriment[53]

XII.40. The proud always want to be happy and to avoid sadness, as in, "Where there is merriment, there is the heart of a fool" (Eccl 7:5). The monk who has come down these two steps of pride in arriving at light-mindedness by way of pride will find that the joy he is always seeking is often disturbed by sadness; he will be upset by the goodness of others. Impatient at his humiliation he flies to false consolations. Anything that shows him his own vileness and the excellence of others checks his curiosity; but on the contrary, he is always ready to notice anything which makes him seem to excel. He uses his curiosity to perceive how he excels others, and he always deceives himself so that he avoids sadness and he can go on being happy.

And so it comes about that anyone who thus continues to juggle joy and sorrow can enjoy only an empty happiness. This is the third

---

51. RB 7.62–66 and RB 7.60–61.
52. *Docendo, non descendendo.*
53. Gra 14; LTR 3.176; SC 37.3; LTR 2.10.

step. Note the signs, which you can recognize in yourself or in anyone else. You will rarely or never see in such a man any signs of groans or tears. You would think to look at him that he was not giving himself a thought, or that he had no sin on his conscience, or that he was purged of his sins. He makes scurrilous gestures.[54] He giggles.[55] He preens himself. He is always joking and ready to laugh at the slightest thing.[56] If anything has happened which would bring contempt on him or cast him down, he wipes it from his memory. And if he notes any good things in himself he will add them up and parade them before his mind's eye. He thinks only of what he wants and he does not ask himself whether he ought to want it. At times he is seized by fits of laughter; he is unable to suppress his foolish mirth. He is like a blown-up bladder which has been punctured and squeezed. As it goes down it squeaks, and the air does not come out everywhere but whistles through the little hole in a series of shrieks. So, the monk who fills his heart with vain and scurrilous thoughts cannot let them out all at once because of the rule of silence, so they burst out at odd moments in giggles.[57] Often he hides his face for shame, purses his lips, clenches his teeth. He still cannot stop laughing and giggling. When he puts his hand in front of his mouth the giggles can still be heard popping out through his nose.

The Fourth Step: Boasting

XIII.41. When vanity has begun to swell the bladder and enlarge it, it makes a bigger hole for the wind to escape. Otherwise it would burst. So the monk, when he cannot express his empty merriment by laughter or gesture, breaks into the words of Elihu, "See, my stomach is like new wine which has no vent; like new wineskins it is ready to burst" (Jb 32:19). Speak or burst! For he is full of talk and the spirit is straining to get out (Jb 32:18). He hungers and thirsts for listeners to whom he can make empty boasts, to whom he can pour out all he feels, and whom he can tell what he is and how great he is.

He finds an occasion to speak. Let us say the subject is literature. He says new things and old (Mt 13:52). His opinions fly about. His

---

54. RB 6.8.
55. On monastic sign language, cf. *Consuetudines Cluniacenses*, II, 4; *De Signis Loquendi*, PL 149.703–5.
56. RB 7.59.
57. RB 6; Perius, *Satires*, ed. W. V. Clausen (Oxford, 1956).

words tumble over one another. He butts in before he is asked. He does not answer other people's questions. He asks the questions himself and he answers them, and he cuts off anyone who tries to speak. When the bell rings for the end of the discussion, even though it has been a long one, he asks for a little more time. He asks permission to come back to the stories later, not so as to edify anyone, but so that he can show off his knowledge (1 Cor 8:1). He may say something edifying, but that is not his intention. He does not care for you to teach, or to learn from you what he himself does not know, but that others should know how much he knows.

If the subject is religion, at once he has dreams and visions to offer. Then he praises fasting, commends vigils, enthuses above all about prayer. He discusses patience, humility, and all the other virtues at great length, but in utter emptiness. Yet if you were to hear him you would say that he "speaks from the fullness of his heart" (Mt 12:34), or "A good man brings forth good things from his good treasure" (Mt 12:35).

If the talk turns to lighter things, he is discovered to be even more talkative, because this is something he really knows about. You would say if you heard him that his mouth was a stream of vanity, a river of scurrility, so that he stirs even solemn and grave minds to merriment. And to cut a long story short, "When there is much talk there is boasting" (Prv 10:19).[58] Here you have the fourth step described and named. Avoid the thing but remember the name. The same warning is appropriate to the fifth step, which I call singularity.

The Fifth Step: Trying to Be Different

XIV.42. When a man has been boasting that he is superior to others it is galling to him not to outdo them in performance, so as to make it obvious that he is more advanced than they are. It is not enough for him to keep the common rule of the monastery and obey his superiors.[59] But he is more interested in seeming to be better than others than in being so. He acts not so as to live better but so as to seem to triumph, so that he can say, "I am not as other men" (Lk 18:11). He

---

58. Cf. Prv 10:19; RB 7.56–58.
59. RB 7.55; cf. SC 19.7; LTR 1.112ff.; SC 64.5; LTR 2.168.

prides himself more on fasting for one day when the others are feasting than on fasting for seven days with the others. One special little
prayer seems to him finer than a night spent in singing psalms.[60] During a meal he often looks up and down the table to see if anyone is
eating less than he, and then he grieves at being outdone and begins
cruelly to deprive himself even of what he used to think it necessary
to eat, for he fears a blow to his reputation more than the pangs of
hunger. If he sees anyone thinner and paler than he is, he despises
himself and cannot rest. And though he cannot see his own face he
wonders what others think of it, and he looks at his hands and arms,
which he can see, feels his ribs, and inspects his shoulders and thighs
so as to test the pallor or color of his face from that of his members.
He is very anxious to perform his own special exercises and lazy
about performing the common ones everyone does. He lies awake in
his bed and sleeps when he is in choir. When the others wake to sing
the psalms of the night office he sleeps on all night. When the others
are resting in the cloister he stays behind by himself to pray in the
chapel.[61] By coughing and groaning and sighing he makes sure that
those outside can hear that he is there in his corner. The simple-
minded are taken in by these special but empty activities, and what
they think to be evidence of his good works. But they do not see his
motive and by canonizing the wretch they confirm him in his error
(Lk 18:11).

The Sixth Step: Arrogance

XV.43. He believes the praises he hears. He is complacent about what
he does. He does not give a thought to his intentions. He puts that from
his mind when he accepts what others think of him. He believes that
he knows more than everybody about everything else, but when they
praise him he believes them rather than his own conscience. As a result
he now not only shows off his piety in what he does and says, but in
his own heart warmly believes that he is holier than others.[62] When he
hears something said in his own praise he thinks it comes not from the
ignorance or kindness of the speaker, but from his own merit, and he
arrogantly takes the credit.

---

60. RB 9.
61. RB 8.3.
62. RB 7.51–54.

The Seventh Step: Presumption[63]

XVI.44. He who thinks himself superior to others, how can he not presume more for himself than others? At meetings he must sit in the most important place. In discussions he speaks first. He comes without being invited. He interferes without being asked. He changes the rules and alters things which have been settled. What he himself has not done or ordained he considers not to have been done right, or to be arranged displeasingly. He judges the judges and prejudges every case. If he is not promoted to be prior[64] he thinks his abbot is jealous of him, or else deceived. If obedience imposes some humble task on him he is indignant. He disdains to do it, thinking that he ought not to be bothered with trivial things. For he feels himself to be fitted for great tasks. But since he is so eager to offer his services and rushes at things rather than taking thought before he acts, he is bound to make mistakes sometimes.

But it is a superior's task to reprove someone who goes wrong. Yet how will he who does not think he is in the wrong, or that he can ever be thought to be in the wrong, confess his fault? So when he is accused of a fault he adds to his sins rather than giving them up. If you see someone answering back when he is reprimanded you will know that he has fallen to the eighth step of pride, which is self-justification.

The Eighth Step: Self-Justification

XVII.45. There are many ways of making excuses (Ps 140:4) for sin.[65] One person will say, "I did not do it." Another will say, "I did it, but it was the right thing to do." Another will admit that it was wrong but say, "It was not very wrong." Another will concede that it was very wrong, but he will say, "I meant well." If he is forced to admit that he did not mean well, he will say as happened in the case of Adam and Eve that someone else persuaded him to do it.[66] If a man defends even his obvious sins in that way, when will he humbly confess to his abbot his hidden sins and the wicked thoughts which come into his heart?[67]

---

63. QH 11.4; LTR 4.451.
64. RB 65.
65. Bernard now lists the "excuses for sin."
66. Cf. Pre 27; LTR 3.272ff.; Gn 3:12–13; Ps 140:4.
67. RB 7.44; cf. *Consuetudines Ordinis Cisterciensis*, III.70, *Nomasticon Cisterciensis*, ed. H. Séjalon (Solesme, 1892), pp. 145ff.

The Ninth Step: Insincere Confession

XVIII.46. Excuses of this sort are judged bad enough for the prophet to call them "words of malice" (Ps 140:4). But false and proud confession is far more dangerous than conscious and persistent self-defense.[68] For some, when they defend their obvious sins, knowing that they will not be believed if they do so, make up a more subtle defense in the form of pretended self-accusation. This is the man "who humbles himself deceitfully while his mind is full of wickedness" (Sir 19:23). His face is downcast; his body is bowed down to the ground; people of this sort wring tears out of themselves if they can. They let their voices catch with sighs and interrupt their words with groans. They not only admit what they have done but even exaggerate their guilt, so that you begin to doubt what you thought of them, and when they confess what you believed them to have done, what seemed certain becomes doubtful. And while they affirm what they do not want to be believed, they hide what they are revealing, and when a praiseworthy confession (Rom 10:10) is heard from their lips, iniquity is still hidden in their hearts (Ps 139:3; Jer 16:17). The result is that he who hears them believes in their humility rather than their veracity, and applies to them the Scripture, "The just man is his own first accuser" (Prv 18:17, Vetus Latina). These men prefer you to think they are untruthful rather than to believe that they lack humility. But in God's eyes they are putting both in jeopardy. If the sin is so obvious that there is no way it can be hidden, they will make great play of penitence, hoping that others will admire their frank confession so much that they forget their sin; nevertheless, their penitence is in the voice not in the heart, and so they do not purge their sins.

XVIII.47. Humility is a glorious thing if it tries to disguise itself with pride so as to avoid punishment! This will soon be perceived by the superior as the deception it is, if he does not take any notice of this prideful humility and refuses to overlook the offense or put off the punishment. An earthen vessel is tested by fire (Sir 27:6), and tribulation makes it clear who is really penitent. A real penitent does not shrink from the labor of doing penance, but whatever hateful task is imposed on him for his sin he patiently embraces without complaint. If obedience forces him to what is hard and goes against his wishes, and even

---

68. Div 40.6; LTR 6¹.239.

if he suffers reproach he has not deserved, he bears it without flagging, so that he shows that he stands on the fourth step of humility. But he whose confession is all pretense, when he is tested by one little punishment cannot simulate humility or hide the fact that he has been pretending up to now. He complains and murmurs and grows angry and proves that far from standing on the fourth step of humility he has sunk to the ninth step of pride which, as we said, can rightly be called insincere confession.

How great do you think will be the confusion in the heart of the proud man when his deception is discovered, his peace gone, his praise diminished, and his sin is still not purged? At last everyone sees what he is; everyone judges him, and they are the more indignant with him when they see that they were wrong in what they thought of him before. Then the superior must not spare him, in case he thinks he can get away with it, for then he would be a stumbling-block to others.

XIX.48. The divine mercy may look on such a man and inspire him to do what is very difficult for him, to submit without a word to the judgment of the community.[69] But if his response is to frown and be insolent, by his rebellion he falls lower and to a more desperate state, to the tenth step, and he who before secretly despised his brothers in his arrogance now openly shows by his disobedience that he despises his superiors.

XIX.49. For you must know that all the steps I have divided into twelve can be put into three groups. In the first six there is contempt for one's brothers. In the next four there is contempt for one's superiors. In the remaining two pride comes to a head in contempt for God. It should also be noted that these two final steps of pride, which are also the first two steps taken by the person who is ascending the ladder of humility, just as they must be climbed before entering the community, so they cannot be descended within the community. It is clear from what it says about the third step in the Rule that they ought to be climbed before entering. "It is the third step when a monk obediently submits himself to a superior for love of God."[70] If then submission is placed at the third step when it is the first thing to happen when someone joins the community as a novice, it follows that the two previous steps are to be understood to have been already climbed. When a monk

---

69. RB 28.
70. RB 7.34.

spurns the agreement of his brothers and the opinion of his superior, how can he remain in the monastery without being a stumbling-block?

The Eleventh Step: Freedom to Sin

XX.50. And so after the tenth step, which is called rebellion, the monk is expelled from his monastery, or leaves it, and at once he is at the eleventh stage. Then he begins to travel roads which seem good to men (Prv 14:12, 16:25)[71] and, unless God blocks his way (cf. Hos 2:6), he will come at their end to the depths of hell, that is, to contempt for God. "When the wicked man reaches the depths of evil he is in contempt" (Prv 18:3).[72] The eleventh step can be called freedom to sin. When he stands there, the monk who recognizes and fears no superior and who has no brothers whom he may respect enjoys doing what he wants the more safely as he does it the more freely; and he does things which in the monastery fear or shame would have held him back from doing. But even if he does not now fear his brothers or the abbot, he is not yet entirely without awe of judgment. Reason, still murmuring faintly, puts this awe in front of him and he still hesitates a little before committing certain sins. Like someone entering a river, he does not plunge, but goes step by step into the torrent of vices.

The Twelfth Step: Habitual Sin

XXI.51. And after he finds that his first sins go unpunished by the terrible judgment of God (Heb 10:27), he freely seeks to enjoy again the pleasures he has experienced. Habit binds him as desire revives, and conscience slumbers.[73] The wretched man is dragged into the depths of evil (Prv 18:3) and handed over captive to the tyranny of the vices as though to be swallowed up in the whirlpool of fleshly desires; and he forgets the fear of God and his own reason. The fool says in his heart, "There is no God" (Ps 13:1).

He cannot tell good from evil now. Nothing holds him back, in mind, hand, or foot, from wrong thoughts, plans, or action. Whatever is in his heart comes to his mouth or his hand. He conceives an idea.

71. Cf. Hum 19.
72. Conv 23; LTR 4.95; Pre 40; LTR 3.280.
73. Conv 5; LTR 4.76.

He chatters about it. He carries it out. He is malevolent, evil-speaking, vile.

As the just man who has climbed all the steps of humility runs toward life with a heart now eager and unburdened because of his good habits, so, because of his bad habits, the wicked man who has descended all the steps does not govern himself with reason and he is not bridled by fear. And so he rashly rushes on to death.

Those in the middle of the climb or the descent are weary and constrained, now struck by fear of the pain of hell, now held back by the force of old habits. Only those at the top or the bottom run unimpeded and without strain. One hurries to death, the other to life. One runs upward, the other downward. Love lifts one up. Lust pulls the other down. In one love and in the other apathy feels the effort nothing. In one perfect love and in the other malice drives out fear (1 Jn 4:18). Truth gives one of them a sense of security, the other gets it from blindness. The twelfth step, then, can be called habitual sin, because the fear of God is lost and replaced by contempt.

XXII.52. Now I would not that anyone should pray for such a one, says the Apostle John (1 Jn 5:16). But surely, Apostle, you are not counseling despair? He who really loves him will still weep. Let him not presume to pray nor cease to sorrow.

What am I saying? If there remains any refuge of hope, is there not a place for prayer?

But hear one who believes, hopes, yet does not pray, "Lord," she said, "If you had been here my brother would not have died" (Jn 11:21). Great is the faith which believed that the Lord would have prevented death by his presence if he had been there. No more than that? Perish the thought that she who believed he could keep someone alive doubted that he could raise him from the dead. "But now," she says, "I know that whatever you ask of God, God will give you" (Jn 11:22). When Jesus asked where they had laid him, she answered, "Come and see" (Jn 11:34). Why did she say that? O Martha, you have given us great signs of faith. Can you be failing in faith? "Come," you said, "and see." Why, if you did not despair, did you not go on to say, "And revive him." But if you are in despair, why do you pester the Master relentlessly? Perhaps faith sometimes receives what prayer is not bold enough to ask for.

As he approaches the body you stop him and say, "Lord by this time he will be stinking; he has been in the tomb for four days" (Jn 11:39). Did you say this in despair, or for a purpose? For the Lord himself, after his resurrection, pretended to be going further when he wanted to remain with the disciples (Lk 24:28). O holy women who are Christ's friends, if you love your brother, why do you not press him to show mercy, him whose power you cannot doubt, and in whose holiness you have absolute trust (Jn 11:3)?

This is their answer. "We pray better by not appearing to pray. We trust the better by seeming not to trust. We show faith by appearing to be uncertain. We show faith and demonstrate our love. He to whom there is no need to say anything knows what we desire (Wis 7:27; Mt 6:8). We know that he can do everything. But this great miracle, so new, so unheard-of even though it is within his power, greatly exceeds anything our humility can deserve. It is enough for us to have brought his power here, to have given his holiness a reason, and we prefer to wait patiently upon his will rather than impudently to ask what he will not perhaps wish to do. Perhaps what our deserving lacks our modesty will supply."

I see Peter, too, weeping after his serious lapse, but I do not hear him praying. Yet I have no doubt that he was forgiven (Mt 26:75; Mk 14:72; Lk 22:61–62).

XXII.53. Learn from the great faith which the Lord's mother had in the wonders he could do. She preserved her modesty in great faith. Learn that modesty is the ornament of faith and that it reproves presumption. "They have no wine," she says (Jn 2:3). How briefly, how reverently she put the problem to him, despite her holy anxiety.

Learn, too, that in such circumstances it is much more holy to complain gently rather than to demand presumptuously, and better to give the shadowy expression of modesty to strong feeling and to speak quietly in prayer in the faith you have. She did not come up to him boldly. She did not speak to him openly and say frankly in everyone's hearing, "I beg you, son, the wine has run out, the guests grow solemn, the Bridegroom is embarrassed—show them what you can do."

Certainly her burning breast and aching heart would have said this or much more, but the holy Mother came to her powerful Son privately. She did not come to test his power but to see what his will might be. "They have no wine," she said. What could be more modest? What could be more trusting? Her faith was secure, her voice low; her desire prevailed.[74] If then she, his mother, forgetting that she was his mother,

<hr />

74. O Assp 10; LTR 5.270.

did not dare to presume to ask for the miracle of the wine, with what barefacedness do I, a vile slave, whose only greatness is to be the servant of mother and Son, presume to ask for the life of one who has been dead for four days?

XIX.54. We read in the Gospel about two blind men who were given their sight. One had lost his sight (Mk 10:46–52; Lk 18:35–43). The other was born blind (Jn 9:1–2). One was blinded, the other congenitally blind. He who was blinded earned wonderful mercy by prayers, but the mercy the other received was the greater and more wonderful, and he felt the kindness of him who gave him light. To him is said, "Your faith has healed you," but not to the other. I read that two recently dead (Mt 9:18–26; Mk 5:21–43; Lk 5:21–43) and a third already dead for four days were resurrected (Jn 11:1–44).[75] But one was revived while she lay in her home, in answer to her father's prayers (Mt 9:18). The other two were restored to life by the great unasked-for gift of love (Lk 1:13; Jn 11:33–36).

XIX.55. If a similar situation should arise (which God forbid) and one of our brothers should die—not in body, but in soul; sinner though I am I will plead with the Savior by my prayers and those of my brothers. If he comes to life again (cf. Lk 15:24) we shall have our brother (Mt 18:15) restored to us as our reward. If we do not deserve to be heard and he is carried out from among us because he cannot endure the company of the living, and they cannot bear his, even then I weep faithfully, but I do not then pray in faith. I do not dare to say openly, "Come, Lord, revive our brother who has died." But I do not cease to cry inwardly trembling, with a heart that has stopped, "If perhaps; if perhaps the Lord may hear the desire of the poor, and hear the words of their hearts with his ears." And this, "Will you not perform miracles upon the dead; will the physicians raise him and praise you?" (Ps 87:11). And of him who is four days dead, "He who is in the grave will not tell of your mercy, and he who is in hell will not speak of your truth" (Ps 87:12).

Meanwhile, the Savior can, if he wishes, come to our help when we are not expecting it and when we have no hope, and, moved by our tears not by our prayers, restore the dead to life or even call back from the grave him who is already dead.

---

75. Jairus's daughter, Mt 9:18–26; Mk 5:22–43; Lk 8:41–56; the son of the widow of Naim, Lk 7:11–17.

I have described as dead the man who, defending his own sins, has rushed down to the eighth step. For the dead do not make confession, any more than someone who does not exist (Sir 17:26). After the tenth step, which is the third from the eighth, he is already swept away by freedom to sin, when he is driven out of the community of the monastery. But when he has gone on to the fourth step after that eighth one, now truly is he said to be four days dead, when, slipping into the fifth stage, he is buried in habitual sin.

XXII.56. Perish the thought that even if we do not presume to pray openly for such, we should not continue to pray for them in our hearts; for Paul, too, grieves for those he knows to have died without repenting (2 Cor 12:21). For even if they cut themselves off from the community's prayers, they cannot sever themselves wholly from the love of their brothers. But they will see how much danger they are in when the Church dare not pray openly for them, although she prays faithfully for Jews, heretics, and pagans. For on Good Friday when she prays for each kind of sinner by name, she makes no mention of the excommunicated.[76]

A NOTE TO THE PERSON TO WHOM THIS IS WRITTEN

XXII.57. You are perhaps saying, brother Geoffrey, that I have done something different from what you asked and I promised, and instead of writing about the steps of humility I have written about the steps of pride.[77] I reply, "I can teach only what I have learned. I did not think I could fittingly describe the steps up when I know more about going down than going up. The blessed Benedict sets the steps of humility before you, which he himself first set out in his heart (Ps 83:6). I have nothing to set before you except the order of my descent. But, if you look carefully, you will find there the way up. If on your way to Rome you meet a man coming from there and ask him the way, how can he do better than show you the way he has come? As he lists the castles, towns and cities, rivers and mountains through which he has traveled,

---

76. On Good Friday the prayers of the faithful are extended and the central action of the Mass is omitted.
77. See Retractation.

as he describes his journey he is telling you what you will find as you go, so that you will recognize each place as you come to it, just as he saw it as he came the other way. Similarly, in these steps of our descent you will perhaps find steps up. As you climb you will read them better in your heart than in this book.

ON CONSIDERATION

In 1145 Eugenius III became Pope. He had once been a monk of Clairvaux and from what Bernard knew of him he had misgivings about his capacity to cope with his new office. During the next decade he wrote first one book, advising Eugenius to set aside time for his spiritual life amidst the pressures of daily business, and then four more.

Bernard chose the title On Consideration because it was the term Gregory the Great had used to describe the bishop's task in his Regula Pastoralis. Bernard himself explains that contemplation is the true and sure perception of the mind, an apprehension of truth in which there is no doubt. Consideration, on the other hand, is searching for truth, active thinking and balancing and judging (Csi ii.5).

The second, third, and fourth books draw Eugenius on to consider what is below him and what is around him; here Bernard declares a view of papal plenitude of power and of the supremacy of spiritual over temporal power that was to be enormously influential in the later Middle Ages, continuing as it did the direction of the changes of the late eleventh century.

Book V deals with the upward aspiration of the soul to the contemplation of heavenly things.[1] Bernard tells Eugenius that he has not known in quite what manner to write to him. He wanted to make his letter personal and to address Eugenius as a close friend; on the other hand, what he has to say concerns issues of general importance, which require a more formal treatment.

---

1. See introduction to this volume.

*He begins with the position in which Eugenius finds him-
self. He has been snatched from the peace of contemplation, the
embrace of Rachel,*[2] *and made Pope (I.1). He has been taken for-
cibly from the solitude of monastic life and now he has no time
for the exercises of his old life. This is a fresh wound and it must
be causing Eugenius pain, but Bernard is afraid that the pain will
numb him so that he no longer feels his loss. That would be natural enough. Acute pain cannot be borne indefinitely, and the
sufferer's capacity to feel is bound to be blunted in time. But it
is important for his soul's health that Eugenius should not forget
Rachel and how he loved her. If his heart grows hard it will destroy him. None with a hard heart has ever been saved (II.3).*

*The way in which Eugenius is living at present is not bal-
anced as it should be between the necessary practical demands of
office and proper attention to his spiritual life. He is allowing his
time and energy to be taken up in listening to litigants "from
morning to night" (III.4).*

*Patience is good, but it is not right to be patient with abuses
(III.4). Service is a good, but it is not right to be the servant of
those who are interested only in their own financial gain (IV.5).
Eugenius must look at his life as a whole and by "consideration"
create a right balance between his duties to others and his spiritual life (V.6). Eugenius has to be a source and spring from
which others may drink to satisfy their spiritual needs; but he is
only a man, and he has spiritual needs too, which he himself must
satisfy (V.6).*

*How is Eugenius to achieve this balance? "I speak not of the
heroic, but of the possible" (VI.7), says Bernard. Eugenius must
distinguish between those matters which are his proper concern
(questions of sin) and those which are unworthy of his attention
(disputes about property) (VI.7). If Eugenius had unlimited time
and energy he could attend to these, too, but as it is, he must not
give himself up wholly to activity (VII.8), for that would be un-
balanced. He must reserve time for solitude in which to be quiet
with God.*

This balance is achieved by "consideration."[3] *Consideration*

---

2. The motif of Leah and Rachel is discussed at length in Zinn.
3. See my *The Thought of Gregory the Great* (Cambridge, 1986).

allows a man to stand away from his own actions and thoughts and assess them. Consideration clears the mind and makes for judiciousness (VII.8). All the virtues encourage balance and moderation. Neither he who indulges to excess nor he who denies himself everything is temperate. Prudence sets a boundary between desire and necessity (VIII.9).

If Eugenius suddenly devotes himself wholeheartedly to consideration it will seem such strange behavior in a Pope that he will annoy many people. He will seem to be criticizing his predecessors implicitly (IX.12). Bernard wants Eugenius to make the change slowly and thoughtfully. He must go on trying cases, but in a way that is appropriate (X.13). Many cases can be handed over to others to judge. The ambitious should not be allowed to thrust themselves and their affairs upon him (X.14). Eugenius should reserve his time for cases that it is proper for him to deal with. He should put the needs of widows and the poor high on the list (X.13).

Here Bernard ends his first book, but Eugenius is promised a second. Bernard was not stirred to write it until after the failure of the Second Crusade. He had been prevailed upon by Eugenius to preach in support of the Crusade in 1146, although at first he had misgivings. His enthusiasm grew so powerful, however, that it became very much his Crusade. Its collapse caused him great pain and bewilderment, and he begins the second book of De Consideratione with an attempt to make sense of what has happened. He can only conclude that the fault lay with the Crusaders: They were not true pilgrims at heart (II.ii.2).

He goes on to look further at the nature of consideration. It is almost but not quite synonymous with contemplation (II.ii.5). Contemplation is direct and intuitive. Consideration involves searching with the mind. (Bernard is not in fact always consistent, and there are instances where the terms seem to be used more or less interchangeably.)

A practical way for Eugenius to conduct this search is for him first to examine himself and then to think about what is below him, what is about him and what is above him. The remaining books of De Consideratione are concerned with these in turn.

Eugenius is Pope. Therefore he must consider himself not only as a private person, but as the holder of high office. He must, in a sense, put himself first. "Let your consideration begin and end with yourself" (II.iii.6), advises Bernard. That is because he must be concerned above all for his own salvation. He must never forget the profession he made as a monk (II.v.8). He set out then to be humble. That humility still befits him in his present high position (II.v.8). His elevation has not made any difference to the standing of his soul. It has simply given him great responsibilities to discharge. He must work at his spiritual life harder than ever. The spiritual labor he must undertake now for others as well as for himself is nothing but the work of a sweating peasant (II.9). He can certainly not afford to relax in luxury or enjoy a life of pomp (II.10). He must consider his failings carefully and do what he can to repair them (II.vii.14).

Books III and IV contain a detailed working out of Eugenius's relations with those who are his subordinates and of his position in the world at large.

I.1 The first of these books, even though they go under the title *On Consideration*, have also had a good deal to say about practical affairs; for they teach or give advice on certain things which are not only for reflection but for action. But this present book is wholly concerned with consideration. Those things which are above you (for they are its subject) require not action but contemplation. There is no way in which you can act upon those things which always exist in the same way for eternity—and some of them from eternity.

I should like you to note carefully, Eugenius, since you are the wisest of men, that whenever your consideration wanders from these things to lesser and visible things, whether in search of knowledge or something for practical use, or to do your duty in administration or action, you go into exile. You do not do so if your consideration concentrates on these higher things, so that through them it seeks what is above. To consider in this way is to come home.

That is a higher and worthier use of present things, for then, according to Paul's wisdom, "The invisible things of God are clearly seen through the things which have been made" (Rom 1:20). Citizens do not need this ladder, but those in exile do. Our author saw this, and made a significant addition to what he said about the invisible being seen through the visible "by the creature of the world" (Rom 1:20). And truly, what need has someone who is already in possession of the throne of a ladder to reach it? The creature of heaven already has means by which he may contemplate invisible things. He sees the Word, and in the Word he sees what has been made through the Word (Jn 1:3). He has no need to beg knowledge from the Creator of what he has made. Nor does he climb down to created things in order to know them, for he sees far better from where he is what they really are in themselves. Therefore he does not need the medium of a bodily sense; he is himself sense and he senses them directly. The best way to see is to do it un-aided; then you know at once everything you wish to know. More: out-side help is unwelcome because to need it is to be less than perfect and not really free.

I.2. Why do you need anything, especially from your inferiors? Surely that would be preposterous and unworthy? It is clearly a dis-honor for a superior to ask the help of inferiors. No man will be per-fectly free from such dishonor until he enters into the freedom of the sons of God (Rom 8:21). They shall all be taught by God (Jn 6:45) and they will be happy in God without the intervention of any creature. This will be a homecoming, when we leave the native land of the body for the realm of spirits. This realm is our God, the greatest Spirit, the great mansion of the blessed spirits. Let neither the bodily sense nor the imagination usurp anything for itself here, for he is truth and wis-dom, virtue, eternity, the supreme Good. For now, we are absent from this place; the place where we are is a vale, and a vale of tears (Ps 83:7), in which sensuality rules and consideration is in exile, in which the bod-ily sense exercises itself freely and effectively, but shows the spiritual eye to be in darkness.[1]

Is it surprising if the stranger needs the help of someone who lives there? Happy is the traveler who in the course of his time on earth can make use of the kindness of the citizens, without which he cannot make the transition, using them rather than enjoying;[2] urging rather than ask-ing; demanding rather than begging.

---

1. On the *regio dissimilitudinis*, see F. Châtillon, *Regio Dissimilitudinis, Mélanges E. Po-déchard* (Lyons, 1945), pp. 85–102.

2. On *uti* and *frui* Bernard would have drawn on Augustine, *De Doctrina Christiana*, I.iii.3, CCSL 32 (Turnholt, 1962).

THE THREE SPECIES OF CONSIDERATION BY
WHICH IT IS POSSIBLE TO ASCEND

II.3. He is great who knows how to empty the senses as though they
were the wealth of those citizens and to use them for the benefit of his
own salvation and that of many. He is no less great who makes himself
steps to climb up to invisible things by studying philosophy. But the
one is sweeter; the other more beneficial. The first is agreed to be happier; the second stronger. But the greatest of all is he who spurns the
use of things which the senses can perceive (as far as human frailty can)
and goes up not by steps but in great leaps beyond our imagining; he
has learned to fly to the heights in contemplation at times.

I think Paul's raptures were like that: raptures, not steps up, for
he himself says that he was "caught up" rather than that he "ascended"
(2 Cor 12:2). That is why he said, "If we are beside ourselves, it is for
God" (2 Cor 5:13). Further, these three come together when consideration, even in the place of its exile (Ps 118:54), is brought higher by
zeal for virtue and with the assistance of grace, and either restrains sensuality so that it does not get above itself, or holds it so that it does not
wander, or flees it, so that it does not corrupt. In the first consideration
is more powerful, in the second freer, in the third purer. Indeed that
flight is made on twin wings of purity and eagerness.

II.4. Do you want me to name each of these species of consideration for you? If it seems acceptable to you, let us call the first practical,
the second scientific, the third speculative.[3] The definitions which I am
about to give will make plain the reasons for describing them in this
way: consideration is practical when it makes use of the senses and the
things the senses perceive in an orderly and coordinated way, so as to
please God. It is scientific when it wisely and carefully searches into
and weighs the signs of God's work in the world. It is speculative when
it retires into itself and, as far as God helps it, frees itself from human
affairs for the contemplation of God.

I think that you are keenly aware that this last is the fruit of the
others. If the others do not lead to this, they are not what they seem to
be. And the first sows much and reaps nothing if it does not look to the
last. The second meanders and makes no progress if it does not direct

---

3. A division drawn from Boethius's *Opuscula Sacra*. See note 14.

itself to the last. Therefore what the first desires, the second scents and the third tastes. The other two lead to the same taste, but more slowly. The first gets there more effortfully, the second more quietly.

III.5. You are saying, "You have told us enough about the way up; you must also tell us where the ascent is leading." If you hope for this you will be disappointed; it is beyond description. Do you think I am going to tell you what the eye has not seen and the ear has not heard and what has not entered the heart of man (1 Cor 2:9)? The Apostle says, "God has revealed it to us through his Spirit" (1 Cor 2:10). Therefore what is above us is not taught us by words but revealed by the Spirit. What words cannot explain, consideration seeks, prayer asks for, a well-led life deserves, purity attains.

Indeed, when I tell you of those things which are above, do not think I am sending you to stare at the sun, or moon, or stars, at the firmament, or the waters which are above the heavens (Ps 148:4). All those things, though they are "above" in place are "below" in dignity of nature. For they are bodies. Your portion is spirit; you will seek in vain for anything above which is not spirit. For God is a spirit (Jn 4:24) and so are the holy angels, and they are above you. But God is superior in nature, the angels in grace. You and the angels have in common that which is best in you, and that is reason. God has no "best" quality; he is wholly one Best. He, and those who are blessed spirits with him, are to be investigated by our consideration in three ways, as though by three paths: by opinion, faith, knowledge. The work of reason is to understand them; faith depends on authority; only opinion rests on a likeness to truth.

Two of these are certain of the truth, but to faith truth is hidden and obscure; to knowledge it is bare and plain. Yet opinion claims no certainty. It seeks truth by trying to discover what is like truth, rather than by grasping it directly.

III.6. Confusion must be avoided, so that faith does not cling to the uncertainty of opinion or call into question again what is firm and fixed by faith. And it is important to know this: that if opinion makes assertions, it is rash. If faith hesitates it is weak. And knowledge, if it tries to break the seal of faith, is considered an intruder, a squinter at majesty (Prv 25:27).

Many have thought their opinion knowledge, and they have been wrong. And yet opinion can be thought to be knowledge. But knowledge cannot be opinion. Why is that? Because the one can be wrong, the other not. Or if it could be deceived, it was not knowledge but opinion. True knowledge not only grasps the truth, but knows that it is the truth.

We can define each of them. Faith is a certain voluntary and confident foretaste of truth not yet apparent. Knowledge is a clear and certain grasp of something unseen. Opinion is holding as true something you do not know to be false.[4] Therefore, as I have said, faith has no doubt, or if it does, it is not faith but opinion.

How then does faith differ from knowledge? In that even though it is no more in doubt than knowledge, we hold what we believe as a mystery, as we do not do with knowledge. When you know something you seek no further. Or if you do, you have not yet "known."

There is nothing we should rather know than what we now believe. Our happiness will be complete when what is already certain to us will be as plain as it is sure.

What We Ought to Contemplate in the Heavenly Spirits

IV.7. Now that we have got these things out of the way, let us direct our consideration to that Jerusalem which is above, our mother (Gal 4:26); and let us carefully and watchfully investigate what is beyond investigation by all the three ways we have mentioned, as far as is lawful, or to the extent that is given to us.

First of all we have discovered by reading and we hold in faith that the citizens of heaven are spirits of power, glorious, blessed, having individuality and ranked in order (2 Jgs 30:16) of dignity from their creation, perfect of their kind, with ethereal bodies, immortal, not created incapable of suffering, but made so (that is, by grace not nature); pure in mind, kindly in affection, devout in piety, perfect in chastity, of one mind in agreement, secure in peace, created by God, dedicated to the praise and worship of God.

People hold different opinions about the bodies of the citizens of heaven, not only whence they come, but whether they have bodies at all. I should not disagree with anyone who said that this was a matter of opinion. That they are endowed with understanding we

---

4. The question of the degree of certainty to be accorded to opinion was discussed among contemporaries. See my *Anselm and a New Generation* (Oxford, 1980), pp. 81ff.

hold not by faith nor by opinion, but by knowledge, for they cannot be without understanding and enjoy the presence of God. Likewise, we know certain of their names because we have heard them, and through these we can grasp and discern something of their merits, dignities, and orders, although human ears do not hear perfectly clearly. What is not learned by hearing is not faith; for "faith comes by hearing" (Rom 10:7). And so we have described these as matters of opinion.

Why are we told these heavenly names, if not to allow us, in faith, to take a view of what they name—angels, archangels, virtues, powers, principalities, dominations, thrones, cherubim, and seraphim: these names. What do they mean? Is there no difference between those spirits which are simply called angels and those called archangels?

IV.8. What does this distinction of orders signify?[5]

Unless you think something else fits better, let us take it that those who are called angels, each of whom is believed to be entrusted with the care of a particular person, are sent to minister, as Paul teaches, to those who are heirs of salvation (Heb 1:14); of these the Savior says, "Their angels always see the Father's face" (Mt 18:10).

Suppose that above these are the archangels who, knowing divine mysteries, are sent only on important and serious occasions. Of these we read that that great archangel Gabriel was sent to Mary (Lk 1:26) for a reason which could not have been more important.

Let us suppose that above them come the virtues,[6] at whose bidding or by whose act signs and wonders appear in the elements or are formed from the elements, to instruct mortal men (Dt 6:22; Ps 134:9, etc.). Perhaps that is why when you read in the Gospel, "There will be signs in the sun, moon and stars" (Lk 21:25), a little after we find, "For the powers of heaven will be moved" (Lk 21:26). These are certainly the spirits through whom powerful signs take place. Let us consider the powers to be above these, whose power checks the powers of darkness (Lk 22:53) and binds the malignity of this air, so that it can do no evil, nor any harm, unless it is for our good.

Above these are, let us say, the principalities, by whose moderation and wisdom every power on earth is set up, ruled, kept

---

5. John Scotus Erigena's renderings of the works of Pseudo-Dionysius are conveniently accessible in PL 111. See especially the *Celestial Hierarchy* on the orders of angels.

6. *Virtus*: power or virtue, here translated virtue to distinguish it from *potestas*.

within bounds, transferred, diminished, altered. Let us suppose the dominations to be ranked still higher, above all these orders, who are their ministering spirits (Heb 1:14). They are masters of the ruler- ship of the principalities, guardians of the powers, the work of the virtues, the revelations of the archangels, the care and provision of the angels.

Let us suppose that the thrones have risen to reaches even higher than these, and that they are called "thrones" because they are seated and God is seated in them. For he cannot be seated upon those who are not themselves seated. Do you ask what I think this "sitting" is? I think it is supreme tranquillity, most placid serenity, the peace which passes all understanding (Phil 4:7). Such is he, the Lord of Sabaoth, who sits upon the throne, judging all things in tranquillity, most placid, most serene, most peaceful. And he has placed thrones for himself, who closely resemble himself.

Let us suppose the cherubim drink from the very fount of wisdom, which is the mouth of the Most High (Sir 24:5), and pour forth a stream of knowledge upon all the citizens of heaven. And let us see whether this is not that of which the prophet spoke, the rushing river which makes glad the city of God (Ps 45:5).

And let us suppose the Seraphim to be those who are aflame with the divine fire, and kindle the other citizens so that each is a burning and shining light, burning with love, shining with knowledge (Jn 5:35).

IV.9. O Eugenius, how good it is for us to be here (Mt 17:4)! But how much better it would be if perhaps we could at some time follow on wholly, whither we have gone in part. We have gone on in mind, but not with our whole mind; with only part, and that too small a part. Our affections lie weighted down by this bodily mass, and they are stuck to the mire by desire; for now only dry and delicate consideration flies before. And yet from that little which is now given consideration freely cries, "Lord, I have loved the beauty of your house and the place of habitation of your glory" (Ps 25:8). What if the soul gathered itself wholly together and, with its affections recalled from all the places where they are held captive (Jer 29:14), (fearing what there is no need to fear, loving what is unworthy of love, grieving over nothing, rejoic- ing over less than nothing), it began to fly in utter freedom and to drive on in the power of the Spirit (Dn 14:35) and to glide along on the fra- grance of grace? Surely when it begins to fly round those shining man- sions and to look more intently into the bosom of Abraham (Lk 16:22) and to see again the souls of the martyrs under the altar (whatever that altar is) (Rv 6:9),[7] wearing the first robe (Lk 15:22) and patiently waiting for the second, will it not say with the prophet, even more insistently, "One thing have I asked of the Lord; this will I seek, that I may dwell in the house of the Lord all the days of my life, that I may see the will of the Lord and visit his temple" (Ps 26:4)? Is not the heart of God to be seen there? Is the perfect and acceptable will of God not manifest there? (Rom 12:2), good in itself, pleasing in its effects, pleasing to those who enjoy it, perfect to the perfect, and the ultimate goal of those who seek? God's heart of mercy (Lk 1:78) is evident there, and the peacefulness of his thoughts (Jer 29:11), and the riches of his salvation (Is 33:6), and the mysteries of good will (Lk 2:16), the secrets of kindness which are hidden from mortals and not clearly glimpsed even by the elect. This is, indeed, for the good of their salvation, so that they do not cease to fear before their love makes them worthy.

IV.10 In these who are called seraphim we can see how he loves whose love arises from no need, but who hates nothing that he has made (Wis 11:25). We can see how he takes care of those he has determined to save; how he carries them along; how he embraces them; how that fire (Dt 4:24; Heb 12:29) burns up the sins the elect have committed in their youth and the chaff of their ignorance, and renders them pure and worthy of his love.

We can see in the cherubim, who are said to be "fullness of knowledge," that the Lord is a God of knowledge (1 Sm 2:3), for in him there is no ignorance of any sort. For he is all light and in him is no darkness at all (1 Jn 1:5). He is all-seeing, and his eye never fails because it is never closed (Ps 16:2). He does not need to move into a light outside himself to see by, because he is the source of his own seeing. We can perceive how he sits on the thrones, as a judge who brings no fear to the innocent and who cannot be circumvented. He does not want to avoid judging, for as we have said, he sees and loves. Nor is it without significance that he sits. It signifies tranquillity. I would like my judgment to come from such a countenance full of love, unable to make a mistake, untroubled.

We see in the dominations how great is God's majesty, at whose nod an empire is set up, whose bounds are universal and eternal.

We see in the principalities the source from which all things come. Just as a door hangs on a hinge, so the universe hangs on his rulership.

---

7. The "altar" of Rv 6:9 was a subject of speculation in medieval exegesis.

We see in the powers that this same Prince powerfully protects those he rules and repels and drives away hostile powers.

We see in the virtues that one force of virtue extends everywhere equally, through which all things have their being as, invisible and motionless, it gives them life and affects them and moves all things for their good, holding them in strength. When it appears to men in uncommon effects, they speak of miracles or prodigies.

Lastly, we can see and wonder at in angels and archangels the truth and reality in experience of that saying, "For he cares about us" (1 Pt 5:7). He does not cease to delight us with visits from such beings, to instruct us by revelations, to whisper advice to us, and to take great care of us to our comfort.

V.11. All this the one and supreme Spirit who created (1 Cor 12:11) them has conferred on these spirits, giving to each as he willed. He works these things in them and gives them these tasks, but to each in a different way. The seraphim burn, but with the fire of God, or rather, with the fire which is God. They love, for this is their special gift, but not as much as God or in the same way. The cherubim shine and are great in knowledge, they participate in truth, though not in the same way as Truth itself, or as much. The thrones sit, but by the beneficence of him who sits in them. They judge with tranquillity (Wis 12:18) but not in the measure or manner of the Bringer of peace (Jn 3:34), the peace which passes all understanding (Phil 4:7). The dominations rule, but under the Lord, and they also serve. What is this compared with his eternal sole dominion? The principalities are princes and they govern, but they themselves are governed, for they would not know how to govern if they were not governed. In the powers, strength is the outstanding quality, but he to whom they owe their strength is strong in a different way, and stronger than they are. Indeed, he is not so much strong as strength itself. The virtues have it as their ministry to stir up the lazy hearts of men by showing them signs. The virtue they have in them brings the signs about. They bring them about, but in comparison with what he does they do nothing. The difference is so great that it is to him alone that the prophets say, "You are God who does marvellous things" (Ps 76:15) and again, concerning him, "He who does great and wonderful things" (Ps 135:4).

V.12. If you say that an angel can be present in us, I have no quarrel with that. I remember that it is written, "An angel spoke in me" (Zec 1:14). Yet there is a difference, and it is this. An angel is "within" when he suggests that we do good. He does not enter to cause us to do good.

He is in us exhorting us to do good, not making us good. God is in us in such a way that he causes something to happen, so that he infuses or, rather, floods us, so that we partake of him. This happens in such a way that a man need not be afraid to say that God is one Spirit with our spirit, even if he is not one person or one substance. For you have, "He who clings to God is one in Spirit with him" (1 Cor 6:17). Therefore the angel is with the soul; God is in the soul. The angel is in the soul as its companion, God as its life.

And so just as the soul sees through the eyes, hears through the ears, smells with the nostrils, tastes with the mouth, and touches with all the rest of the body, so God does different things through different spirits, for example, in some showing his love, in others his knowledge, in others more of what he does, just as the manifestation of the Spirit is made to each for his benefit (1 Cor 12:7). Who is this we speak of so familiarly, but who is in reality so far off? How do we speak of him in our talk when he is hidden in his majesty and completely beyond our seeing and feeling?

Hear what he himself says to men: "Just as the heavens are exalted above the earth, so are my ways higher than your ways and my thoughts than your thoughts" (Is 55:9). We are said to love; so is God, and many more things of that sort. But God loves as Love itself; he knows as Truth itself. He sits as Equity, rules as Majesty, governs as Prince, keeps safe as Salvation, works as Strength, reveals as Light, is with us as Holiness. All these things the angels do, and so do we; but in a far lowlier way, and not because of the good we are but because of the good we share.

What Is to Be Contemplated in the Essence of God. The Heresy of Those Who Say "God Is God in His Divinity, But the Divinity Is Not Itself God: God Is One"[8]

VI.13. Pass beyond those spirits for now and you may perhaps be able to say with the Bride, "Almost as soon as I had passed them I found him whom my soul loves" (Sg 3:4). Who is he? I cannot think of any

---

8. The debate to which Bernard refers here concerned the teaching of Gilbert of Poitiers. For a discussion, see the introduction to N. M. Häring's edition of Gilbert of Poitiers's *Commentaries on Boethius* (Toronto, 1966).

better way to put it than to say that he is "He who is" (Ex 3:14). This is what he wanted to be said of him. He enjoined Moses to say this to the people, "He who is has sent me to you" (Ex 3:14). Rightly indeed. Nothing is more fitting to the eternity which God is. If you say that God is good or great or blessed or wise or anything of that sort, it is all summed up by saying that he "is." For to him, to be is what it is to be all these things. If you were to add a hundred such things you would not have gone beyond saying that he is. If you said those things you would not have added anything. If you did not mention them you would have subtracted nothing.

If you have now seen how unique and how supreme his being is, surely you consider that in comparison with him, whatever is not this being rather fails to exist than exists?

What is God? That without which nothing exists (Jn 1:3). Just as nothing exists without him, so he cannot exist without himself. He exists for himself and for all, and so in some way he alone exists who is his own existence and that of everything else.

What is God? The beginning. This is what he called himself (Jn 8:25). Many things are called beginnings, but that is because something comes after them. If you look back and see that one thing precedes another, you will call that the beginning. So if you are seeking the true and absolute beginning, it is necessary for you to discover that which has no beginning. That from which everything began had itself no beginning. For if it had a beginning it must have had a source. Nothing begins from itself—unless perhaps someone thinks that that which was not could have given a beginning to its own existence. Or that something existed before it existed? But since reason does not accept either of these things, it is clear that nothing exists as its own beginning. And indeed what had its beginning from something else was not first. Therefore the true Beginning did not have a beginning in any way, but began wholly from itself.

VI.14. What is God? A Being for whom the ages have not come or gone, and are coeternal with him. What is God? He "from whom and through whom and in whom are all things" (Rom 11:36; 1 Cor 8:6). "From whom" are all things through creation, not as from a source. "Through whom" are all things (in case you think the Author and the Creator are not one and the same). "In whom" are all things, not as in a place, but as if "in power." "From whom" are all things, as from one beginning, the Author of all things. "Through whom" are all things, lest we think the Maker is not the beginning. "In whom" are all things (in case we think there is some third thing, a place). "From whom," that is, not of whom, for God is not material.

He is the efficient not the material cause.[9] In vain do the philosophers search for matter. God did not need matter. He did not look for a workshop or a craftsman. He himself made everything through himself and in himself. Whence? From nothing. For if he made it from anything, he did not make that something, and thus he did not make everything. Perish the thought that from his incorrupt and incorruptible substance he should make so many corruptible things, good though they are.

Do you ask where he is if all things are in him? I can say no more than this: What place can hold him? Do you ask where he is not? That, too, I cannot say. What place is without God? God is beyond understanding (Jer 32:19). But you have grasped something if you have realized this about him: that he who is not enclosed in any place is nowhere and he who is not excluded from any place is everywhere. In his own sublime and incomprehensible way, just as all things are in him (Col 1:16–7), so he is in all things (1 Cor 15:28). As the Evangelist says, "He was in the world" (Jn 1:10). Yet he is now where he was before the world began. There is nowhere further to ask about. There was nothing but God and so he was in himself (Jn 1:3).

VII.15. What is God? He is that than which nothing better[10] can be thought. If you think that is correct you should not hold that there is anything from which God is and which is not itself God. For if there were such a thing it would undoubtedly be the better. How could it not be better than God if it is not God and yet is that which causes God to be? But it is better for us to say that that divinity by which they say that God is, is nothing other than God. For there is nothing in God but God. "What?" they say. "Do you deny that God has divinity?" No, but that which he is, he is. "Do you deny that he is God by divinity?" No, but that divinity is nothing but what he himself is.[11]

If you have found something else, if the Trinity which is God assists me, I shall rise up boldly against it. The earth has far corners to

---

9. This division of types of causes had become a commonplace; Abelard could not trace it to its Greek origin, but he discusses it in *Theologia Christiana*, II.28, ed. M. Buytaert, CCCM XII (Turnholt, 1969), pp. 144 *et alibi*.

10. Gilbert Crispin, abbot of Westminster, adapts Anselm's *dictum* that God is that than which nothing greater can be thought, and speaks, as Bernard does here, of *melius*. See *The Works of Gilbert Crispin*, ed. A. S. Abulafia and G. R. Evans (London, 1986).

11. See note 8.

limit it. That is not what God is like. God is a Trinity. God is each of the three Persons. If it pleases you to add a fourth divinity, I am already convinced that this person who is not God is not worthy of worship. I think you agree, for "You shall worship the Lord your God and him only shall you serve" (Lk 4:8). It is a glorious divinity which does not dare to claim divine honor for itself. But it is better that we reject this fourth than receive it without honor. Many things are said to be in God, and in a most true and Catholic[12] way, but the many are one. Otherwise, if we were to think them separate, we should not have a fourness but a hundredfold. For example, we call God great, good, just, and innumerable things of that sort, but unless you consider all to be one in God and with God, you will have a multiple God.

VII.16. I can think of a better God than this God of yours. You ask what God? Pure simplicity. True judgment puts a simple nature higher than a compound one. I know what they are accustomed to reply to this. They say, "We do not attribute many things to God as conditions of his existence, but only this one: divinity." You therefore assert, if not a multiple God, at least a dual one, and you have not arrived at pure simplicity, nor at that than which nothing better can be thought. That which is under even one form is not simple, just as she who has known even one man is not a virgin. I speak with confidence. He who is even double shall not be my God. For I have a better. Certainly I should put this dual God before a numerous and multiple one, but I despise such a God in comparison with a simple God. My God is universal. He does not have this or that attribute, any more than he possesses these or those. He is who he is (Ex 3:14), not what he is.

He is pure, simple, whole, perfect, constant to himself, with nothing about him which is temporal or local or involved in the particularities of created things. He gives up nothing of himself to such things. There is nothing of his which can be counted, nothing which can be made to add up to a total of one. He is one, but not a unity of many things. He is not made of parts like a body, or diffused in feelings like a soul. He is not a substance with forms, like all things which are made (Jn 1:3), not a single form as he seems to these thinkers to be.[13] Great praise be to God that he is claimed to be made free of forms by a single form! This is to say that everything else is under many forms and God

---

12. *Catholicus* was often used for *Christianus* in the twelfth century.
13. The reference is to Gilbert of Poitiers and his disciples. See N. M. Häring's introduction to his edition of *Gilbert of Poitiers, Commentaries on Boethius* (Toronto, 1966).

is under only one. What is this? Shall he by whose beneficence all things exist himself bow in acknowledgement to another's beneficence? That praise, as they say, amounts to blasphemy. Is it not greater to be in need of nothing than of one thing? Have reverence enough for God to attribute to him what is greater. If your thinking cannot ascend so high, how can you place God lower? He is his own form; he is his own essence. For now I look up to his level and if another higher should appear I would rather grant him to be that. Surely we need not fear that thought will fly higher than he? However high it goes he is beyond it. To look for the Most High below the highest point man's thought can reach is ridiculous. To put him at that point is impious. He is to be sought beyond it, not this side of it.

VII.17. Climb, if you can, to a still loftier thought and God will be exalted (cf. Ps 63:7–8). God is not formed; he is form. He is not affected; he is feeling. He is not a composite; he is pure simplicity. And you know exactly what I mean by simple: It is the same as one. God is as simple as one. He is one as nothing else is. If it can be put this way, he is "one-est." The sun is one, for there is no other sun. The moon is one, again because there is no other. He is one in that way, but more so. What is more than that? He is one in himself.

You wish this to be explained to you? He is always the same, and in the same way. The sun is not one like that, nor the moon. Both declare that they are not, for one moves and the other wanes. God is not only one to himself; he is one in himself. There is nothing in him but himself. He does not change with time. Nor does his substance alter. Hence Boethius says of him, "This is truly one in which there is no number, nothing but what it is. For it cannot be made subject to forms because it is a form."[14] Compare this with everything else which can be said to be one and nothing else will seem one.

Yet God is a Trinity. What then? Have we made nonsense of what has been said about unity by bringing in Trinity? No. But we establish what the unity is. We say that he is Father, Son, and Holy Spirit, yet not three Gods but one. What is this number without number, so to speak? If it is three how can it not be a number? If it is one, how is it a number? "But I have," you say, "something I can number and something I cannot." The substance is one but the Persons are three. Is that

---

14. Boethius, *De Trinitate*, 2, *Theological Tractates*, ed. H. F. Stewart, E. K. Rand, and S. J. Tester (London, 1973).

startling or incomprehensible? Not if the Persons are thought of apart from the substance. Now since those three Persons are that substance and that substance is those three Persons, who can deny that there is number? For they are truly three. But who can number them? For truly they are one.

But if you think that is easily explained, tell me what you have numbered in speaking of three. Natures? There is one. Essences? There is one. Substances?[15] There is one. Deities? There is one. "I number not these but the Persons," you say, which are not that one nature, one essence, one substance, one divinity. You are a Catholic. You will not say this.

VIII.18. The Catholic Church believes that the properties of the Persons are no other than the Persons themselves, and that the Persons are no other than one God, one divine substance, one divine nature, one divine and supreme majesty. Number them if you can, either the Persons without the substance (which is what they are) or the properties without the Persons (which are what they are). But if anyone tries to divide the Persons from the substance or the properties from the Persons, I do not know how he who goes so much too far in numbering can profess himself a worshiper of the Trinity. And so we speak of three, but not to the prejudice of unity. We speak of one, but not to the confusion of Trinity. For these names are not empty, nor are they words without meaning.

Does someone ask how this may be (Jn 3:9)? Let it be enough for him to believe this, not as something which is clear to reason, nor as something which is a matter of uncertain opinion, but as something of which he is convinced by faith. This is a great mystery (Eph 5:32) and to be revered, not peered into. How is there plurality in unity or unity in plurality? It is rash to enquire into this; it is devout to believe it; to know it is life, and life eternal (Jn 17:3). Therefore, Eugenius, if you consider it of value, think how many kinds of "one" there are, so that the supremacy of this unique "one" may be more obvious.

There is what can be called a collective unity, as when we make a pile of many stones. There is a constituted unity (1 Cor 12:12,12:20), as where a body is constituted of many members or when many parts make a whole of some sort. There is conjugal unity by which two cease to be two and become one flesh (Gn 2:24; Mk 19:5–6; 1 Cor 6:16). There

---

15. Augustine uses *natura*, *essentia*, *substantia* interchangeably.

is unity of nature as when soul and flesh make one man. There is moral unity by which a virtuous man tries to free himself from instability and inconsistency and always to be at one with himself. There is a unity of consent, when through charity many men are of one mind and one spirit (Acts 4:32). There is a unity of devotion, when the soul, clinging to God with all its desires, is one in spirit with him (1 Cor 6:17). There is a unity of deigning, by which our clay was assumed by the Word of God in a single Person.

VIII.19. What are all these compared with that supreme and, so to speak, "unique" One, where shared substance makes unity. If you compare any of them to that unity it will be in some way one, but there will be no comparison between them. Therefore among all the things which are rightly said to be one, the unity of the Trinity is first, in which three Persons are one substance. It excels, putting it into second place, that unity by which three substances are one Person in Christ. Moreover, these and the others which can be said to be one are called one in imitation of that supreme unity, not by comparison with it, as true and sober consideration demonstrates. Nor are we led away from professing this unity by asserting that it is a unity of three, for in this Trinity we do not find any multiplicity, any more than there is solitude in its unity. Therefore when I say "one" the number of the Trinity does not disturb me, for it does not multiply the essence or change it or divide it. Again, when I say "three," the idea of unity does not argue against me, for this unity does not confuse the three entities or beings, or reduce them to singularity.

IX.20. I tell you that I think the same of that unity to which I have attributed the honor of being second to this among other "ones." I say that in Christ the Word, the soul and the body are one Person without confusion of essences, and that without prejudice to the unity of Person they keep their numerical distinctness. Nor would I deny that this unity is of that sort by which the soul and the body are one man.[16] It was indeed appropriate that that mystery brought about for man should fit his constitution so closely and in a way so like it. It was appropriate, too, that it should be like that supreme unity which is in God and is God, so that in the same way as in him three Persons are one essence, so the three essences should, on the contrary, be one person. Do you not see how beautifully he is placed between the two unities, he who

---

16. See H. Denzinger, *Enchiridion Symbolorum* (Rome, 1967), p. 42.

is made the Mediator between God and man, the man Christ Jesus (1 Tim 2:5)? Most lovely fittingness, I say, that the mystery of salvation should correspond to both by an appropriate similarity, that is, both to the Savior and to the saved. Thus this unity stands in the middle between the two unities, lowlier than the one, higher than the other, and as much lower than the one as it is higher than the other.

IX.21. That Person, Christ, in whom God and man are one[17], is in himself such a great and powerful expression of unity that you would not go wrong if you were to predicate either of the other, truly and in a Catholic way pronouncing God to be man and man to be God. You cannot (except by talking nonsense) predicate the body of the soul or the soul of the body in the same way, even though body and soul are similarly one man. It is not suprising that the soul is not equally able to bind to itself a body by the mere intention of giving it life, strong though that is, and to hold a body by its affections, as divinity has done in the case of that man who was predestined to be the Son of God in power (Rom 1:14). Divine predestination is a long and powerful chain to bind, stretching from eternity. What is longer than eternity? What is more powerful than divinity? That is why this unity cannot be dissolved even by death, though body and soul are separated by death. Perhaps this is what he felt who said that he was unworthy to loose the strap of his sandal (Mk 1:7).

X.22. It would not seem inappropriate to me if someone linked with these three essences in Christ those three measures of flour in the Gospel (Mt 13:3; Lk 13:21), which, mixed and leavened, make one bread. How well the woman leavened them, so that the Word was not separated from the body or the soul even at the division of body and soul. Even in separation there remained inseparable unity. For the separation in part which took place could not break that unity which remained in all three. Whether body and soul were joined or divided, the unity of Person continued in all three. One and the same Christ, one and the same Person, was the Word, the soul and the body, even after death. It was in the Virgin's womb, as I think, that this mingling and leavening took place, and that Woman who mingled also leavened—for perhaps I should not go far astray in identifying this leaven as Mary's faith. She who truly believes is truly blessed, for what the Lord said to her was fulfilled in her (Lk 1:45). These things would not have been

---

17. *Ibid.*

fulfilled unless, as the Lord said, they were all leavened and unleavened perpetually (Mt 13:33), keeping for us, in death as in life, the one perfect Mediator of God and men with his divinity, the Man Christ Jesus (1 Tm 2:5).

Concerning Those Who Assert That the Flesh of Christ Is Something New Created in the Virgin, and Not Taken from the Flesh of the Virgin

X.23. We must take note in this wonderful mystery of the marvellous and most fitting degrees of distinction, according to the number of measures of meal: new, old, eternal. The new is the soul, which we believe to be created from nothing at the moment it is infused. The old is the flesh, which we know is passed on from the first man, that is, from Adam. The eternal is the Word, which is, with undoubted truth, asserted to have been coeternal with the Father from eternity, and begotten by him. And in these you will see, if you look carefully, a triple kind of divine power (2 Mc 7:28). Something is made from nothing; something new is made from something old, something everlasting and blessed from something damned and dead. What does this have to do with our salvation? A great deal in every way (Rom 3:2). First, because having been brought to nothing by our sin, we are created new again by this in some way, so that there is a sense in which we are the beginning of his creation (Jas 1:18). Second, because we have been freed from the old slavery and made sons of God (Rom 8:21) and we walk in newness of spirit (Rom 6:4, 7:6). Lastly, because we are called from the power of darkness (Col 1:13) to the kingdom of eternal brightness in which even now he has caused us to sit, in Christ (Eph 2:6). Let those who try to separate us from the flesh of Christ be cut off from us, for wickedly asserting that the flesh of Christ was created newly (2 Cor 5:17) in the Virgin and not taken from her. Long before that prophetic spirit spoke beautifully about this view, or rather, blasphemy, of the wicked, when he said, "A shoot shall come forth from the root of Jesse and a flower spring up from his root" (Is 11:1). He could have said, "and a flower from the shoot," but he preferred "from the root" in order to show that the shoot and the flower had the same origin. Therefore flesh was assumed from the origin from which the Virgin came forth and was not created new in the Virgin; for it was derived from the same root.

The Many Expressions of Divine Contemplation

XI.24. Perhaps you will groan if we ask again what God is: both because we have asked that question so often already, and because you doubt whether we are going to find an answer. I tell you, Father Eugenius, it is only God who can never be sought in vain (Is 45:19), even when he cannot be found. Let your own experience convince you of that, not, believe an expert, not myself, but the Holy One, who said, "Lord you are good to those who hope in you, to the soul which seeks you" (Lam 3:25).

What, then, is God? He is the purpose to which the universe looks, the salvation of the elect. What he is to himself, only he knows. What is God? All-powerful will, benevolent virtue, eternal light, changeless reason, supreme blessedness. He creates minds to share in himself, gives them life, so that they may experience him, causes them to desire him, enlarges them to grasp him, justifies them so that they may deserve him, stirs them to zeal, ripens them to fruition, directs them to equity, forms them in benevolence, moderates them to make them wise, strengthens them to virtue, visits them to console, enlightens them with knowledge, sustains them to immortality, fills them with happiness, surrounds them with safety.

God Is No Less the Punishment of the Proud Than the Glory of the Humble

XII.25. What is God? He is not less the punishment of the wicked than the glory of the humble. He is, as it were, the rational principle of equity, unchanging and never compromising; indeed, he reaches everywhere, and every evil which meets him must be confounded (Wis 8:1). Is it not obvious that everything which is swollen or distorted must be shaken to pieces when it is thrown against it? Woe to anything which comes up against a righteousness which, because it is also fortitude, does not know how to give way. What is contrary and opposed to evil will as always to be striving and clashing, but for nothing. Woe to rebellious wills, which get only punishment when they oppose themselves. What is a worse punishment than always to will what will never be and to be constantly opposing what will always be? What is condemned like a will given up to this compulsion to desire and to turn away, so that it experiences both only perversely, and, for that reason, wretchedly? It will never have what it wants and it will endure forever what it does not want. It is wholly just that he who is never drawn to what is right should never attain what he wants. Who makes this so? The righteous Lord our God, who deals with the perverse in their own perverse way (Ps 91:16, 17:27). Right and wrong never agree, for they are opposed (Gal 5:17), even when they do not harm one another. The harm they do is to one another, certainly not to God. "It is hard for you," he says, "to kick against the goad" (Acts 9:15). It is not for the goad that it is hard, but for him who kicks. God is also the punishment of the wily man, for he is light. What is so hateful as light to obscene and profligate minds? Truly, "everyone who does evil hates the light" (Jn 3:20). But, I say, can they not avoid it? No. It shines in the darkness and the darkness does not comprehend it (Jn 1:5). The light sees the darkness, because for light to shine is to see. But the light is not seen in turn by the darkness, and the darkness does not comprehend it. It is seen so that it can be confounded; it does not see, for if it did it would be comforted. It is seen not only by the light but in the light. By whom? By everyone who sees, so that the multitude of witnesses may add to their confusion. But out of so large a number of spectators no eye causes each more trouble than his own. From no scrutiny in heaven or on earth (1 Cor 8:5) would a heavy conscience be more glad to flee, and from none is he less able to flee. The darkness does not hide even itself. Those who see nothing else see themselves. The works of darkness pursue them (Rom 13:12), and they have no place to hide from them (Ps 18:7), not even in darkness.

This is the worm which does not die (Mk 9:43), the memory of things past (Wis 11:13). Once it is put into a person, or rather, born in a person through sin, it clings there stubbornly, and it is never afterward to be removed. It never stops gnawing at the conscience. Feeding on this food which is never exhausted, it draws out its life. I am filled with horror by this gnawing worm, and by such a living death. I am filled with horror at the thought of falling into the hands of this living (Heb 10:31) death, this dying life.

XII.26. This is the second death (Rv 20:14) which never actually kills, but is always killing. Who can grant that they die once and not allow that they die forever? Those who say to the mountains, "Fall upon us" and to the hills, "cover us" (Lk 23:30), what is it they wish to end but death, or else avoid through the kindness of death? It is said, "They will call upon death but death will not come" (Jb 3:21). See this more clearly. It is agreed that the soul is immortal and that it will never exist without its memory, or else it would not be the soul any longer.[18] So long as the soul lasts, the memory lasts. But in what condition? Defiled with shameful acts, disgusting with crimes, swollen with vanity, scruffy and neglected with contempt. What was has passed away (2 Cor 5:17), but it is both past and not past? It has passed from the hand but not the mind. What is done cannot be undone. Even if it was done in time, what has been done lasts for eternity. What you have done wrong and remember for eternity must gnaw away for eternity. Thus you will know from experience how true is the saying, "I will stand before you and accuse you" (Ps 49:21). The Lord has spoken (Dt 4:10) and everyone who is opposed to him must be opposed to himself, so that in the end he complains, "O guardian of men, why have you set me against you. Why have I become a burden to myself" (Jb 7:20).

That is how it is, Eugenius. No being can be opposed to God and in harmony with itself. Whoever God accuses, accuses himself. Surely there will be no way in the next life in which reason can ignore the truth or the soul without its body and gathered into itself, ignore the eye of reason. How could it, when death has sent to sleep and imprisoned the senses through which the soul used to rush out from itself into the transient beauty of this world (1 Cor 7:31)? Do you see that everything is ready to bring confusion on vile men when they were brought forth to become a spectacle to God, the angels and men themselves (1 Cor 4:9)? Oh, how badly placed are all the wicked! They are set in opposition to this torrent of absolute justice and exposed to the light of naked truth. Surely this is what it is to be perpetually tossed about and perpetually confounded? The prophet says, "Destroy them with a double destruction, O Lord our God" (Jer 17:8).

What Is the Length and Breadth and Height and Depth?

XIII.27. What is God? He is the length and breadth and height and depth (Eph 3:18). "What!" you say. "Are you taking to teaching quaternity, which you abominated before?" Not at all. I did and do abominate it. I seem to have listed many things, but they are one. The one God has been described, but so that we can understand, not as he

---

18. The origin of the soul was a topic of contemporary debate, touched on in the *Sentences of the school of Laon*, O. Lottin, *ed. cit.*

is in himself. The divisions are for our benefit. They are not in him. There are different words, many paths, but they signify One; One is sought by many paths. In that quaternity no divisions of substance are expressed, no dimensions, such as we perceive by the senses, no distinction of persons, such as we adore in the Trinity, no counting of properties, such as those we attribute to the Persons individually, although they are not distinct from the Persons. To put it another way, these four are one in God and the one is four. But we cannot grasp the simplicity of God. While we strive to understand what he is as one, he appears to us as fourfold. This is because we see through a glass darkly (1 Cor 13:12); that is the only way we can see in this life. But when we see him face to face we shall see him as he is (1 Cor 13:12; 1 Jn 3:2). Then the uncertain vision of our souls will not falter, however hard we strain to see, or fragment into its own multiplicity. It will draw together, unite and conform itself to the unity of God, or rather to God who is unity, so they will be face to face with one another. Indeed, we shall be like him because we shall see him as he is (1 Jn 3:2). This is the blessed vision for which he rightly longed who said, "My face has sought you, your face, Lord, do I seek" (Ps 26:8).

For now, the search is still going on. So let us climb into the four-horse chariot. For we are still weak and feeble and we need a vehicle of that sort, in order to know him by whom we are known (Phil 3:12). He is the reason for the vehicle. For we have this instruction from the Charioteer himself, he who first showed us this chariot, so that we might desire "to comprehend with all the saints what is the length and breadth and height and depth" (Eph 3:18). He says "comprehend" not "know" so that we should not be content to be curious for knowledge, but seek with all our power to comprehend. The reward lies not in knowing but in comprehending. To put it another way, as someone says, it is a sin for someone to know what is good and not to do it (Jas 4:17). And Paul himself says in another place, "So run that you may comprehend" (1 Cor 9:24). (I shall explain in a moment what it means to "comprehend.")

XIII.28. What, then, is God? He is "length," I say. What is that? Eternity. Eternity is so long that it has no end of place or time. He is also breadth (Eph 3:18). And what is that? Love. And who shall draw boundaries to God's love, for he hates nothing that he has made (Wis 11:25)? Indeed, he causes his sun to rise upon the good and the wicked and rain falls upon the just and the unjust (Mt 5:45). Therefore his bosom enfolds even his enemies. And not satisfied with that, it stretches to infinity. He goes beyond every bound not only of love but of knowledge, as the Apostle goes on to say, "And to know the love of Christ, which passes all understanding" (Eph 3:19). What more can I say? He is eternal, or perhaps even greater, eternity itself. Do you see that the width is as great as the length? Would that you could see not only what it is like but what it actually is! To be breadth is to be depth. The one no less than two; the two no more than one. God is eternity; "God is love" (1 Jn 4:16). He is length without extension, breadth without distension. In both equally he exceeds local and temporal limits, but by the freedom of his nature, not by the vastness of his substance. He who made everything according to measure (Wis 11:21) is immense in this way, and although he is immense, this is the measure of his immensity.

XII.29. Again, what is God? "The height and the depth." In one he is above all, in the other, he is within all. It is clear that nowhere in the Godhead is equality limited. It stands square on all sides and is utterly consistent. Consider his power as the height and his wisdom as the depth. They correspond to one another symmetrically, and while the height is beyond reach the depth is equally beyond seeing into. Paul wonders at it and exclaims, "O height of the riches of the wisdom and knowledge of God; how inscrutable are his judgments, and his ways are beyond searching out" (Rom 11:33). Let us exclaim with Paul, gazing upon the most simple unity of those attributes with God and in God. O powerful wisdom, reaching everywhere in strength. O wise power, disposing all things sweetly! One reality, many effects, different acts (1 Cor 12:6). And this one reality is length because it is eternity, breadth because it is love, height because it is majesty, depth because it is wisdom.

XIV.30. We know this. But surely we do not think we have comprehended it? Argument does not comprehend these things but holiness, if that which is incomprehensible can be comprehended in any way.

But if it could not, the Apostle would not have said that we should comprehend with all the saints (Rom 11:33). So the saints comprehend it. Do you ask how? If you are holy[19], you have comprehended it and you know. If not, be holy and you will know from your own experience. Holy love makes a man holy, and it is twofold: holy fear (Ps 18:10)

19. Augustine discusses the memory and other powers of the soul in *De Trinitate*, X, ed. W. J. Mountain and Fr. Glorie, CCSL 50 (Turnholt, 1968).

of the Lord and holy love. The soul moved entirely by these grasps as if with its two arms, embraces, hugs, holds, and says, "I have him and I will not let him go" (Sg 3:4). And fear responds to the height and depth, love to the breadth and length. For what is so to be feared as the power which cannot be resisted, the wisdom from which you cannot hide? If either of these were lacking, God could be feared less. But it is fitting that you should fear him whose eye is ceaselessly seeing everything, and in whose powerful hand all things lie.

Again, what is so lovable as love itself, by which you love and are loved? Eternity makes it more lovable by being joined to it, for since it does not cease (1 Cor 13:8) it casts out suspicion (1 Jn 4:18). Love, then, with perseverance and long-suffering, and you will have length. Extend your love to your enemies and you will have breadth. Be fearful with all care, and you have grasped the height and depth (Eph 3:18).

XIV.31. But if you prefer, four attributes of your own correspond to the divine four: if you marvel, if you fear, if you burn, if you endure. Marvel at the height of majesty. Fear the abyss of judgment. To burn you must love. Eternity requires perseverance in enduring.

Who will wonder but he who contemplates the glory of God (Acts 7:55)? Who will fear, but he who looks into the depths of wisdom (1 Cor 2:10)? Who will burn but he who meditates on the love of God? Who will continue and persevere in love but he who emulates the eternity of love? Surely perseverance is an image of eternity? It is to perseverance alone that eternity is given—or rather it is perseverance alone that gives a man to eternity, as the Lord says, "He who perseveres to the end shall be saved" (Mt 10:22).

XIV.32. And now, notice that in these four are four kinds of contemplation. The first and greatest is to wonder at majesty. This demands a heart made pure, so that, freed from vices and released from sin, it can ascend easily to heavenly things. Sometimes this contemplation holds the watcher rapt in amazement and ecstasy, if only for a moment. A second kind of contemplation is necessary for this man. He needs to look on the judgments of God. While this contemplation strikes fear into the onlooker because it is indeed frightening, it drives out vices, strengthens virtues, initiates into wisdom, protects humility. Humility is the true and solid foundation of the virtues. For if humility were to collapse, the building-up of the virtues will fall down. The third kind of contemplation is occupied (or rather at leisure) in remembering kindnesses and, so as to avoid ingratitude, it urges him who remembers to love his Benefactor. Of such says the prophet, speaking to the Lord,

"They shall declare the memory of the abundance of youth sweetness" (Ps 144:7). The fourth contemplation, which forgets what is past, rests wholly in the expectation of what is promised (Phil 3:13), which nourishes patience and nerves the arm of perseverance, for what is promised is eternal. I think it is now easy to compare our four terms with those of the Apostle. For meditation on the promises covers length; remembrance of blessing, width; contemplation of majesty, height; examination of judgments, depth (Eph 3:18). He must still be sought who has not yet been found (Mt 7:7) fully, but he is perhaps sought more worthily and found more easily by prayer than discussion. So let this be the end of the book but not of the search.

ON LOVING GOD

*Aimeric, cardinal deacon of the Church of Rome from 1121 and
chancellor from 1126, was a good friend to Clairvaux. Bernard
wrote him more than a dozen letters. At some time between 1125,
when Bernard wrote the letter to the Carthusians with which he
ends his treatise, and Aimeric's death in 1141, Aimeric asked him
for a book on loving God.*

*Early in the 1120s Bernard had already written on the love of
God in the context of the monastic life, in a letter to the monks of
the Grande Chartreuse, written at their request. His thinking in
the* De Diligendo Deo *is close to what he said there, although developed in more detail. He had evidently been pleased with the way
he had expressed the central ideas in this letter, for he instructed
that it be copied at the end of the new treatise. The whole treatise,
including the letter, is translated here as Bernard himself would
have wished. The letter is integral to what he has to say.*[1]

PROLOGUE

To the illustrious lord Aimeric, cardinal deacon and chancellor of the
See of Rome, Bernard, called abbot of Clairvaux,[1] wishes that he may
live for the Lord and die in the Lord.

---

1. See Introduction to this volume.
1. In referring to himself modestly in this way Bernard is following a convention of
classical and medieval rhetoric.

You usually ask me for prayers, not answers to questions. And indeed I confess that I am not worthy to offer either. Yet prayer is my profession, even if I do not live as though it were. As to the task you have given me, to tell the truth it seems to me that I lack the diligence and ability it requires. Still, I assure you that I am glad that you are asking for spiritual in return for wordly gifts (1 Cor 9:11). It is only that you could have asked someone richer in spiritual gifts than I.

Because it is the habit both of the educated and of the uneducated to make this sort of excuse, you would be hard put to it to know whether it is prompted by genuine inability or self-excusing modesty, were it not that the execution of the task will make it plain. Accept from my poverty what I have, or I shall be thought a philosopher because of my silence.

I do not promise to answer everything you ask—only to tell you what God will give me to say about loving him. This subject tastes sweeter, and is treated with more confidence, and is more profitable to whoever hears, than any other. Your other questions you must keep for those better qualified to answer them.

I.1. You wish then to hear from me why and how God ought to be loved. I answer: The cause of loving God is God himself.[2] The way to love him is without measure.[3] Is this not enough? Perhaps it is, but only for the wise. Yet I owe something to the unwise, too (Rom 1:14), and it is usual to add something for their benefit to what is sufficient for the wise man.[4] And so, for the sake of those who are slower, I shall not find it tedious to go into each point at length, if not more deeply.

For two reasons, then, I say that God is to be loved for his own sake. No one can be more justly loved, or with greater benefit. Indeed, when it is asked why God ought to be loved, the question has two possible meanings. We may wonder which is the real question: whether God is to be loved because he deserves it, or because it is for our good. I give the same answer to both: There seems to me no good reason to love him which does not lie in himself.

So let us first see how he deserves our love.

---

2. Cf. William of St. Thierry, *The Nature and Dignity of Love*, 3, PL 184.382.

3. This pun makes use of a phrase in a letter to Augustine. See Letter 109 from Severus, PL 33.419.

4. *Sat est dictum sapienti*, "a word to the wise" is a commonplace in classical authors. See Plautus, *Persa*, 4.7(19); Terence, *Phormio*, 3.3(8), for examples.

How God Is to Be Loved for His Own Sake

He who gave himself to us when we did not deserve it certainly deserves a great deal from us (Gal 1:4). What better thing could he give us than himself? And so if we bring God's deserving into question in asking why God should be loved, we have the chief reason for loving him in this, "That he first loved us" (1 Jn 4:9–10). Surely he deserves to be loved in return when we think of who loves, whom he loves, how much he loves. Is it not he whom every spirit confesses (1 Jn 4:2) saying, "You are my God for you do not need the goods I have" (Ps 15:2)?

This divine love is true love, for it is the love of one who wants nothing for himself (1 Cor 13:5). To whom is such pure love shown?[5] "When we were still his enemies," it says, "he reconciled us to himself" (Rom 5:10). So, in utmost generosity, God loved even his enemies.

But how much did he love? St. John says, "God so loved the world that he gave his only-begotten Son" (Jn 3:16). St. Paul says, "He did not spare his own Son, but gave him up for us" (Rom 8:32). The Son, too, said of himself, "No one has greater love than the man who lays down his life for his friends" (Jn 15:13). Thus the righteous deserved to be loved by the wicked, the highest and all-powerful by the weak (Rom 5:6–7).

But someone says,[6] "That is true for men but not for angels." It is true; he who came to man's help in his great need preserved the angels from that need. he who did not allow men to remain as they were, out of an equal love gave the angels the grace not to fall into such a need.[7]

II.2. To those who see these things clearly, I think it will be evident why God is to be loved—and why he deserves to be loved. But if unbelievers hide these facts, God is always able to make their ingratitude plain by the innumerable kindnesses he showers on men for their benefit and which are quite obviously his gifts. For who else provides food for everyone who eats, light for seeing, air to breathe? It would be foolish to want to list them when I have just said that they are innumerable. Let it be enough to give the chief ones, bread, sun, and air, as examples. I say "chief" not because they are more excellent than

---

5. The Latin text has *puritas*, but the reference is clearly to purity of love.
6. This device of the pretended interruption was often used by lecturers in the twelfth century.
7. Cf. Gra 29; LTR III.187.

other gifts, but because they are more necessary, for they are bodily necessities.

You must look for higher goods in the higher part of yourself, that is, the soul. These higher goods are dignity, knowledge, virtue. Man's dignity is his free will, which is the gift by which he is superior to the animals and even rules them (Gn 1:26). Man's knowledge is that by which he recognizes that he possesses this dignity, but that it does not originate in himself. His virtue is that by which he seeks eagerly for his Creator, and when he finds him, holds to him with all his might.

II.3. Each of these three has two aspects.

Dignity is not only a natural privilege. It is also the power of dominion, for all living things on earth can be seen to stand in fear of man (Gn 9:2). Knowledge, too, is twofold, for we know both that we possess this dignity and whatever else we have that is good, and that they do not originate in ourselves. Virtue can equally be seen to have two aspects. By it we seek our Maker and when we have found him we cling to him so that we cannot be separated from him.

Dignity is nothing without knowledge, and knowledge can even be a stumbling-block without virtue. This is the reason for both these things. What glory is it to have what you do not know you have? And to know what you have, but not to know that it does not originate with you is to have glory, but not before God (Rom 4:2). To him who glories in himself the Apostle says, "What do you have that you have not received? But if you have received it, why do you boast as if you had not received it?" (1 Cor 4:7). He does not simply say, "Why do you boast?" He adds, "As if you had not received," so as to emphasize that the guilt lies not in boasting of something, but in doing so as if it was not a gift which had been received. This sort of thing is rightly called vainglory, because it does not rest on a solid foundation of truth. St. Paul points out the difference between truth and vainglory. "He who boasts, let him boast in the Lord" (1 Cor 1:31; 2 Cor 10:17; cf. Jer 9:23–24), that is, in the truth. For the Lord himself is truth (Jn 14:6).

II.4. There are two things you should know: first, what you are; second, that you are not what you are by your own power. Then you will boast, but not in vain. It says that if you do not know yourself, you should go and follow the flocks of your companions (Sg 1:6–7).[8] This is what actually happens. When man has a high honor bestowed on him

---

8. Cf. SC 32.10; LTR 1.233.

but does not appreciate it, he is deservedly compared with the beasts with whom he shares his present mortality and state of corruption (Jn 14:6).

It happens, too, when a man does not appreciate the gift of reason and spends his time with herds of unreasoning beasts; and when he ignores the glory which is within him, and models himself on the outward things his senses perceive; and when he is so carried away by curiosity[9] that he becomes no different from any other animal, because he does not see that he has received anything more than they have.

And so we should greatly fear that ignorance which makes us think less of ourselves than we should. But no less, indeed rather more, should we fear that ignorance which makes us think ourselves better than we are. This is what happens when we are deceived into thinking that some good in us originates with ourselves.

But you should avoid and detest even more than these two that presumption[10] by which, in full knowledge and deliberately, you dare to seek your own glory in good things which are not your own and which you know perfectly well are not yours by any power of your own. Thus you unashamedly steal another's glory. For the first ignorance has no glory. The second has a glory, but not in God's eyes (Rom 4:2). But this third evil which is committed knowingly is an act of treason against God.

This arrogance [11]born of the last ignorance is worse and more dangerous because while the second kind of ignorance causes us to ignore God, this leads us to despise him. And it is worse and more disgusting than the first because while the first makes us the companions of beasts, this throws us into fellowship with demons. It is pride, the greatest sin, to use gifts you have been given as though you were born with them, and to arrogate to yourself the glory which belongs to the generous giver.

II.5. With these two, dignity and knowledge, must go virtue, which is the fruit of both. Through virtue we seek and cling to the Giver of all good things and give him the glory he deserves for all that he has given. But he who knows how to do what is right and does not do it will receive many lashes (Lk 12:47). Why? Because "He did not want to understand how to behave well" (Ps 35:4). More than that, "He

---

9. For Bernard curiosity is the first step of pride (Hum 28).
10. For Bernard presumption is the seventh step of pride (Hum 44).
11. For Bernard arrogance is the sixth step of pride (Hum 43).

plotted wickedness upon his bed" (Ps 35:5). He endeavors like a wicked servant to snatch and steal away the good Lord's glory for himself, the glory due for the good qualities which he knows quite certainly do not originate with himself, because God has given him that knowledge.

It is perfectly obvious then that without knowledge dignity is utterly useless, and that knowledge without virtue is to be condemned. Truly the man of virtue, in whom knowledge is not to be condemned and dignity is not fruitless, cries to God and freely confesses, "Not to us, Lord, but to your name be the glory" (Ps 113:9). That is, "We credit ourselves with no knowledge or dignity; we ascribe it all to your name, for it all comes from you."

II.6. We have wandered too far from our subject in striving to show that those who do not know Christ are without excuse: for they are taught enough by natural law (cf. Rom 1:19ff.; 2:14–5) and the good perceptions of their bodily senses to oblige them to love God for his own sake. To sum up what has been said: Is there anyone, even an unbeliever, who does not know that he has received the necessities of bodily life in this world which we mentioned earlier—by means of which he survives, sees and breathes—from no other but him who gives food to all flesh (Ps 135:25), who causes his sun to rise on the good and the wicked alike, and the rain to fall on the just and the unjust (Mt 5:45)? Again, what man however wicked would think that that human dignity which shines in his soul came from any Author but he who says in Genesis, "Let us make man in our own image and likeness" (Gn 1:26)? Who can think that the Giver of knowledge is anyone but he who teaches man knowledge (Ps 93:10)? And who either thinks he has received the gift of virtue from any but the hand of that same Lord of virtues, or hopes to have it from any other source?

And so God deserves to be loved for himself, even by the unbeliever (Rom 3:2), for even if he does not know Christ, he knows himself.[12] No one, not even an unbeliever, can be excused, if he does not love God with all his heart, all his mind, and all his strength (Mk 12:30). An inborn sense of justice in him, which reason recognizes, cries out that he ought to love him with all his powers, for he knows that he owes him everything.[13]

Yet it is difficult for anyone, once he has received from God the

---

12. On *scito teipsum*, see the introduction to *Peter Abelard's Ethics*, ed D. Luscombe (Oxford, 1971).

13. The play on *debeat/debere* is lost in English.

power to will freely, to give up his will wholly to God and not rather to will things for himself. Perhaps it is impossible. he is tempted to treat what he has been given as his own, and clutch it to himself; as it is written, "Everyone seeks his own" (Phil 2:21), and again, "The thoughts and feelings of men are inclined to evil" (Gn 8:21).

III.7. On the contrary, the faithful know how utterly they stand in need of Jesus and him crucified (1 Cor 2:2). They wonder at and reach out to that supreme love of his which passes all knowledge (Eph 3:19).[14] They are ashamed not to respond to such love and deserving with the little they have to give.

The more surely you know yourself loved, the easier you will find it to love in return. Those to whom less has been given love less (Lk 7:47). The Jew and the pagan are not moved by such wounds of love as the Church experiences. She says, "I am wounded by love" (Sg 2:5), and again, "Surround me with flowers, pile up apples around me, for I am sick with love" (Sg 3:11). The Church sees King Solomon in the crown which his mother had placed on his head (Sg 3:11).[15] She sees the Father's only Son carrying his Cross (Jn 19:17). She sees the Lord of majesty (1 Cor 2:8)[16] struck and spat upon. She sees the Author of life and glory (Acts 3:15) transfixed by nails, wounded by a lance (Jn 19:34), smeared with abuse (Lam 3:30), and finally laying down his precious life for his friends (Jer 12:7; Jn 15:13). She sees these things, and the sword of love pierces her soul more deeply (cf. Lk 2:35), and she says, "Surround me with flowers, pile up apples around me, for I am sick with love" (Sg 2:5).

WHERE DO THE POMEGRANATES COME FROM?

These are beyond a doubt the pomegranate fruits which the Bride brought into her Beloved's garden (Sg 6:10). They were picked from the Tree of Life (Gn 2:22), and their taste had been transmuted to that of the heavenly bread, and their color to that of Christ's blood. At last she sees the death of death and death's author defeated (Heb 2:14). She sees captivity led captive (Eph 4:8) from hell to earth and from earth to heaven, so that at the name of Jesus every knee may bow, in heaven,

---

14. Cf. Csi 5.28; LTR 3.491.
15. Cf. Div 50; LTR 6^i. 270–71.
16. Bernard uses the Old Latin translation of the Bible here.

on earth, and in hell (Phil 2:10). Under the ancient curse (Heb 6:8) the earth had produced thorns and thistles; now she sees it burst into bloom again under the renewed grace of a new blessing. And as she beholds all this, she remembers the verse "My flesh has bloomed again, and willingly shall I praise him" (Ps 27:7).[17] She desires to add to the pomegranate fruits which she gathered from the tree of the Cross some of the flowers of the resurrection whose fragrance more than anything else invites the Bridegroom to visit her more often.

III.8. Next she says, "You are fair, my Beloved, and beautiful. Our bed is strewn with flowers" (Sg 1:15). By the mention of the bed she makes it plain enough what she desires; and when she says that it is strewn with flowers she indicates clearly why she hopes to be granted her desire: not for her own merits,[18] but for the sake of flowers from the field the Lord has blessed (Gn 27:27). Christ delighted in flowers. He wanted to be conceived and to grow up in Nazareth (Lk 1:26ff.).[19] The heavenly Bridegroom takes such pleasure in these fragrances that he comes often and willingly to the chamber of the heart in which he finds such fruits piled up and such flowers strewn. Where, that is, he sees constant reflection on the grace of the Passion and the glory of the resurrection. There he is present constantly and willingly.

The tokens of the Passion are like last year's fruits, the fruits that is of all the time past which was spent under the dominion of sin and death (cf. Rom 5:21). In the fullness of time they appear (Gal 4:4). But see, the signs of the resurrection are like the flowers of a new age, blooming in a new summer of grace; and their fruit will be the general resurrection which is to come at the last, and which will last for ever.[20] "Now," it says, "winter is over. The rain is past and gone. Flowers appear in our land" (Sg 2:11–12). This means that summer has come, with him who changed the coldness of death into the warm spring of a new life. "Behold," he says, "I will make all things new" (Rv 21:5). His flesh was sown in death; it flowered again in the resurrection (1 Cor 15:42). His fragrance makes the dry grass grow green again in the fields of our "valley." What was cold becomes warm again. What was dead comes to life again.

---

17. *Versiculus:* Bernard is not referring to a "verse" in quite the modern sense. The Bible was divided into verses it seems by Stephen Langton at the end of the twelfth century.

18. Bernard discusses merits in SC 68.6; LTR 2.200.

19. Nazareth was traditionally derived etymologically from "flower." Cf. Tpl 13; LTR 3.225.

20. On the fruits of the Passion and resurrection, see Ann 1.4; LTR 5.15.

III.9. In the freshness of these flowers and fruits and the beauty of the field which gives off so sweet a scent, the Father himself takes delight in the Son who is making all things new, so that he says, "Behold the odor of my Son is like that of a rich field which the Lord has blessed" (Gn 27:27): a rich field indeed, of whose fullness we have all received (Jn 1:16).

The Bride enjoys a greater freedom, for she may gather fruit and pick the flowers when she wishes (Sg 7:13). With these she strews her conscience within, so that when the Bridegroom comes the couch of her heart may give off a sweet fragrance.

It befits us, too, to fortify our own hearts with the testimony of faith, if we want Christ to be a frequent guest (Eph 3:17): faith both in the mercy of him who died for us, and in the power of him who rose again, as David said, "I have heard these two things: Power is of God and mercy is yours, Lord" (Ps 61:12–13). And so "the testimonies" of both these things "are utterly believable" (Ps 92:5). Christ died for our sins and rose again to make us righteous (Rom 4:25). For our protection he ascended (Mk 16:19) and sent the Holy Spirit to be our Comforter (Jn 16:7; Acts 9:31). He will one day return to bring us fulfilment (cf. Acts 1:11). He showed his mercy in dying, his power in the resurrection, and both in the remainder of his actions.

III.10. With these fruits and flowers the Bride begs to be surrounded and nourished now. I believe that she does so sensing that the warmth of her love can easily cool if it is not encouraged and supported until she is led into the chamber (Sg 2:5; 3:4), where she will be held in the long-desired embrace (Prv 7:18), so that she can say, "His left hand is under my head and his right hand has embraced me" (Sg 2:6).

Then she will know and experience indeed all the testimonies of love which she has received at his first coming,[21] as though from the left hand of the Beloved, and far less sweet and of less worth than the embrace of his right hand (Ps 30:20). She will experience what she has heard, "The flesh is of no value; it is the spirit which gives life" (Jn 6:64). She will prove in reality what she has heard, "My spirit is sweeter than honey, and my inheritance than honey and the honeycomb" (Sir 24:27), and what follows: "The memory of me will endure forever" (Sir 24:28). This means that as long as this world lasts, in which one generation is succeeded by another (Eccl 1:4), God's chosen ones will not be without

---

21. Cf. Adv. 4.9; LTR 4.182.

the consolation of memory until they can enjoy the feast of God's presence. Thus it is written, "They will broadcast the memory of your sweetness" (Ps 144:7), referring undoubtedly to those of whom it is said just before this passage, "Generation after generation will praise your works" (Ps 144:4). And so memory is for the generations of this world; presence belongs to the kingdom of heaven. Those who are chosen already enjoy the glory of his presence there; the generation which is still on its pilgrimage is comforted in the meantime by memory.

IV.11. It is important to note which generation takes comfort in remembering God. It is not the wicked and stubborn generation (Ps 77:8), to whom it is said, "Woe to you who are rich; you have your consolation" (Lk 6:24), but rather the generation which can say, "My soul refused to be comforted" (Ps 76:3). This is truly our attitude if we add what follows, "I remembered the Lord and rejoiced" (Ps 76:4). It is indeed right that those who take no delight in present things should be sustained by the recollection of what is to come, and those who refuse to be consoled by plentiful but mutable things should find joy in thinking of eternity. This is the generation of those who seek the Lord (Ps 23:6), who do not look for their own advantage (1 Cor 13:15), but seek the face of the God of Jacob.

In the meantime memory is sweet for those who long for God's presence. It does not satisfy their longing but intensifies it (cf. Mt 5:6). He himself bears witness to the manner of his feeding, "He who eats me will hunger for more" (Sir 24:29). And he who is fed by God says, "I shall be satisfied at the sight of your glory" (Ps 16:15).

Blessed are those who are hungry and thirsty for righteousness now (Mt 5:6), for they alone will be satisfied one day. Woe to you, wicked and perverse generation! Woe to you, stupid and foolish people (Jer 4:22; 5:21), who do not trouble to think of the past, and who fear the future! Not even now do you want to be freed from the snare of the hunters (Ps 90:3, 123:7), for those who wish to become rich in this world fall into the devil's net (1 Tm 6:9). Even then you cannot avoid the harsh words (cf. Jn 6:61). Oh, the harsh and cruel sentence, "Go, you who are cursed, into everlasting fire!" (Mt 25:41). These words are harsher and more dreadful than that which is repeated every day for us in Church in the memorial of his Passion, "He who eats my flesh and drinks my blood has eternal life" (Jn 6:55). That is, "He who remembers my death and mortifies his members on earth after my example (Col 3:5) has eternal life" (Jn 3:36). That means, "If we suffer together, you shall reign with me" (Rom 8:17; 2 Tim 2:12).

And yet many today shrink back at these words and desert him (Jn 6:67; 18:6), and answer not in words but by their actions, "This is a hard saying. Who can listen to it?" (Jn 6:61). The generation which did not discipline its heart and whose spirit is not in good credit with God (Ps 77:8), but which hopes instead in unreliable riches (1 Tm 6:17), feels oppressed by the story of the Cross (1 Cor 1:18), and thinks it burdensome to remember the Passion. How will it ever bear the weight of his words when it actually hears them, "Go, you who are cursed, into everlasting fire, which is prepared for the Devil and his angels" (Mt 25:41)? This stone will crush him on whom it falls (Mt 21:44).

But truly the generation of the righteous (Ps 111:2) will be blessed, those who, whether away from him or in his presence (2 Cor 5:9), strive with the Apostle to please God. They will hear, "Come, you blessed of my Father," and so forth (Mt 25:34).

Then the generation which did not discipline its heart (Ps 77:8) will learn too late how easy and sweet in comparison with that sorrow was Christ's burden (Mt 11:30), from which they withdrew their stiff necks (Dt 9:13, 31:27) as if it were a rough hard load.

O wretched slaves of mammon (Mt 6:24), you cannot simultaneously glory in the Cross of our Lord Jesus Christ (Gal 6:14) and hope for a treasury of money or chase after gold (1 Tm 6:17), and taste how sweet the Lord is (Ps 33:9). So then, you will doubtless find him whom you did not find sweet to remember severe indeed when you stand before him in person.

IV.12. By contrast the faithful soul sighs deeply for his presence and rests peacefully in the thought of him, and until it is fit to have the glory of God revealed to it face to face (2 Cor 3:18), it glories in the ignominy of the Cross (Gal 6:14). So then does the Bride and Dove of Christ wait. In the meantime she rests upon her inheritance; for there fall to her lot (Ps 67:14) now in the present, in the recollection of the abundance of your sweetness (Ps 144:7) Lord Jesus, silvery wings (Ps 67:14), candid with innocence and purity. She places her hope in the joy she will feel at the sight of your face (Ps 15:11). Then even her back will gleam gold (Ps 67:4), when she is led with delight into the splendor of the saints (Ps 109:3). There the rays of wisdom will illuminate her more brightly still.

Rightly indeed does she glory now and say, "His left hand is beneath my head and his right hand embraces me" (Sg 2:6). His left hand stands for the recollection of his love, than which nothing is greater, for he laid down his life for his friends (Jn 15:13). His right hand signifies the blessed vision which he promised to his friends, and the joys of the presence of his majesty. Rightly, too, that vision of God which makes us resemble him, that inestimable delight in the divine presence is thought of as the "right hand," of which the Psalmist sings in delight, "In your right hand are everlasting joys" (Ps 15:11). In the "left hand" we rightly "place" that wonderful love which is recollected and is always to be remembered, for the Bride leans upon it and rests until evil is past (Ps 56:2).

IV.13. Rightly then is the left hand of the Bridegroom under the Bride's head, upon which he supports her leaning head. This leaning is the intention of her mind, and he supports it so that it may not bend or incline toward fleshly and worldly desires (Gal 5:16; Ti 2:12). For the body, which is corruptible, weighs down the soul, and the earthly dwelling of the soul hems it in and keeps it preoccupied with many thoughts (Wis 9:15).[22]

What is the result of contemplating such great mercy and mercy so undeserved, such generous and proven love, such unlooked-for condescension, such persistent gentleness, such astonishing sweetness? To what, I ask, will all these wonderfully draw and deeply attract the thoughtful mind when it considers them carefully and is wholly set at liberty from unworthy love? It will despise everything else, everything which will get in the way of that desire. The Bride surely runs eagerly in the odor of these perfumes, and loves ardently (Sg 1:3). Yet even when she has fallen wholly in love she thinks she loves too little because she is loved so much. And she is right. What can repay so great a love and such a lover? It is as if a little speck of dust (Is 40:15) were to marshal itself to return a love which is ever before it in Majesty and which can be seen to bend all its power on the work of salvation. The words "God so loved the world that he gave his only begotten Son" (Jn 3:16) were certainly spoken of the Father, and, "He gave himself up to death" (Is 53:12) was undoubtedly said of the Son (Jn 14:26). And it is said of the Holy Spirit, "The Paraclete, the Holy Spirit, whom my Father will send in my name, he will teach you all things and will cause you to remember all that I have said to you" (Jn 14:26). God, then, loves, and loves with all his being, for the whole Trinity loves—if the word "whole" can be used of the infinite, the incomprehensible, absolute Being.

---

22. Wis 9:15; cf. Gra 37.41; LTR 3.192–93; Conv 30; LTR 4.106.

V.14. I believe that he who understands this will recognize clearly enough why God is to be loved, that is, why he deserves to be loved. Because the Son is not his, the unbeliever has neither the Father nor the Holy Spirit (1 Jn 5:12). For "He who does not honor the Son does not honor the Father who sent him" (Jn 5:53). Nor does he honor the Holy Spirit whom the Son sent (Jn 15:26, 16:7). And so it is not surprising that a man should love the less someone whom he knows less well (cf. Lk 7:47). Nevertheless, the unbeliever is aware that he owes him everything, because he knows that he is the Author of everything.

But then what of me? What do I owe, who hold my God to be not only the generous Giver of my life, its beneficent Governor, its holy Comforter, its careful Director, and above all these its most liberal Redeemer, everlasting Protector, Defender, Glorifier? It is written, "With him is plentiful redemption" (Ps 129:7), and again, "He entered the sanctuary once and for all, when he had won eternal salvation" (Heb 9:12). And, on conversion, "He will not forsake his own; they shall be kept safe forever" (Ps 36:28). And the Gospel says about the riches he brings, "They will pour into your lap good measure and full and pressed down and running over" (Lk 6:38). And again, "eye has not seen or ear heard, nor has it entered the mind of man, what God has prepared for those who love him" (1 Cor 2:9). And about glorification, "We wait for the Savior, our Lord Jesus Christ, who will renew the body of our lowliness and make it like his glorified body" (Phil 3:20–21). And that, "The sufferings of this time are not to be compared with the glory which is to come, which will be revealed in us" (Rom 8:18), and again, "That which is but a brief and light trouble in this present life will work in us beyond its weight, for eternal life, as we contemplate not the things which are seen but the things which are unseen" (2 Cor 4:17–18).

IV.5. What shall I give to God in return for all these things (Ps 115:12)? Reason and natural justice press the unbeliever to give himself up wholly to him from whom he has everything, and to love him with all his heart. Faith urges me to love more than that him whom I know to have given me not only myself but his own self. When the age of faith had not yet come God had not made himself known in the flesh, died on the Cross, risen from the tomb, returned to the Father, or proved his great love for us (Rom 5:8), about which I have said so much; when he had not yet commanded man to love the Lord his God with all his heart, with all his soul, and with all his strength (Dt 6:5; Mt 12:30), that is, with all he is, all he knows, all he can do.

God is not unjust when he claims his works and his gifts for himself (Heb 6:10). Why should the work of an artist not love its master,
if it has the ability to do so? Why should it not love him with all its
might, since it can do nothing except by his gift?

In addition, the fact that man was created gratuitously, out of
nothing—and in such dignity—makes the duty of love still clearer and
demonstrates further the justice of God's demand. Besides, think of the
greatness of the additional kindness when he saved man and beast (Ps
35:7–8). How did God multiply his mercy then? We, I emphasize, ex-
changed our glory for the likeness of a calf which eats grass (Ps 105:20),
and have become like brute beasts through our sins (Ps 48:13, 21). If I
owe all that I am in return for my creation, what am I to add in return
for being remade, and remade in this way? For I was not remade as
easily as I was made. It is written not only of me, but of everything that
was made (Jn 1:3), "He spoke and they were made" (Ps 148:5). But he
who made me by speaking once said a great deal more to remake me,
and did miracles, and endured hardship, and not only hardship but humiliation. "What then shall I give the Lord for all that he has given me?
(Ps 115:2)? In the first act he gave me myself; in the second he gave
himself; and when he did that he gave me back myself. Given and given
again, I owe myself in return for myself, twice over. What am I to give
God in return for himself? For even if I could give myself a thousand
times over, what am I to God (cf. Jb 9:3, 9:14)?

How God Should Be Loved

VI.16. First see in what measure God deserves to be loved by us, and
how he deserves to be loved without measure. For (to repeat briefly
what I have said) "he first loved us" (1 Jn 4:10). He loved—with such
love, and so much and so generously—us who are so insignificant and
who are what we are. I remember that I said at the beginning that the
way to love God was to love without measure. Now since the love
which is directed to God is directed to something immense, something
infinite (for God is both immense and infinite)—who, I ask, ought to
draw a line to our love or measure it out? And what about the fact that
our love itself is not freely given but given in payment for a debt? So
immensity loves; eternity loves; the love which passes knowledge gives
itself (Eph 3:19); God loves, whose greatness knows no bounds (Ps
114:3), whose wisdom cannot be counted (Ps 146:5), whose peace

passes all understanding (Phil 4:7), and do we measure out our response?

"I will love you, Lord, my strength, my fortress, my refuge, my deliverer" (Ps 17:2–3), you who are everything I can desire and love. My God, my Helper, I shall love you in proportion to your gift and my capacity, less indeed than is just, but to do that is beyond me. Even though I cannot love you as much as I ought, still I cannot love you more than I am able. I shall be able to love you more only when you deign to give me more; and even then you can never find my love worthy. "Your eyes have seen my imperfection," and "all shall be written down in your book" (Ps 138:16), all who do what they can, even if they cannot do all that they should. It is clear, I think, how much God ought to be loved, and for what merit in him. For his own merit, I say, but to whom is it really clear how great that is? Who can say? Who can feel it?

VII.17. Now let us see how he is to be loved for our benefit. How far does our perception of him fall short of what he is? We must not keep silent about what we can see clearly, even if all is not clear to us. Above, when we proposed to seek why and how God is to be loved, I said that there were two meanings of the question with which we began. We asked why he should be loved, meaning by what merit of his or for what benefit of ours. Both questions can, it seems, be asked. After speaking of God's merit, not as he deserves, but as well as I am able, it remains for me to say something about the reward, as far as it will be given to me to do.

That God Is Not Loved without Reward

God is not loved without reward, even though he should be loved without thought of reward. True charity cannot be empty, but it does not seek profit, "For it does not seek its own benefit" (1 Cor 13:5). It is an affection, not a contract. It is not given or received by agreement. It is given freely; it makes us spontaneous. True love is content. It has its reward in what it loves. For if you seem to love something, but really love it for the sake of something else, you actually love what you are pursuing as your real end, not that which is a means to it. Paul did not preach in order to eat; he ate in order to preach. He loved not the food but the Gospel (1 Cor 9:18).

True love does not ask for a reward but it deserves it. A reward is offered to him who does not yet love; it is owed to him who loves; it is given to him who perseveres. When we are trying to persuade people about lesser matters, it is not the willing but the unwilling that we woo with promises and rewards. Who would think a man ought to be paid for doing what he wants to do? No one, for example, pays a hungry man to eat, or a thirsty man to drink, or a mother to feed the child of her womb (Is 49:15). Who would think of getting someone to fence his vine or dig round his tree or build himself a house by begging him to do it, or paying him a fee? How much more does the soul that loves God ask for no reward but God? Certainly, if that is not all it asks, it does not love God.

VI.18. It is always natural for every rational being to desire what it sees to be finer and to direct its energies toward it. It is never satisfied with anything which lacks what it judges it should have. For example, a man who has a beautiful wife looks at a lovelier woman with a discontented eye or mind. He who is dressed in fine clothes wants better. He who is very rich envies a richer man.

Today you see many men who already have great wealth and possessions still laboring day by day to add one field to another (Is 5:8) and to extend their boundaries (Ex 34:24)—with greed which knows no bounds. And you see those who have houses worthy of a king and vast palaces, nevertheless adding house to house every day (Is 5:8), and building with a restless love of novelty, knocking down what they build, altering rectangles to rounds.[23] And what of men in high positions? Do we not see them striving with all their might to reach still higher positions; their ambition is never satisfied. There is no end to it all because the highest and the best is not to be found in any of these things. If a man cannot be at peace until he has the highest and best, is it surprising that he is not content with inferior and worse things? It is folly and extreme madness always to be longing for things which cannot only never satisfy but cannot even blunt the appetite; however much you have of such things you still desire what you have not yet attained; you are always restlessly sighing after what is missing.

When the wandering mind is always rushing about in empty effort among the various and deceptive delights of the world, it grows weary and remains dissatisfied. It is like a starving man who thinks that what-

---

23. Horace, *Ep.* 1.1(100), ed. H. Rushton Fairclough (London, 1970).

ever he is stuffing himself with is nothing in comparison with what remains to be eaten; he is always anxiously wanting what he has not got
rather than enjoying what he has. For who can have everything? That
little which a man obtains by all his effort, he possesses in fear. He does
not know what he will lose and when.

Thus the perverted will which is aiming for the best and trying to
make speed toward that which will fully satisfy it fails in its endeavor.
Vanity makes fun of it, bringing it into these twisted paths; sin deceives
itself with lies (Ps 26:12). If you really wish to have what you desire,
that is, if you wish to lay hold of that which leaves nothing further to
be desired, what need is there to bother with these other things? If you
do, you are running along winding roads, and you will be dead long
before you reach what you desire by this route.

VI.19. The wicked therefore walk round in this circle (Ps 11:9),
naturally wanting what will satisfy their wants, and foolishly thrusting
away the means of attaining it—that is, of attaining not consumption
but consummation. In this way they wear themselves out with pointless effort and do not reach the end of happy fulfillment. They delight
in the beauty of the creature rather than of the Creator (Rom 1:23).
They lust for each and every experience more than they desire to come
to the Lord of all. And indeed if they could ever do all they set themselves to do, they would succeed—if anyone could indeed obtain everything without the Source of all things.

For by that law of human desire which causes man to hunger
more for the things he does not have than for the things he has, and
to spurn what he has for the sake of things he does not possess, soon
he has obtained and cast aside everything in heaven and on earth
(Eph 1:10). In the end, I do not doubt that he will rush toward the
only thing he now lacks—the God of all. There he will rest, for just
as there is no rest this side of heaven, so on the other side, nothing
can disturb his rest.

Then he will surely say, "It is good for me to cling to God" (Ps
72:28). He will say, "What is there for me in heaven, and what have I
desired on earth?" (Ps 72:25). And again, "God of my heart, God, my
lot for ever" (Ps 72:26). So therefore as I said, whoever desires the greatest good can reach it, if he can first gain all the other things he wants
which fall short of it.

VI.20. But that is quite impossible. Life is too short. Our strength
is insufficient. There are too many temptations. Those who struggle on
are exhausted by the length of the roads and the uselessness of their

efforts. They wish to obtain all they want, but they are unable to reach the end of their desires. If they would only be content with reaching it all in thought and not insist on experiencing it! That they can easily do, and it would not be pointless, for man's mind is quicker than his senses and it sees further and the senses dare not touch anything which the mind has not already examined and approved. I think this is what is meant by the text "Test everything, and hold on to what is good" (1 Thes 5:21). The mind looks ahead, and if it does not give permission the senses must not pursue what they want. If they did, you would not go up the mountain of the Lord, nor stand in his holy place (Ps 23:3–4), and you would have received your rational soul in vain; you would be following your sense like a dumb beast without any resistance from your lazy reason. Those whose reason does not keep ahead of their feet run, but not on the road (cf. Is 59:8). They spurn the Apostle's advice. They do not run to win (1 Cor 9:24). When will they reach him whom they put off coming to until they have tried everything else? The desire to possess everything first is a winding road and a circle to go round and round forever.

VI.21. The just man is not like that. When he hears about the wicked behavior of those who are going round and round (Ps 30:14)—for there are many traveling the wide road which leads to death (Mt 7:13)—he chooses for himself the royal road and turns neither to right nor to left (Nm 20:17, 21:22). Finally, the prophet bears witness, "The path of the just is straight and straightforward to walk on" (Is 26:7). It is men such as this who take the shortcut to salvation and avoid the troublesome and unrewarding roundabout way, choosing the brief and abbreviating word (Rom 9:28). They do not want to have everything they see. On the contrary, they sell all they have and give it to the poor (Mt 19:21). "Blessed are the poor," indeed, "for theirs is the kingdom of heaven" (Mt 5:3). Everyone runs (1 Cor 9:24), but we must distinguish between the runners. For "the Lord knows the way of the just; the way of the wicked will perish" (Ps 1:6). So a little is better to the just than all their wealth is to the wicked (Ps 36:16), for indeed—as Wisdom says and the foolish man discovers—"He who loves money will not be satisfied by money" (cf. Eccl 5:9). But those who hunger and thirst after righteousness will be satisfied (Mt 5:6).

Righteousness is the natural and vital food of the rational soul. Money cannot diminish the mind's hunger; more than air is needed to satisfy that of the body. If a hungry man opens his mouth to the wind and you see him blow out his cheeks with air in the hope of satisfying his hunger, will you not think he is mad? So it is no less a madness if you think the rational soul can be satisfied and not merely "puffed up" by bodily things. What do bodily things mean to the soul? The body cannot feed on spiritual things or the soul on bodily things. "Bless the Lord, my soul. He satisfies your desire with good things" (Ps 102:1, 5). He satisfies it with good things, stirs it to goodness, keeps it in goodness, anticipates, sustains, fulfills. He causes you to desire and he himself satisfies your desire.

VI.22. I said before that God is the cause of loving God. I spoke the truth, for he is both the efficient and the final cause. He himself provides the occasion. He himself creates the longing. He himself fulfills the desire. He himself causes himself to be (or rather, to be made) such that he should be loved. He hopes to be so happily loved that no one will love him in vain. His love both prepares and rewards ours (cf. 1 Jn 4:19). Kindly, he leads the way. He repays us justly. He is our sweet hope. He is riches to all who call upon him (Rom 10:12). There is nothing better than himself. He gave himself in merit. He keeps himself to be our reward. He gives himself as food for holy souls (Wis 3:13). He sold himself to redeem the captives (Lam 3:25).

Lord, you are good to the soul which seeks you. What are you then to the soul which finds? But this is the most wonderful thing, that no one can seek you who has not already found you. You therefore seek to be found so that you may be sought for, sought so that you may be found. You can be sought, and found, but not forestalled. For even if we say "In the morning my prayer will forestall you" (Ps 87:14), it is certain that every prayer which is not inspired is half-hearted.

Now let us see where our love begins, for we have seen where it finds its end.

VIII.23 Love is one of the four natural passions.[24] They are well enough known; there is no need to name them. It is clearly right that what is natural should be at the service of the Lord of nature. That is why the first and great commandment is, "You shall love the Lord your God" (Mt 22:37).

---

24. Cf. SV 85.5; LTR 2.310; QH 14.19; LTR 4.414; Div 50.2; LTR 6⁶.271; Quad 2.3; LTR 4.321; cf. Juvenal, *Satires*, 1:85–86, ed. W. V. Clausen (Oxford, 1959).

THE FIRST DEGREE OF LOVE: WHEN MAN LOVES HIMSELF FOR HIS OWN SAKE

But because nature has become rather frail and weak, man is driven by necessity to serve nature first. This results in bodily love, by which man loves himself for his own sake. He does not yet know anything but himself, as it is written, "First came what is animal, then what is spiritual" (1 Cor 15:46). This love is not imposed by rule but is innate in nature. For who hates his own flesh (Eph 5:29)? But if that same love begins to get out of proportion and headstrong, as often happens, and it ceases to be satisfied to run in the narrow channel of its needs, but floods out on all sides into the fields of pleasure, then the overflow can be stopped at once by the commandment "You shall love your neighbor as yourself" (Mt 22:39).

It is wholly right that he who is your fellow in nature (2 Pt 1:4) should not be cut off from you in grace, especially in that grace which is innate in nature. If a man feels it a heavy burden to help his brothers in their need and to share in their pleasures, let him keep his desires in check all by himself if he does not want to fall into sin. He can indulge himself as much as he likes as long as he remembers to show an equal tolerance to his neighbor. O man, the law of life and discipline impose restraint (Sir 45:6) to prevent you chasing after your desires until you perish (Sir 18:30), and to save you from making of nature's good things a way to serve the soul's enemy through lust.

Is it not much more right and honest to share nature's goods with your fellow man, that is, your neighbor, than with an enemy? If you take the advice of Wisdom and turn away from your pleasures (Sir 18:30) and make yourself content with food and clothing as the Apostle teaches (1 Tm 6:8), soon you will find that your love is not impeded by carnal desires which fight against the soul (1 Pt 2:11). I think you will not find it a burden to share with your fellow man what you withhold from the enemy of your soul. Then will your love be sober and just, when you do not deny your brother what he needs from the pleasures you have denied yourself. It is in this way that bodily love is shared, when it is extended to the community.

VIII.24. But what are you to do if when you share with your neighbor you yourself are left without something you need? What but ask in full faith (Acts 4:29, 28:31) from him who gives generously to everyone and does not grudge (Jas 1:5), who opens his hand and pours blessing on every creature (Ps 144:16). There is no doubt that he will come to your aid generously when you are in need, since he is so generous in time of plenty. Scripture says, "First seek the Kingdom of God and his justice and all these things will be added to you" (Mt 6:33; Lk 12:31). He promises without being asked to give what is needed to whoever is not greedy for himself and loves his neighbor. This is to seek the kingdom of God and to implore his help against the tyranny of sin, to take on the yoke of chastity and sobriety rather than to let sin rule in your mortal body (Rom 6:12). More: This is righteousness, to share what is common to your nature with him who has the same gift of nature.

VIII.25. But to love one's neighbor with perfect justice it is necessary to be prompted by God. How can you love your neighbor with purity if you do not love him in God? But he who does not love God cannot love in God. You must first love God, so that in him you can love your neighbor too (Mk 12:30–31).

God therefore brings about your love for him, just as he causes other goods. This is how he does it: He who made nature also protects it. For it was so created that it needs its Creator as its Protector, so that what could not have come into existence without him cannot continue in existence without him. So that no rational creature might be in ignorance of this fact and (dreadful thought) claim for himself the gifts of the Creator, that same Creator willed by a high and saving counsel that man should endure tribulation; then when man fails and God comes to his aid and sets him free, man will honor God as he deserves. For this is what he says, "Call upon me in the day of tribulation. I will deliver you, and you shall honor me" (Ps 49:15). And so in that way it comes about that man who is a bodily animal (1 Cor 2:14), and does not know how to love anything but himself, begins to love God for his own benefit, because he learns from frequent experience that in God he can do everything which is good for him (Phil 4:13), and that without him he can do nothing (Jn 15:5).

THE SECOND DEGREE OF LOVE, WHEN MAN LOVES GOD FOR HIS OWN GOOD

IX.26. Man therefore loves God, but as yet he loves him for his own sake, not God's. Nevertheless the wise man ought to know what he can do by himself and what he can do only with God's help; then you will avoid hurting him who keeps you from harm.

If a man has a great many tribulations and as a result he frequently turns to God and frequently experiences God's liberation, surely even if he had a breast of iron or a heart of stone (Ez 11:19; 36:26), he must soften toward the generosity of the Redeemer and love God not only for his own benefit, but for himself?

THE THIRD DEGREE OF LOVE: WHEN MAN LOVES GOD FOR GOD'S SAKE

Man's frequent needs make it necessary for him to call upon God often, and to taste by frequent contact, and to discover by tasting how sweet the Lord is (Ps 33:9). It is in this way that the taste of his own sweetness leads us to love God in purity more than our need alone would prompt us to do. The Samaritans set us an example when they said to the woman who told them the Lord was there, "Now we believe, not because of your words, but because we have heard him for ourselves and we know that truly he is the Savior of the world" (Jn 4:42). In the same way, I urge, let us follow their example and rightly say to our flesh, "Now we love God not because he meets your needs; but we have tasted and we know how sweet the Lord is" (Ps 33:9).

There is a need of the flesh which speaks out, and the body tells by its actions of the kindnesses it has experienced. And so it will not be difficult for the man who has had that experience to keep the commandment to love his neighbor (Mk 12:31). He truly loves God, and therefore he loves what is God's. He loves chastely, and to the chaste it is no burden to keep the commandments; the heart grows purer in the obedience of love, as it is written (1 Pt 1:22). Such a man loves justly and willingly keeps the just law.

This love is acceptable because it is given freely. It is chaste because it is not made up of words or talk, but of truth and action (1 Jn 3:18). It is just because it gives back what it has received. For he who loves in this way loves as he is loved. He loves, seeking in return not what is his own (1 Cor 13:5), but what is Jesus Christ's, just as he has sought not his own but our good, or rather, our very selves (2 Cor 12:14). He who says, "We trust in the Lord for he is good" (Ps 117:1) loves in this way. He who trusts in the Lord not because he is good to him but simply because he is good truly loves God for God's sake and not for his own. He of whom it is said, "He will praise you when you do him favors" (Ps 48:19) does not love in this way.

That is the third degree of love, in which God is already loved for his own sake.

The Fourth Degree of Love: When Man Loves Himself for the Sake of God

X.27. Happy is he who has been found worthy to attain to the fourth degree, where man loves himself only for God's sake. "O God, your justice is like the mountains of God" (Ps 35:7). That love is a mountain, and a high mountain of God. Truly, "a rich and fertile mountain" (Ps 67:16). "Who will climb the mountain of the Lord" (Ps 23:3)? "Who will give me wings like a dove, and I shall fly there and rest" (Ps 54:7)? That place was made a place of peace and it has its dwelling-place in Sion (Ps 75:3). "Alas for me, my exile has been prolonged!" (Ps 119:5). When will flesh and blood (Mt 16:17), this vessel of clay (2 Cor 4:7), this earthly dwelling (Wis 9:15), grasp this? When will it experience this kind of love, so that the mind, drunk with divine love and forgetting itself, making itself like a broken vessel (Ps 30:13), throw itself wholly on God and, clinging to God (1 Cor 6:17), become one with him in spirit and say, "My body and my heart have fainted, O God of my heart; God, my part in eternity" (Ps 72:26)? I should call him blessed and holy to whom it is given to experience even for a single instant something which is rare indeed in this life. To lose yourself as though you did not exist and to have no sense of yourself, to be emptied out of yourself (Phil 2:7) and almost annihilated, belongs to heavenly not to human love.

And if indeed any mortal is rapt for a moment or is, so to speak, admitted for a moment to this union, at once the world presses itself on him (Gal 1:4), the day's wickedness troubles him, the mortal body weighs him down, bodily needs distract him, he fails because of the weakness of his corruption and—more powerfully than these—brotherly love calls him back. Alas, he is forced to come back to himself, to fall again into his affairs, and to cry out wretchedly, "Lord, I endure violence; fight back for me" (Is 38:14), and, "Unhappy man that I am, who will free me from the body of this death?" (Rom 7:24).

IX.28. But since Scripture says that God made everything for himself (Prv 16:4; Rv 4:11) there will be a time when he will cause everything to conform to its Maker and be in harmony with him. In the meantime, we must make this our desire: that as God himself willed that everything should be for himself, so we, too, will that nothing, not

even ourselves, may be or have been except for him, that is according
to his will, not ours. The satisfaction of our needs will not bring us
happiness, not chance delights, as does the sight of his will being fulfilled in us and in everything which concerns us. This is what we ask
every day in prayer when we say, "Your will be done, on earth as it is
in heaven" (Mt 6:10). O holy and chaste love! O sweet and tender affection! O pure and sinless intention of the will—the more pure and
sinless in that there is no mixture of self-will in it, the more sweet and
tender in that everything it feels is divine.

To love in this way is to become like God.[25] As a drop of water
seems to disappear completely in a quantity of wine, taking the wine's
flavor and color; as red-hot iron becomes indistinguishable from the
glow of fire and its own original form disappears; as air suffused with
the light of the sun seems transformed into the brightness of the light,
as if it were itself light rather than merely lit up; so, in those who are
holy, it is necessary for human affection to dissolve in some ineffable
way, and be poured into the will of God. How will God be all in all (1
Cor 15:26) if anything of man remains in man? The substance remains,
but in another form, with another glory, another power.

When will this be? Who will see this? Who will possess it? "When
shall I come and when shall I appear in God's presence" (Ps 41:3)? O
Lord my God, "My heart said to you, 'My face has sought you. Lord,
I will seek your face' " (Ps 26:8). Shall I see your holy temple (Ps 26:4)?

IX.29. I think that cannot be until I do as I am bid. "Love the Lord
your God with all your heart and with all your soul and with all your
strength" (Mk 12:30). Then the mind will not have to think of the body.
The soul will no longer have to give the body life and feeling, and its
power will be set free of these ties and strengthened by the power of
God. For it is impossible to draw together all that is in you and turn
toward the face of God as long as the care of the weak and miserable
body demands one's attention. So it is in a spiritual and immortal body,
a perfect body, beautiful and at peace and subject to the spirit in all
things, that the soul hopes to attain the fourth degree of love, or rather,
to be caught up to it; for it lies in God's power to give to whom he will.
It is not to be obtained by human effort. That, I say, is when a man
will easily reach the fourth degree: when no entanglements of the flesh

---

25. On *deificatio*, see Augustine, Letter 10:2, ed. A. L. Goldbacher, CSEL 34 (Vienna),
pp. 4–5.

hold him back and no troubles will disturb him, as he hurries with great speed and eagerness to the joy of the Lord (Mt 25:21; 25).

But do we not think that the holy martyrs received this grace while they were still in their victorious bodies—at least in part? They were so moved within by the great force of their love that they were able to expose their bodies to outward torments and think nothing of them. The sensation of outward pain could do no more than whisper across the surface of their tranquillity; it could not disturb it.

XI.30. But what of those who are already free of the body? We believe that they are wholly immersed in that sea of eternal light and bright eternity.

What Is Impossible for Souls before the Resurrection

It is not in dispute that they want their bodies back; if they thus desire and hope for them, it is clear that they have not wholly turned from themselves, for it is evident that they are still clinging to something which is their own, even if their desires return to it only a very little. Until death is swallowed up in victory (1 Cor 15:54), and the everlasting light invades the farthest bounds of night and shines everywhere—so that heavenly glory gleams even in bodies—these souls cannot wholly remove themselves and transport themselves to God. They are still too much bound to their bodies, if not in life and feeling, certainly in natural affection. They do not wish to be complete without them, and indeed they cannot.

And so before the restoration of their bodies souls will not lose themselves, as they will when they are perfect and reach their highest state. If they did so the soul would be complete without its body, and would cease to want it.

The body is not laid down nor resumed except for the good of the soul. "Precious in God's sight is the death of his saints" (Ps 115:15).

If death is precious, what must life be, and life such as that? It need not be surprising that the glorified body should seem to confer something on the soul, for it was of use to it when it was weak and mortal. Oh, how truly did he speak who said that all things work together for good to those who love God (Rom 8:28)! Its weak body helps the soul to love God; it helps it when it is dead; it helps it when it is resurrected, first in producing fruits of patience, secondly in bringing peace, thirdly in bringing completeness. Truly the soul does not want to be perfected without that which it feels has served it well in every condition.

XI.31. It is clear that the flesh is a good and faithful companion to the good spirit. It helps it if it is burdened, or if it does not help, it relieves it; at any rate, it is an aid and not a burden. The first state is full of labor, but fruitful (Mt 3:8); the second is a time of waiting, but without weariness; the third is glorious. Listen to the Bridegroom in the Song holding out this threefold invitation: "Eat," he says, "and drink, friends; be intoxicated, dearest" (Sg 5:1).[26] He calls those who are laboring in the body to eat. Those who have set aside their bodies he calls to drink. Those who have resumed their bodies, he encourages to drink their fill. These he calls "dearest," for they are filled to overflowing with love. For there is this difference between these and those others he calls "friends," not "dearest," so that those who groan because they are still laboring in the flesh are held dear for the love they have; those who are free from the weight of the flesh (2 Cor 5:4) are more dear because they are made more ready and quicker to love. More than both are they called "dearest" (and so they are) (1 Jn 3:1) who, having received the second garment, are in their resurrected bodies in glory. They burn the more eagerly and fiercely with love for God because nothing is now left to them which can trouble them or hold them back in any way. Neither of the first two states can claim that. For in the first the body is born along with labor, and in the second, too, it is awaited with no small desire.

XI.32. First, then, the faithful soul eats its bread, but alas, in the sweat of its brow (Gn 3:19). While in the flesh the soul moves by faith (2 Cor 5:7), which must act through love (Gal 5:6), for if it does not, it is dead (Jas 2:20).

This work is food, as the Lord says, "My food is to do the will of my Father" (Jn 4:34). When it is free of the flesh, the soul no longer feeds on the bread of sorrow (Ps 126:2), but having eaten it is allowed to drink deeply of the wine of love, but not the pure wine, for as it says in the Song of Songs in the person of the Bride, "I drank my wine mixed with milk" (Sg 5:1). The soul mixes the sweetness of natural affection with the wine of divine love when it desires to resume its glorified body. The soul therefore burns when it has drunk the wine of holy charity,

---

26. Cf. Gra 9; LTR 3.172; Div 41.12, 87.4; LTR 6¹.253, 331.

but not to the point of intoxication, for the admixture of this milk tempers it for the moment. Intoxication overthrows minds and makes them forget everything. The soul which is still concerned with the restoration of its body is not forgetting itself completely. But after it finds the only thing it needs, what is to prevent it from taking leave of itself altogether and going to God, and becoming as much unlike itself as it is given to it to be like God? Then only is the soul allowed to drink from the goblet of wisdom, of which we read, "How splendid is my cup which intoxicates me" (Ps 22:5). Is it surprising if the soul is then intoxicated by the riches of God's dwelling (Ps 35:9)? No longer tormented by wordly cares, it safely drinks the pure new wine with Christ in his Father's house (Mt 26:29; Mk 14:25).

XI.33. Wisdom presides over this threefold banquet (Prv 9:1ff.) of love, feeding those who labor, giving drink to those at rest, and intoxicating those who rule. As at a banquet in this world, food is served before drink, as the order of nature requires, and Wisdom keeps to it.

First, up to the time of our death, we eat the work of our hands (Ps 127:2), when we chew effortfully what has to be swallowed. After death, in the spiritual life, we drink with ease whatever we are offered. Then, when our bodies are resurrected, we are intoxicated by immortal life, abounding in wonderful plenty. This is what the Bridegroom means in the Song, "Eat and drink, friends; be intoxicated, dearest" (Sg 5:1).

Dearest indeed, who are intoxicated with love. Intoxicated indeed, who deserve to be present at the wedding feast of the Lord (Rv 19:9), eating and drinking at his table in his kingdom (Lk 22:30), when he takes his Church to him in glory, without blemish or wrinkle or any defect (Eph 5:27). Then will he intoxicate his dearest ones with the torrent of his delight (Ps 35:9), for in the most passionate and most chaste embrace of Bridegroom and Bride, the rush of the river makes glad the city of God (Ps 45:5). I think this is no other than that which the Son of God, who waits on us as he goes (Lk 12:37), promised: "The just are feasting and rejoicing in the sight of God, and they delight in their gladness" (Ps 67:4). Here is fullness without disgust, insatiable curiosity which is not restless, an eternal and endless desire which knows no lack, and lastly, that sober intoxication (Acts 2:15) which does not come from drinking too much, which is no reeking of wine, but a burning for God.

From this point that fourth degree of love can be possessed forever, when God is loved alone and above all, for now we do not love ourselves except for his sake; he is himself the reward of those who love him, the eternal reward of those who love him for eternity.[27]

Prologue to the Letter Which Follows[28]

XII.34. I remember that some time ago I wrote a letter to the holy Carthusian brothers in which, among other matters, I discussed these same four degrees. Perhaps I said other things in it about love, much as I have talked of it here. For that reason I think it may be helpful to include it here, especially since it is easier to transcribe what I have already to hand, ready dictated, than to compose something new.

Here Begins the Letter on Love Written To the Holy Brothers of La Chartreuse

True and sincere charity, I say, must be said to proceed wholly from a pure heart, a good conscience, unfeigned faith (1 Tm 1:5), by which we love our neighbor's good as our own. For he who loves himself most, or solely, does not love the good purely, because he loves it for his sake, not for its own. And such a man cannot obey the prophet who says, "Praise the Lord, for he is good" (Ps 117:1). He praises the Lord perhaps, because he is good to him, but not simply because he is good. Let him take note that the same prophet utters a reproach to him, "He will acknowledge you when you do him good" (Ps 48:19).

There are some who praise God for his power, some who praise him for his goodness to them, and some who praise him simply because he is good. The first is a slave, fearful on his own account. The second is mercenary, and desires profit for himself. The third is a son who honors his father. Both he who is fearful and he who is greedy act for themselves. Only he who loves like a son does not seek his own (1 Cor 13:5). I think this text speaks of this kind of love. "The law of the Lord is spotless. It converts souls" (Ps 18:8), for it alone can turn the mind from love of itself and the world and direct it to God. Neither fear nor love of self can convert the soul. They change the appearance of one's deeds

---

27. SC 83.4; LTR 2.300.
28. *Ep.* 11.3–9.

from time to time, but never one's character. A slave can sometimes do God's work, but because he does not do it of his own free will he remains in his former state of hard-heartedness. The hireling can do it, too, but because he does not do it for nothing he can be convicted of being led by his own desire. Where there is self-interest there is the desire to be allowed special terms.[29] Where that is present there is a corner, and in corners you will find rust and dirt (Ez 24:12–13).[30] Let the slave, then, have his law (Rom 2:14), the very fear by which he is constrained. Let the mercenary have his greed, by which he is held back when he is enticed and tugged at by temptation (Jas 1:14). But neither of these is without spot, and they cannot convert souls. Love truly converts souls because it makes them willing.

XII.35. I have called love "unspotted" because it keeps nothing for itself. For if a man holds nothing as his own, all he has belongs to God. What belongs to God cannot be unclean. Therefore love is the immaculate law of God, and it seeks not its own profit but what benefits many (1 Cor 10:33; 13:5). It is called the law of the Lord because he himself lives by it, and also because no one can possess it except by his gift. It does not seem absurd for me to say that even God lives by the law, for I have said that the law is nothing else but love. For what preserves the supreme and ineffable unity in the blessed Trinity but love? Love is the law then, and the law of the Lord, which in some manner holds and unites the Trinity in unity in the bond of peace (Eph 4:3). But let no one think that I am taking this love as a quality, or an accident. If I did, I should be saying—perish the thought—that there is something in God which is not God. But it is that divine substance which is in no way other than itself, as John says, "God is love" (1 Jn 4:8).

It is love indeed, then, and it is God, and it is the gift of God (Eph 2:8). And so love gives love; the substance gives rise to the accident. Where it signifies the giver, it is the name of a substance. Where it signifies the gift, it is a quality. This is the eternal law, creating and governing the universe. All things were made in weight and measure and number (Wis 11:20), according to this law. Nothing is left outside this law. Even the Law of all is not outside this law, for the law is nothing but itself, by which even if it does not create itself, yet it rules itself.

XIII.36. The slave and the mercenary have a law which is not

---

29. The fifth step of pride. Hum 42; LTR 3.48–49.
30. LTR 5.208; sermon for the sixth Sunday after Pentecost.

from God. One does not love God. The other loves something more than God. They have a law which is not of the Lord (Rom 2:14). And indeed each of us can make his own law, but no one can cause it to be independent of the changeless order of the eternal law. I should say that someone had made his own law when he puts his own will before the common and eternal law, wickedly wishing to imitate his Creator, so that just as God is a law unto himself, he too wants to rule himself and make his own will law. Alas! A heavy and unendurable burden lies on all the sons of Adam (Sir 40:1; Acts 15:10), bowing our necks and bending them, bringing our life to hell (Ps 87:4). "Unhappy man that I am, who will free me from the body of this death?" (Rom 7:24), by which I am made to tremble and am almost crushed, so that, "If the Lord did not help me, my soul would soon be in hell" (Ps 93:17).

Weighed down by this burden groaned he who said, "Why have you set me against you? I have become a burden to myself" (Jb 7:20). Where he said, "So that I have become a burden to myself" he shows that he had been his own law, and that no one but himself had brought that about. But he said, first, addressing himself to God, "Why have you set me against you?" indicating that he had not escaped the law of God.

It is the property of the everlasting and just law of God that he who is not willing to be ruled gently is ruled painfully by himself, and he who is not willing of his own free will to take up the gentle yoke and light burden of love (Mt 11:30) will bear against his will the insupportable burden of his own will (Mt 23:4). And so in a wonderful and just way, the everlasting law has captured him who runs from it and set him in opposition to it, and at the same time it has kept him in subjection to it. Yet he does not remain with God in his light and rest and glory, because he is subject to force and exiled from happiness. O Lord my God, "why do you not take away my sin, and why do you not remove my wickedness?" (Jb 7:21) so that, freed from the heavy burden of my own will, I may breathe freely under the light load of love, and not be coerced by slavish fear or attracted by mercenary greed, but be moved by your spirit (Rom 7:21), the spirit of freedom (2 Cor 3:17) by which your children live, and which bears witness to my spirit that I, too, am one of your sons (Rom 8:14; 16), that there is the same law for us both, and I may be myself what you are in this world (1 Jn 4:17). Those who do what the Apostle says, "Owe no one anything but the debt of love" (Rom 13:8)—they are undoubtedly as God is and in this world they are neither slaves not hirelings, but sons.

XIV.37. And so the sons are not outside the law, unless perhaps someone wants to put a different interpretation on the text "The law is not made for the righteous" (1 Tm 1:9). But you must know that law given in a spirit of slavery by fear is different from the law of freedom given in gentleness. Children are not under fear, but they cannot survive without love.

Do you wish to hear why there is no law for those who are good? Scripture says, "You have not received the spirit of slavery again in fear" (Rom 8:15). Hear then the just man saying of himself that he is not under the law and yet not free of the law. "I have become," he says, "as if I were under the law with those who are bound by the law, although I am not outside the law of God but bound by that of Christ" (1 Cor 9:20–21). So it is not right to say, "The just have no law," or, "The just are outside the law," but "The law is not made for the just," that is, it is not imposed on them against their will, but freely given to them when they are willing, and inspired by goodness (1 Tm 1:9). So the Lord says beautifully, "Take my yoke upon you" (Mt 11:29), as if he said, "I do not impose it on the unwilling; but you take it if you want to; otherwise you will find not rest but labor for your souls."

XIV.38. The law of love is good and sweet. It is not only borne lightly and easily, but it also makes bearable the laws which make men into slaves and hirelings. It does not destroy them; it fulfills them. As the Lord says, "I have not come to take away the law, but to fulfill it" (Mt 5:17). It tempers the slave's law and makes the hireling's law orderly. It lightens both. For there will never be any love without fear but chaste love. There will never be love without greed unless it is kept within bounds. Therefore love fulfills the slave's law when it overflows in devotion. It fulfill's the hireling's law when it sets limits to greed.

Devotion mixed with fear does not remove the fear but purifies it. Punishment is lifted, for while law was servitude it could not function without it. Fear remains forever, but a pure and filial fear (Ps 18:10). For we read that "perfect love casts out fear" (1 Jn 4:18). This is to be understood to refer to the punishment which is never absent from servile fear, as I have said—by that mode of speaking by which the cause is often given for the effect.[31]

Greed is brought to order when love overshadows it and evils are condemned and what is better is preferred to what is merely good, and

---

31. *Usus loquendi* is a favorite expression of Augustine and of Anselm of Canterbury.

the good is desired only for the sake of what is better. When by the grace of God this is fully achieved, the body is loved, and all the goods of the body for the sake of the soul, and the goods of the soul for the sake of God, and God for his own sake.

XV.39. But truly, since we are carnal and born of carnal desire (Rom 7:14), it is unavoidable that our desire and love should begin with the body and if it is rightly directed, it will then proceed by grace through certain stages, until the spirit is fulfilled (Gal 3:3). For "The spiritual does not come first but the animal, and then the spiritual" (1 Cor 15:46). And first it is necessary for us to bear an earthly likeness, before we have a heavenly likeness (1 Cor 15:49). In the first instance therefore man loves himself for himself. He is a bodily creature, and he cannot see beyond himself. But since he sees that he cannot be the author of his own existence he begins to inquire after God by faith (Heb 11:6) because he needs him, and he begins to love him. And so he comes to love God in the second degree, but still for himself and not for God's sake. But then when he begins to worship him, and to keep coming to him because he needs him, God gradually begins to make himself known to him through his thinking, reading, prayer, and obedience. By this growing familiarity God causes him truly to feel his sweetness. In this way, when he has tasted how sweet the Lord is (Ps 33:9), he passes to the third stage, where he loves God, not now for himself, but for God's sake. Truly he remains for a long time in that state, and I do not know whether the fourth stage, where a man comes to love himself only for God's sake, is fully attained by anyone in this life.

If anyone has experienced it, let him say so. To me it seems impossible. But I have no doubt that that is how it will be when the good and faithful servant is led into the joy of his Lord (Mt 25:21) and intoxicated by the riches of the house of God (Ps 35:9). It will be as though in some miraculous way he forgets himself and as though going out of himself altogether comes wholly to God, and afterward holds fast to him, one with him in spirit (1 Cor 6:17). I think this is what the prophet felt when he said, "I shall enter into the power of the Lord. Lord, I shall be mindful of your justice" (Ps 70:16). He knew well that when he entered into the spiritual power of the Lord he would have cast off all the weaknesses of the flesh. He would no longer need to give it a thought. In the spirit, he would have eyes for nothing but God's justice.

Then surely the individual members of Christ (1 Cor 6:15) can say for themselves what Paul said of their Head, "And if we have known Christ according to the flesh we have not known him" (1 Cor 5:16). No one knows himself according to the flesh, for "flesh and blood will not possess the kingdom of God" (1 Cor 15:50). That is not because the flesh will not exist as a substance in the future, but because every need of the flesh will vanish and fleshly love will be absorbed in the love of the spirit, and the weak human affections we have now will be changed into divine affections.

Then the net of love, which ceaselessly drags every kind of fish from the great wide sea, will be drawn in to shore; the bad will be cast out and he will keep only the good (Mt 13:47–48). If in this life he enfolds every kind of fish within the folds of his wide-ranging love, and for the time being it wraps itself round them all (1 Cor 9:19), drawing all in, both those who are against him and those who are for him. Making them in some way all his own he does not only rejoice with those who rejoice. He weeps with those who weep (Rom 12:15). But when the net is drawn to shore, all that has been suffered in sadness will be thrown out like rotten fish, and he will keep only what pleases him and is a joy.

But surely even then Paul (to take an example) will either be made weak with the weak or burn for those who are made to suffer when scandal and weakness no longer exist (2 Cor 11:29; cf. 1 Cor 9:22)? Will he grieve for those who do not repent, when there is neither sinner nor penitent (2 Cor 12:21)? Perish the thought that he should weep for those who have been condemned to eternal fire with the devil and his angels (Mt 25:41) when he is in that city the rush of whose river brings joy (Ps 45:5) and whose gates the Lord loves more than all the tents of Jacob (Ps 86:2). Even if there is now sometimes rejoicing in victory, yet there is strain in battle and life is in danger. Yet in that land which is home there is no more sorrow or adversity, as the song says, "Just as the dwelling-place of all who rejoice is in you" (Ps 86:7), and again, "Everlasting joy will be theirs" (Ps 61:7). Finally, how can mercy be remembered when the only thought is of God's justice (Ps 70:16)? There will be no place for wretchedness, no time for mercy; there will then surely be no feeling of compassion.[32]

---

32. See the concluding passages of Augustine's *City of God;* CCSL 47 (Turnholt, 1955), 2 vols.

Sermons on

The Song of Songs

Bernard always had a special love for the Song of Songs. Early in his monastic career, when he made himself ill by overwork, he spent some time in a hut in the monastery garden resting and convalescing. William of St. Thierry spent some time with him there, himself convalescent, and they talked of the Song of Songs so as to pass the time in a constructive way.[1] The themes of the Song of Songs were always in his mind as he wrote and preached, and in 1135 he began a series of sermons that was to continue, with breaks while he was absent from Clairvaux, until his death in 1153.

He found matter there for reflection on current affairs, on his own personal experiences, on human life and the love of God. It proved both a book about the present and particular and a hymn to eternal things. He points out in Sermon 30 (1ff.) [not in this volume] that there must be points of likeness between self-knowledge and knowledge of God (*iam in aliquo similis*) or we could not learn from one about the other, as God clearly intends us to do.

This is a consistent emphasis in Bernard's spirituality. He preaches the value of man in God's eyes, but at the same time he sees that value as lying in God himself, through the union with God that the perfect among men will one day enjoy. Self-knowledge is worthwhile, but only because it will be swallowed up in the knowledge and love of God. The kiss of contemplation is a participation in the life and love of the Trinity. Human dignity consists in man's capacity to return to God, to become again the being God made.

The "likeness" is portrayed in the Song of Songs as the bond

---

1. VP I.vii.32–33; PL 185.246C; VP I.xi.59; PL 185.258–59. See Introduction to this volume.

between Bridegroom and Bride. The bond holds not by any act
of man, but by the action of divine grace.

It is a likeness that can never be finally lost. Even in exile,
in the "region of unlikeness," the soul retains an inborn resem-
blance to God (Sermon 27.6).

Among the sermons translated here are the opening series,
on the "Kiss" of the soul and her Bridegroom and, some of the
later sermons, in which Bernard conveys most vividly the quality
of his personal experience of rapture in contemplation.

SERMON I

To you, brothers, I shall say what I should not say to those who are in
the world, or at least I shall say it in a different way. The preacher who
follows the Apostle Paul's method of teaching will give them milk to
drink, not solid food (1 Cor 3:1–2; Heb 5:12–4). Before those who are
spiritually minded more solid food must be set, as the Apostle himself
teaches by his own example. "We speak," he says, "not in the words of
those learned in human wisdom, but in words taught by the Spirit. We
teach spiritual things to those who are spiritual" (1 Cor 2:13). Again,
"We speak wisdom to those who are mature in the faith" (1 Cor 2:6),
among whom I am sure I can number you, unless you have studied
divine teaching so long, mortified your senses and meditated day and
night on the law of God, all in vain (Ps 1:2).

And so be ready to eat not milk but bread. In Solomon there is
bread, and bread that is fine and flavorsome. I speak of the book which
is called the Song of Songs. Let it be brought forth, then, if you please,
and broken.

I.2. Now if I am not mistaken, through the grace of God you have
been taught well enough by the words of Ecclesiastes to know and despise the vanity of this world. And what about Proverbs? Surely your
life and conduct have been sufficiently amended and directed by the
teaching found there?[1] You have already tasted these two, loaves you

---

1. The notion that Solomon had written three books of graduated difficulty by which
the soul could progress from practical goodness in daily life to the contemplation of the highest
spiritual truth and the love of God is a commonplace of medieval exegesis, borrowed from
Origen.

have accepted as being provided by a friend from his store (Lk 11:5). Come for the third loaf, too, so that perhaps you may recognize what is best (Phil 1:10).

There are only two evils—or two chief evils—which war against the soul: an empty love of the world and too much self-love (1 Pt 2:11). The two books we have mentioned can cure both diseases. One uproots wickedness and excess of body and of conduct with the hoe of self-control. The other, by the light of reason, shrewdly perceives that all the glory of the world has a deceptive look, and distinguishes it unerringly from solid truth. More than that, it sets the fear of God and the keeping of his commandments above all human pursuits and worldly desires (Eccl 12:13). And so it should. For the first is the beginning of wisdom (Ps 111:10) and the second its fulfillment. For it is obvious that there is no true and perfect wisdom except in turning from evil and doing good (Ps 36:27; Prv 3:7). And no one can turn wholly from evil without the fear of God, nor is any work good unless it is done according to the commandments.

I.3. Taking it that these two evils have been put from us as a result of reading these two books, we may fittingly go on to this holy, contemplative discourse which, the fruit of the first two, feeds only seriously inclined ears and minds.

II.1. Before the flesh has been subdued and the spirit set free by the pursuit of truth, before the glories of the world and its entanglements have been seen for what they are, and put from us, it is presumptuous of us to attempt the study of what is holy, for we are impure. Just as a light shines unseen on blind or closed eyes, so the man who is an animal does not see the things which belong to the spirit of God (1 Cor 2:14). For the Holy Spirit teaches only the truth (Wis 1:5), and has nothing to do with the life of a man who lacks self-discipline. He will have no part in the emptiness of the world, because he is the Spirit of Truth (Jn 14:17). What does the wisdom from above have to do with worldly wisdom (Jas 3:17; 1 Cor 3:19), which is foolishness in God's eyes? Or the wisdom of the flesh, which is hostile to God (Rom 8:7)? But I think that the friend who comes with us will have no cause for complaint against us when he has shared this third loaf.

II.4. But who will break it? Here is the Master of the household. Know the Lord in the breaking of bread (Lk 24:35). Who else is the right person to do it? I should not dare to do it myself. Look upon me as someone from whom you expect nothing.

For I am one of those who are expecting; I beg with you for food for my soul, the nourishment of the Spirit. Poor and needy indeed, I knock at the door which, "when he opens it, no one can close" (Rv 3:7), asking for help so that I may understand the mystery of this most profound discourse. "The eyes of us all are turned upon you in hope, Lord" (Ps 144:15). "The little children beg for bread; no one gives it to them" (Lam 4:4). They trust that they will receive it from your merciful love. O most Kind, break your bread for those who are hungering for it; by my hands, if you will allow, but by your own power.

III.5. Tell us, I beg, by whom, about whom, and to whom is said, "Let him kiss me with the kiss of his mouth"?[2] Why this sudden and abrupt beginning in the middle of a speech? For he breaks into words as if he had mentioned a speaker in the text, to whom this speaker is replying as she demands a kiss. Then again, if she asks for or demands a kiss from someone, why does she clearly and specifically say "with his mouth," as if lovers were in the habit of kissing with anything but the mouth, or with mouths which are not their own? Yet she does not say, "Let him kiss me with his mouth," but, more intimately, "with the kiss of his mouth."

What a delightful way of putting it (Ps 103:34)! We begin with a kiss, and the lovely face of Scripture readily attracts the reader and leads him on, so that he delights to search into what lies hidden in it even if it costs him effort, and no difficulty can weary him where the sweetness of the discourse eases the labor. Surely this way of "beginning without a beginning," this freshness of expression in so old a book, must capture the reader's attention? It is clear that this work was not written by human wit, but was composed by the art of the Spirit. As a result, even if it is difficult to understand, it is nevertheless a source of delight to him who looks into it.

IV.6. But what now? Shall we leave out the title? No! Not even one iota may be omitted (Mt 5:18), when we are instructed to collect the fragments in case they are lost (Jn 6:12). This is the title: "The Beginning of the Song of Songs of Solomon."

Observe first the name of the Peacemaker, "Solomon"; that is appropriate at the beginning of a book which opens with the sign of peace, the kiss. And note, too, that only minds at peace are invited by this kind of opening to understand the Scriptures, minds which master the dis-

---

2. In classical rhetorical textbooks orators were taught to inquire in trying a case in court, by whom the offense was committed, whom it concerned and to whom it was done, and so on.

turbances caused by the vices and the tumults of care within themselves.

IV.7. Again, the title says not simply "Song," but "Song of Songs." Do not think that that is unimportant. I have read many songs in Scripture, and I do not remember any with that title.

Israel sang a song to the Lord (Ex 15:1–19) because he had escaped the sword and yoke of Pharaoh, and the twofold miracle of the Red Sea both freed and avenged him. The song he sang is not called "The Song of Songs," but, if I remember correctly, Scripture says, "Israel sang this song to the Lord" (Ex 15:1).

Deborah sang (Jgs 5:1) and Judith sang (Jdt 16:1), and the mother of Samuel sang (1 Sm 2:1), and some of the prophets sang, too (cf. Is 5:1–2, 26:1–10). And none of them is said to have called his song the "Song of Songs." You will find, if I am not mistaken, that each sang in gratitude for himself or on behalf of his own people, for a victory, for example, for escape from danger, or for something longed-for which had been given. And so then many have sung, each for his own reason, so that they should not be found ungrateful for God's goodness to them, as in, "He gives thanks to you, O God, for blessing him" (Ps 48:19).

But King Solomon, singular in wisdom, sublime in glory, rich in possessions, secure in peace, is not known to have been in need of any benefit for whose granting he would have sung this song. Nor does Scripture itself anywhere say that he did.

8. And so, divinely inspired, he sang the praises of Christ and the Church, of the gift of holy love and the mystery of eternal union with God. And at the same time he expressed the longing of the holy soul, its wedding song; and exulting in the Spirit, he composed a joyful song.

Yet it is in figurative language. It is not surprising that he veiled his face like Moses (Ex 34:33; 2 Cor 3:13). It must have shone no less than Moses' face did when he met God face to face, for in those days there was no one, or almost no one, who could bear the glory of the face of God unveiled (2 Cor 3:18). Therefore I think this wedding song is given its title because it is excellent, and that is why it alone is deservedly called "The Song of Songs," just as he in whose honor it is sung is alone called "King of Kings and Lord of Lords" (1 Tm 6:15).

V.9. If you consider your own experience, surely it is in the victory by which your faith overcomes the world (1 Jn 5:4), and "in your leaving the lake of wretchedness and the filth of the marsh" (Ps 39:3) that you sing to the Lord himself a new song because he has done marvellous works (Ps 97:1)?

Again, when he began to "set your feet upon a rock and direct your steps" (Ps 39:3–4), I think that then, too, there was a new song in your mouth, a song to our God for his gift of newness of life. When you repented, he not only forgave your sins, but also promised rewards; did you not then sing of the Lord's ways, rejoicing the more in the hope of good things to come (Rom 12:12), for great is the glory of the Lord (Ps 137:5)?

And when, perhaps, he illuminates some passage in Scripture which was closed or obscure to you, then you cannot resist delighting his ears with the voice of exultation and praise (Ps 4:5), the sound of one who feasts in gratitude for the food of the bread of heaven he has given you.

And in the daily trials and battles from which those who live a holy life in Christ are never free, for they come from the world, the flesh, and the devil (2 Tm 3:12), you learn by your experience that the life of man on earth is an endless battle (Jb 7:1), and it is necessary to renew your song every day, for every victory that is won: each time temptation is overcome, or vice subdued, or a danger that threatens avoided, or the trap of the tempter detected, or a long-standing passion of the soul cured once and for all, or a virtue which has been longed for very much for a long time and often prayed for obtained at last by the gift of God. How can you not, just as often (in the words of the prophet) "give thanks and sound the voice of praise" (Is 51:3)? Otherwise when the time of judgment comes, he will be thought ungrateful who cannot say to God, "Your statutes were my song in the place of my exile" (Ps 118:54).

V.10. I think you will recognize from your own experience those psalms which are called not "The Song of Songs," but "a song of steps." Each of you, according to the steps he has taken upward in his heart (Ps 83:6), may choose one of these songs to praise and give glory to him who leads you on. How else is this passage to be taken, "There are shouts of exultation and safety in the tents of the just" (Ps 117:15)? And still more that beautiful and most saving exhortation of the Apostle, "Singing songs and psalms to the Lord in your hearts with psalms, hymns, and spiritual canticles" (Eph 5:19)?

VI.11. But there is a song which, in its singular dignity and sweetness, outshines all those we have recalled, and every other there may be, and rightly have I called it "The Song of Songs," because it is itself the fruit of all the others. This sort of song only the touch of the Holy Spirit teaches (1 Jn 2:27), and it is learned by experience alone. Let

those who have experienced it enjoy it; let those who have not burn
with desire, not so much to know it as to experience it. It is not a noise
made aloud, but the very music of the heart. It is not a sound from the
lips but a stirring of joy, not a harmony of voices but of wills. It is not
heard outwardly, nor does it sound in public (Is 42:2). Only he who
sings it hears it, and he to whom it is sung—the Bride and the Bridegroom. It is a wedding song indeed, expressing the embrace of chaste
and joyful souls, the concord of their lives and the mutual exchange of
their love.

VI.12. For the rest, it is not for the souls of children and novices
to sing or to hear, or for those who have recently turned from a worldly
life, but those who are making progress and have disciplined themselves
to study, and who have, with God's help, reached, as it were, the age
for marriage (I mean the "age" of deserving, not of years), and is made
fit for the heavenly Bridegroom. This is a union which we shall describe
more fully in due course. But the hour is passing and poverty and our
Rule demand that we go out to work.[3] Today we have been talking
about the title. Tomorrow, with God's help, we shall go on to speak
about the kiss.

SERMON 2

On the Kiss

I.1. When I reflect, as I often do, on the ardor with which the patriarchs longed for the incarnation of Christ, I am pierced with sorrow
and shame. And now I can scarcely contain my tears, so ashamed am
I of the lukewarmness and lethargy of the present times. For which of
us is filled with joy at the realization of this grace as the holy men of
old were moved to desire by the promise of it?

Soon now we shall be rejoicing at the celebration of his birth (Lk
1:14). But would that it were really for his birth! How I pray that that
burning desire and longing in the hearts of these holy men of old may
be aroused in me by these words: "Let him kiss me with the kiss of his
mouth" (Sg 1:1). In those days a spiritual man could sense in the Spirit
how great would be the grace released by the touch of those lips (Ps

---

3. RB 48.

44:3). For that reason, speaking in the desire prompted by the Spirit (Is 26:8), he said, "Let him kiss me with the kiss of his mouth," desiring with all his heart that he would not be deprived of a share in that sweetness.

I.2. The good men of those days could say, "Of what use to me are the words the prophets have uttered? Rather, let him who is beautiful beyond the children of men (Ps 44:3) kiss me with the kiss of his mouth. I am no longer content with what Moses says, for he sounds to me like someone who cannot speak well" (Ex 4:10). Isaiah is "a man of unclean lips" (Is 6:5). Jeremiah is a child who does not know how to speak (Jn 1:6). All the prophets are empty to me.

But he, he of whom they speak, let *him* speak to me. Let him kiss me with the kiss of his mouth. Let him not speak to me in them or through them, for they are "a watery darkness, a dense cloud" (Ps 17:12). But let him kiss me with the kiss of his mouth, whose gracious presence and eloquence of wonderful teaching causes a "spring of living water" to well up in me to eternal life (Jn 4:14). Shall I not find that a richer grace is poured out upon me from him whom the Father has anointed with the oil of gladness more than all his companions, if he will deign to kiss me with the kiss of his mouth (Ps 44:8)? His living and effective word (Heb 4:12) is a kiss; not a meeting of lips, which can sometimes be deceptive about the state of the heart, but a full infusion of joys, a revelation of secrets, a wonderful and inseparable mingling of the light from above and the mind on which it is shed, which, when it is joined with God, is one spirit with him (1 Cor 6:17).

It is with good reason, then, that I have nothing to do with dreams and visions, reject figures and mysteries, and even the beauty of angels seems tedious to me. For my Jesus outshines them so far in his beauty and loveliness (Ps 44:5). That is why I ask him, not any other, angel or man, to kiss me with the kiss of his mouth.

II.2. I do not presume to think that I shall be kissed by his mouth. That is the unique felicity and singular prerogative of the humanity he assumed. But, more humbly, I ask to be kissed by the kiss of his mouth, which is shared by many, those who can say, "Indeed from his fullness we have all received" (Jn 1:16).

II.3. Listen carefully here. The mouth which kisses signifies the Word who assumes human nature; the flesh which is assumed is the recipient of the kiss; the kiss, which is of both giver and receiver, is the Person which is of both, the Mediator between God and man, the Man Christ Jesus (1 Tm 2:5).

For this reason, none of the saints presumed to say, "Let him kiss me with his mouth," but, "with the kiss of his mouth," thus acknowledging that prerogative of him on whom uniquely once and for all the Mouth of the Word was pressed, when the whole fullness of the divinity gave itself to him in the body (Col 2:9).

O happy kiss, and wonder of amazing self-humbling which is not a mere meeting of lips, but the union of God with man. The touch of lips signifies the bringing together of souls. But this conjoining of natures unites the human with the divine and makes peace between earth and heaven (Col 1:20). "For he himself is our peace, who made the two one" (Eph 2:14). This was the kiss for which the holy men of old longed, the more so because they foresaw the joy and exultation (Sir 15:6) of finding their treasure in him, and discovering all the treasures of wisdom and knowledge in him (Col 2:3), and they longed to receive of his fullness (Jn 1:16).

II.4. I think that what I have said pleases you. But listen to another meaning.

III.4. The holy men who lived before the coming of the Savior understood that God had in mind a plan to bring peace to the race of mortal men (Jer 29:11). For the Word would do nothing on earth which he did not reveal to his servants the prophets (Am 3:7). But this Word was hidden from many (Lk 18:34), for at that time faith was rare upon the earth and hope was very faint even in the hearts of many of those who were waiting for the redemption of Israel (Lk 2:38). Those who foreknew also proclaimed that Christ would come in the flesh and that with him would come peace. That is why one of them says, "There will be peace when he comes to our earth" (cf. Mi 5:5). By divine inspiration they preached faithfully that men were to be saved through the grace of God. John, the forerunner of the Lord, recognized that this was to be fulfilled in his own time, and he declared, "Grace and truth have come through Jesus Christ" (Jn 1:17), and all Christian peoples now experience the truth of what he said.

III.5. In those days, although the prophets foretold peace, the faith of the people continually wavered because there was no one to redeem or save them (Ps 7:3), for the Author of peace delayed his coming (Mt 25:5). So men complained at the delay, because the Prince of Peace (Is 9:6), who had been so often proclaimed, had not yet come, as had been promised by the holy men who were his prophets from of old (Lk 1:70).

They began to lose faith in the promises and they demanded the kiss, the sign of the promise of reconciliation. It was as if one of the people were to answer the messengers of peace, "How much longer are you going to keep us waiting?" (Jn 10:24). You foretell a peace which does not come. You promise good things and there is still confusion (Jer 14:19). See, many times and in many ways (Heb 1:1) angels announced to the patriarchs and our fathers proclaimed to us (Ps 43:2), saying, "Peace. And there is no peace" (Jer 6:14). If God wants me to believe in his benevolent will which he has so often spoken of through the prophets but not yet shown in action, "Let him kiss me with the kiss of his mouth," and so by this sign of peace make peace secure. For how am I to go on believing in mere words? They need to be confirmed by deeds. Let him confirm that his messengers spoke the truth, if they were his messengers, and let him follow them in person, as they have so often promised; for they can do nothing without him. He sent a boy bearing a staff (Jn 15:5)[1] but no voice or life (2 Kgs 4:26–31).

I do not rise up or awaken; I am not shaken free of the dust (Is 52:2); I do not breathe in hope, if the prophet himself does not come down and kiss me with the kiss of his mouth.

III.6. Here we must add that he who makes himself our Mediator with God is the Son of God and he is himself God. What is man that he should take notice of him, or the son of man, that he should think of him? (Ps 143:3). Where am I to find the faith to dare to trust in such majesty? How, I say, shall I, who am dust and ashes, presume to think that God cares about me (Sir 10:9)? He loves his Father. He does not need me, nor my possessions (Ps 15:2). How then shall I be sure that he will never fail me?

If it is true, as you prophets say, that God has the intention of showing mercy, and thinks to make himself manifest for our reassurance (Ps 76:8), let him make a covenant of peace (Sir 45:30), an everlasting covenant with me (Is 61:8) by the kiss of his mouth.

If he is not going to go back on what he has said (Ps 88:35), let him empty himself, humble himself (Phil 2:7), bend low and "kiss me with the kiss of his mouth." If the Mediator is to be acceptable to both sides, let God the Son of God become man; let him become the son of man, and make me sure of him with the kiss of his mouth. When I know that the Mediator who is the Son of God is mine, then I shall accept him trustingly. Then there can be no mistrust. For he is brother to my flesh

---

1. John the Baptist.

(Gn 37:27). For I think that bone of my bone and flesh of my flesh cannot spurn me (Gn 2:23).

III.7. So, therefore, the old complaint went on about this most sacred kiss, that is, the mystery of the incarnation of the Word, while faith faints with weariness because of its long and troubled waiting, and the faithless people murmured against the promises of God because they were worn out by waiting. Am I making this up? Do you not recognize that this is what Scripture says, "Here are complaints and the loud murmur of voices, order on order, waiting on waiting, a little here, a little there" (Is 28:10)? Here are anxious prayers full of piety, "Give their reward, Lord, to those who wait on you, so that your prophets may be found faithful" (Sir 36:18). Again, "Bring about what the prophets of old prophesied in your name" (Sir 36:17). Here are sweet promises full of consolation, "Behold the Lord will appear; and he will not lie. If he seems slow, wait for him, for he will come, and that soon" (Hb 2:3). Again, "The time of his coming is near and his days will not be prolonged" (Is 14:1), and, from the Person of him who was promised, "Behold," he says, "I am running toward you like a river of peace, and like a stream in flood with the glory of the nations" (Is 66:12).

In these words, both the urgency of the preachers and the lack of faith of the people is clear enough. And so the people murmured and faith wavered and, as Isaiah puts it, "The messengers of peace weep bitterly" (Is 33:7). Therefore, because Christ delayed his coming lest the whole human race should perish in desperation while they thought their weak mortality condemned them and they did not trust that God would bring them the so-often promised reconciliation with him, those holy men who were made sure by the Spirit looked for the certainty that his presence could bring, and urgently demanded a sign that the covenant was about to be renewed for the sake of the weak in the faith.

IV.8. O Root of Jesse, who stand as a sign to the peoples (Is 11:10), how many kings and prophets wanted to see you and did not (Lk 10:24)? Simeon is the happiest of them all because by God's mercy he was still bearing fruit in old age. For he rejoiced to think that he would see the sign so long desired. He saw it and was glad (Jn 8:56). When he had received the kiss of peace he departed in peace, but first he proclaimed aloud that Jesus was born, a sign that would be rejected (Lk 2:25–34).

And so it was. The sign of peace arose and was rejected, by those who hate peace (Ps 119:7). For what is peace to men of goodwill (Lk 2:14) is a stone to make men stumble, a rock for the wicked to fall over

(1 Pt 2:8). "Herod was troubled, and all Jerusalem with him" (Mt 2:3). He came to his own and his own did not receive him (Jn 1:11). Happy those shepherds keeping watch at night who were found worthy to be shown the sign of this vision (Lk 23:8). For even at that time he was hiding himself from the wise and prudent and revealing himself to the simple (Mt 11:25; Lk 10:21). Herod wanted to see him (Lk 23:8), but because he did not want to see him out of goodwill, he did not deserve to see him.

The sign of peace was given only to men of goodwill; the only sign which was given to Herod and his like is the sign of Jonah and the prophet (Mt 12:39). The angel said to the shepherds, "This is a sign for you" (Lk 2:12), you who are humble, you who are obedient, you who are not haughty (Rom 12:16), you who are keeping vigil and meditating on God's law day and night (Ps 1:2). "This is a sign for you," he said.

What is this sign? The sign the angels promised, the sign the people asked for, the sign the prophets foretold, the Lord Jesus has now made, and he shows it to you; the sign in which unbelievers receive the faith, the faint-hearted hope, the perfect security. This is your sign.

What is it a sign of? Indulgence, grace, peace, the peace which will have no end (Is 9:7). It is this sign: "You will find a baby wrapped in swaddling clothes and lying in a manger" (Lk 2:12). But this baby is God himself, reconciling the world to himself in him (2 Cor 5:19). He will die for your sins and rise again to make you just (Rom 4:25), so that, made just by faith, you may be at peace with God (Rom 5:1).

This was the sign of faith that the prophet once asked Achaz the king to ask of the Lord his God, either from the heavens or from the depths of hell (Is 7:11). But the wicked king refused, not believing, wretched man, that in this sign the heights would be joined to the depths in peace. This came to pass when the Lord descended even to hell, and greeted those who dwell there with a holy kiss (1 Cor 16:20), so that even they received the sign of peace, and then he returned to heaven and made it possible for the spirits there to share the same sign in everlasting joy.

IV.9. We must come to the end of this sermon. But let me sum up briefly what I have said. It seems clear that this holy kiss was given to the world for two reasons: to give the weak faith and to satisfy the desire of the perfect. This kiss is no other than the Mediator between God and men, the man Christ Jesus (1 Tm 2:5), who with the Father and the Holy Spirit lives and reigns world without end, Amen.

SERMON 3

Today we read the book of experience. Let us turn to ourselves and let each of us search his own conscience about what is said. I want to investigate whether it has been given to any of you to say, "Let him kiss me with the kiss of his mouth" (Sg 1:1). Few can say this wholeheartedly. But if anyone once receives the spiritual kiss of Christ's mouth he seeks eagerly to have it again and again. I think no one can know what it is except he who has received it. It is a hidden manna (Rv 2:17), and he who eats it hungers for more (Sir 24:23). It is a sealed-up fountain (Sg 4:12), to which no stranger has access, but he who drinks from it thirsts for more and he alone (Sir 24:29).

Hear the demand of one who has experienced it: "Restore to me the joy of your salvation" (Ps 50:14). But a soul like mine, burdened with sins, cannot dare to say that, while it is still crippled by fleshly passions (2 Tm 3:6), and while it does not feel the sweetness of the Spirit, and is almost wholly unfamiliar with and inexperienced in inner joys.

I.2. But I should like to point out to the man who is like this that there is a place for him on the road to salvation. He may not rashly lift his face to the face of the most serene Bridegroom, but he can throw himself timidly at the feet of the most severe Lord with me, and with the Publican (Lk 18:13) tremble on the earth and not look up to heaven, in case he is dazzled by the light. Eyes that are used to darkness will be blinded by light (Prv 25:27), and wrapped again in a darkness deeper than before. You who are such a soul, do not think that position despicable in which the sinner laid down her sins and put on the garment of holiness. There the Ethiopian changed her skin (Jer 13:23) and, restored to a new brightness, she could reply faithfully and truthfully to those who reproached her (Ps 118:42), "I am black but I am beautiful, daughters of Jerusalem" (Sg 1:4).

Are you wondering how she was able to change like this, or how she deserved it? You shall hear in a few words. She wept bitterly (Lk 22:62) and sighed deeply from her inmost heart, and her sobs shook her one by one, and the evils within her came forth. The heavenly Physician came quickly to help her, for "his Word runs swiftly" (Ps 147:15).

Surely the Word of God is not a medicine? Indeed it is, strong and powerful, searching out the heart and mind (Ps 7:10). "God's word is living and effective, and more penetrating that any two-edged sword, penetrating to the place where soul and spirit meet, and separating the marrow; it judges the thoughts" (Heb 4:12).

O wretch, prostrate yourself like this blessed penitent, so that you can cease to be miserable. Prostrate yourself on the ground, embrace his feet, plead with kisses, water them with tears (Lk 7:37–50). Wash not only him but yourself, and you will become one of the flock of shorn ewes as they come up from the washing (Sg 4:2). Even then you will not dare to lift your face, swollen with shame and grief, until you hear him say, "Your sins are forgiven" (Lk 7:48), and "Awake, awake captive daughter of Sion, awake, shake off the dust" (Is 52:1–2).

II.3. Though you have given a first kiss to the feet, do not presume to rise at once to kiss the mouth. You must come to that by way of another, intermediate kiss, on the hand. This is the reason for that kiss: "If Jesus says to me, 'Your sins are forgiven,' what is the good of that unless I cease to sin? I have taken off my filthy garment. If I put it on again, what progress have I made?" (Sg 5:3). If I dirty again the feet that I have washed, surely the washing is valueless? Filthy with every sort of vice, I have lain for a long time in the slough of the mire (Ps 39:3). If I return to it again it is worse than my first falling into it. I remember that he who healed me himself said to me, "Behold you are healed; go and sin no more, lest worse befall you" (Jn 5:14).

It is necessary that he who gives the will to repent should add the virtue of continence lest I should do things to repent of worse than the first (Lk 11:26). Woe is me even if I repent, if he immediately takes away the hand without which I can do nothing (Jn 15:5). Nothing, I say, because without him I cannot repent, or contain my sin. For that reason I listen to Wisdom's advice, "Do not repeat yourself at your prayers" (Sir 7:15). I fear the Judge's reaction to the tree which did not bear good fruit (Mt 3:10). For these reasons I am not fully satisfied by the first grace, by which I repent of my sins, unless I receive the second, too, so that I may bear worthy fruits of repentance (Lk 3:8), and not return like a dog to his vomit (Prv 26:11).

II.4. There remains to consider what I must seek and receive before I may presume to touch higher and more sacred things (Mt 7:8). I do not want to be there all at once. I want to proceed a step at a time. The sinner's impudence displeases God as much as the penitent's modesty pleases him. You will please him more readily if you live within your limits and do not seek things too high for you (Sir 3:22). It is a long leap and a difficult one from the foot to the mouth, and that way of getting there is not appropriate.

How then, should you go? Should you who were recently covered in filth touch the holy lips? Yesterday dragged out of the mire, do you present yourself today to the face of glory? Let your way be by the hand. The hand first touched you and now lifts you up. How will it lift you up? By giving you the grace to aspire. What is that? The sweetness of temperance and the fruits of worthy repentance (Lk 3:8), which are the works of holiness; these can lift you from the mire (Ps 112:7) to the hope of daring greater things. When you receive this grace you kiss his hand. Give the glory not to yourself but to him (Ps 113:9). Give it once and again, both for the forgiveness of sins and for the virtues that are given. Otherwise you will need to fortify yourself against such darts as these, "What do you have that you have not received? If you have received, why do you glory as though you had not?" (1 Cor 4:7).

III.5. Now at last, having the experience of the divine kindness in these two kisses, perhaps you will not feel diffident of presuming to what is holier. The more you grow in grace, the more you are enlarged in faith. Thus it is that you will love more ardently and press more confidently for that which you know you still lack. For, "to him who knocks it shall be opened" (Lk 11:10). I believe that that supreme kiss of the highest condescension and wonderful sweetness will not be denied to him who so loves.

This is the way; this is the order. First we cast ourselves at his feet and deplore before God who made us (Ps 94:6) the evil we have done. Secondly, we reach out for the hand which will lift us up, which will strengthen our trembling knees (Is 35:3). Last, when we have obtained that, with many prayers and tears, then perhaps we shall dare to lift our faces to the mouth which is so divinely beautiful, fearing and trembling, not only to gaze on it, but even to kiss it. For "Christ the Lord is a Spirit before our face" (Lam 4:20). When we are joined with him in a holy kiss we are made one with him in spirit through his kindness (1 Cor 6:17).

III.6. My heart rightly says to you, Lord Jesus, "My face has sought you; your face, Lord do I seek" (Ps 26:8). In the morning you showed me your mercy (Ps 142:8). When I lay in the dust to kiss your footprints you forgave my evil life. Later in the day you gave joy to your servant's soul (Ps 85:4), when, with the kiss of your hand, you gave him grace to live a good life. And now what remains, O good Lord, except that now in full light, while I am in fervor of spirit, you should admit me to the kiss of your mouth, and grant me the full joy of your presence

(Ps 15:11). Show me, O sweetest and most serene, "Show me where you feed, where you lie down in the noonday" (Sg 1:6).

Brothers, it is good for us to be here (Lk 9:33), but the duties of the day call us away. These guests whose arrival has just been announced to us oblige me to break off my sermon rather than bring it to an end. So I am going to our guests, so as not to neglect the duty of charity of which we have been speaking—lest we hear it said of us, "They do not practice what they preach" (Mt 23:3). In the meantime, pray that the words of my mouth may be pleasing to God (Ps 118:108), for your edification and for his praise and glory (1 Pt 1:7).

SERMON 4

I.1. Yesterday's sermon outlined the progression of the soul in three stages, by means of the image of three kisses. You have not forgotten? Today, I shall continue the argument, as far as God in his goodness may allow his poor one (Ps 67:11). We said, if you remember, that those kisses are given to the feet, the hands, the mouth, one after the other. The first comes at the beginning of our Christian life. The second is given to those who are making progress. The third is a rare experience, given only to the perfect.

The Scripture we are trying to expound begins from this last alone, and we have added the other two for its sake. Whether it was necessary, you shall judge. For I think that the way the word is presented requires it. It would be surprising if you did not see that there was something else, other kisses, which she who said "He kisses me with the kiss of his mouth" (Sg 1:1) wanted to distinguish from the kiss of the mouth. Why, then, when she could have said simply, "He kisses me," did she distinctly and pointedly add, contrary to ordinary usage, "with the kiss of his mouth," unless it was to show that the supreme kiss she wanted was not the only one?

Surely we say in her place, "Kiss me," or "Give me a kiss"? No one adds, "with your mouth," or "with the kiss of your mouth." What? When we are going to kiss one another we do not have to say what we want when we offer our lips to one another. To take an example: St. John simply says when he describes the kiss that Judas gave the Lord, "And he kissed him" (Mk 14:45). He does not add, "with his mouth" or "with the kiss of his mouth." So with everyone who speaks or writes.

There are, then, these three affections or stages of progress in the soul. They are well enough known and obvious to those who have experienced them. First there is the forgiveness of sins; then the grace to do good; then the presence of him who forgives, the benefactor, is experienced as strongly as it can be in a fragile body.

I.2. Hear why I called the first and second stages "kisses." We all know that a kiss is a sign of peace. If, as Scripture says, "our sins separate us from God" (Is 59:2), peace is lost between us. When, therefore, we make satisfaction and are reconciled with the removal of the sin which was separating us, the favor we receive can surely only be called a kiss. And then there is no better place for receiving this kiss than the feet. The satisfaction we make for our sins of pride ought to be humble and lowly.

II.3. But when God grants us the grace of a sweet familiarity with him, so that we can live better lives in accordance with that relationship, we lift our heads from the dust with greater confidence, so as to kiss the hand of our benefactor, as people do. But in receiving this gift we seek not our own glory but that of the giver, and we ascribe his gifts to him and not to ourselves. Otherwise, if you glory in yourself and not in the Lord (1 Cor 1:31) you will be kissing your own hand not his. That, Job says, is the great sin, and a denial of God (Jb 31:28). If then Scripture bears witness that to seek one's own glory (Jn 7:18) is to kiss one's own hand, then he who gives the glory to God is not improperly said to kiss God's hand (Jn 9:24). We see that this is even among men. Slaves kiss the feet of the masters they have offended when they ask their pardon, and the poor kiss the hands of the rich when they receive gifts from them.

III.4. Truly, since "God is a Spirit" (Jn 4:24), his simple substance cannot have bodily members. Perhaps you will not accept all this, but demand that I show you these hands and feet of God and so support what I say about the kiss of the feet and the hands.

But what if I, in my turn, ask about the mouth of God, for Scripture certainly speaks of the kiss of a mouth? Show me how God has a mouth. Either he has a mouth, hands, and feet, or he has none of these things. But God has a mouth by which he teaches men knowledge (Ps 93:10), and a hand by which he gives food to all flesh (Ps 135:25), and he has feet, for which the earth is a footstool (Is 66:1). When the sinners of the earth turn from their sins and are humbled it is to these feet that they come with a kiss.

God has all these not by nature, but we understand them as ways by which we can come to him. A truly humble desire to confess casts us down before him as if at his feet. A burning devotion to God discovers renewal and refreshment in him as at the touch of his hand. A joyous contemplation finds rest in him in the rapture which is the kiss of his mouth.

He who governs all is all things to all, yet he has no particularities. All that we can say of him in himself is that "he dwells in inaccessible light" (1 Tm 6:16). His peace is beyond our understanding (Phil 4:7). His wisdom is beyond measure (Ps 146:5) and his greatness has no bounds (Ps 144:3). No man can see him and live (Ex 33:20).

Yet he who is the ground of all being is not far from each of us (Acts 17:27), for without him is nothing (Jn 1:3). But, to make you wonder more: Nothing is more present than he and nothing is more incomprehensible. What is more present to anyone than his own being? And what is more incomprehensible than the Being of all things? I say that God is the Being of all things not because they are the same as him, but because "from him and through him and in him are all things" (Rom 11:36). He is, as their Creator, the Being of all things that are made. But he is the cause, not the stuff of their being.

In this way, this majesty has deigned to be present to his creatures, to be all in all things to all living things throughout their life; to all rational creatures the light of understanding; virtue to those who use their reason rightly; glory to those who conquer.

III.5. In all this creating, governing, administration, moving and causing motion, renewing and strengthening, he needs no bodily instruments, for by his word alone he created all bodies and spirits. Souls need bodies and bodies needed senses by which to know and affect one another. But the Omnipotent is not like that. By the swift action of his will he chose to create and ordain things. He can do what he will, as much as he wills, and without the help of any bodily members. Do you think he needs the help of bodily senses to understand what he has created? Nothing at all can hide from him, or flees the light of his presence. Sense-awareness can never be the vehicle of his knowledge. Not only does he know all things without a body; he also causes the pure in heart to know him in this way.

I have said a good deal about this, so as to make it clear. But perhaps now that I must stop for today, we should postpone more discussion until tomorrow.

Sermon 5

I.1. There are four sorts of spirits, as you know: those of beasts, our own, those of angels, and the Spirit which created them all. Only one of these needs no body, or anything like a body, for its own sake or anyone else's sake, and that is he whom every bodily or spiritual creature rightly confesses, saying, "You are my God because you have no need of my goods" (Ps 15:2).

First, it is clear that the animal spirit needs a body so much that it cannot exist without it. When an animal dies its spirit[1] ceases to live at the same moment as the body. But we live after the death of the body. Nevertheless, only through the body does the way, the ascent to the life of blessedness, lie open to us. He who said, "The invisible things of God are understood through the things he has made" (Rom 1:20) realized that. Those things which are made, that is, those bodily and visible things, come to our knowledge only through the bodily senses. The spiritual creature which we are has a body which is necessary to it, and without which it cannot reach that knowledge which is the only way to the knowledge the blessed have.

If any of you objects that baptized infants who die and who leave their bodies without any knowledge of bodily things are believed to enter the blessed life nevertheless, I answer briefly that this is a gift of grace, not of nature. It is out of place to talk of miracles here; I am speaking about nature.

I.2. There is a true and truly divine saying which will show you beyond doubt that the heavenly spirits need bodies. "Are they not all ministering spirits, sent to minister to those who are heirs to salvation" (Heb 1:14)? How are they to carry out their ministry without bodies, especially to those who live in the body? Only bodies can go from place to place as sure and well-known authority proves that angels do.[2] They were seen by the patriarchs, entered their dwellings, ate, had their feet washed. So both the lower and the higher spirits need bodies of their own, not for themselves, but so that they can give help to others.

I.3. Animals are created to serve man's bodily and temporal needs. In the course of time, the spirits of animals pass away; they die

---

1. The animal soul is not rational or immortal, but it shares with the human soul the property of giving life to the body. Bernard is drawing on Augustine here.
2. Cf. Gn 19:1, 32:1; Ex 14:19; Mt 4:11, 13:49. It was assumed that motion from place to place is impossible without a body.

with the body. A slave does not remain in the house forever. Those who use him well will find that their use of this temporal service will have its outcome in an eternal reward. The angel, in freedom of spirit, eagerly takes care over the duties of his office and shows himself a willing servant in helping mortals to future blessing, as fellow-citizens with him for eternity and co-heirs of the joy of heaven.

Therefore both animals and angels need bodies, one to serve us as it is its nature to do, the other to help us because he loves us. I do not see how their bodies can help them in eternity. For the irrational soul, even if it perceives bodily things through the body, is surely not able to make use of the body's help to progress from the bodily and material things of which his senses tell him to an understanding of spiritual truths? Yet by its bodily and temporal service the body is known to help those who turn all their use of temporal things to eternal ends, and who live in this world as though they had no dealings with it (1 Cor 7:31).

I.4. The heavenly spirit, without the help of a body or the perceptions of its senses, is able to understand the highest truths and to penetrate their depths by the kinship of its nature and its liveliness. The Apostle knew that. When he said, "The invisible things of God are understood through the things he has made," he added, "by the creature of the world" (Rom 1:20). For this is not true for the heavenly creature. The spirit which is wrapped in flesh and dwells on earth makes progress by thinking about the things the senses can perceive and gradually, little by little, it comes to know what the dweller in heaven grasps quickly and easily by his inborn subtlety and the sublimity of his being. It relies on no aid from the bodily senses or any part of the body, and its understanding owes nothing to any bodily thing. For why should he search the evidence of the senses for what he can read in the book of life (Phil 4:3), and without contradiction or difficulty? Why should he labor, covered in sweat, to separate the grain from the chaff, to squeeze wine from grapes and oil from olives, if he has all these things in plenty ready to hand? Who will beg his living among strangers when he has all the bread he needs at home (Lk 15:17)? Who will bother to dig a well and search with hard effort for springs of water in the depths of the earth when a bubbling fountain is pouring out clear water for him? Neither angelic spirits nor those of beasts can make any use of bodily help for their own benefit in attaining the knowledge which makes a creature spiritually blessed. The one is not capable of it because of his innate stupidity; the angel does not need it because he has the privilege of a more excellent glory.

I.5. The spirit of man, which has its place between the highest and the lowest, has an obvious need for a body, for two reasons. Without it the soul cannot act for its own benefit, or do good to others. For, not to mention the other members of the body or their duties, how are you to teach a listener except with your tongue or hear instruction without ears?

I.6. And so, because the brute spirit cannot give the service its nature owes without the help of the body, and the spiritual and heavenly creature cannot fulfil its ministry of love without a body, and the rational soul cannot act for its own and its neighbor's salvation without a body, it is clear that every created spirit needs a body, whether to help or both to help and be helped.

What about those living things which seem to be no use to themselves, or to man either? They are beautiful to look at, even if they are useless. Their usefulness lies rather in providing food for reflection than in anything they do. Even if they are found to be harmful and even damaging to the salvation of man in this world, there is some way in which their bodies can work together for good for those he has called to be holy according to his purpose (Rom 8:28). If they are no good for work or food they make man use his wits and learn from the things God has made, as all exercise of the reason does, about the mysteries of God (Rom 1:20). For both the devil and his company, whose intentions are always evil, are always trying to do harm to those who try to be good. To them it is said, "Who can hurt you if you strive to do good?" (1 Pt 3:13). God forbid that they should be able to harm you. The truth rather is that despite themselves they help you, and work together for good.

II.7. As for the rest, I do not want you to press me to tell you whether the bodies of angels are a part of their nature as men's bodies are to men; whether, even though they are immortal, they have an animal nature like that of man, which is not immortal in this life; or whether they change and alter these bodies into whatever form or appearance they wish, making them dense and solid when they want to be visible, while at the same time they are impalpable in reality because of the subtlety of their nature and substance, and wholly beyond our seeing; or whether they remain simple spiritual substances and assume bodies when they need them and put them off again to dissolve into the matter from which they were formed when the task is done. The Fathers seem to have held different opinions.[3] I myself do not see clearly what to say, and I confess that I am unsure. But I think that your spiritual progress would not be much helped by knowing.

II.8. But note that no created spirit can act upon our minds by itself, that is, without the intermediary of the instrument of the body. It cannot mingle with us or flood us, to give us knowledge or add to what we know, or to make us good or better. No angel and no beast can do that to me; I cannot do it myself. Even the angels cannot influence one another in that way.

III.8. That prerogative is unique to the Supreme and Boundless, who alone, when he teaches angels or men, does not need to speak with his mouth in their ears (Ps 93:10). He pours himself out directly and makes himself known. Himself pure, he is seen by the pure. Alone, he has no need of anyone. Alone he is sufficient unto himself and for all, by his own will alone.

III.9. Yet there are vast and countless effects which he has through his creatures, bodily or spiritual; but he uses them as one who gives them commands, not as one who begs them to act. For example, he uses my bodily tongue now to do his work of teaching you, when he could undoubtedly do so more easily and sweetly himself. He does it as a concession, not because he needs to do it. He acts in this way for your good, and to bestow merit on me, not because he needs to do so.

Every man must remember this when he does good, in case he is tempted to give the glory to himself and not to God (1 Cor 1:31).

There is the further case, of the person—evil angel or wicked man—who does good deeds despite himself; it is evident that any good he does, does not benefit himself, for no good can benefit anyone whose will is set against it. He is therefore to be credited only with "dispensing" good, but, I do not know why, we find the good which comes through a wicked man sweeter and more welcome. That is why God does good to the good through the wicked; it does not mean that he needs their help in doing good.

III.10. Who can doubt that God has even less need of creatures which have neither sense nor reason? But these have a share in doing good, and so it is clear that all things serve him (Ps 118:91) who can

---

3. On the sources of the views Bernard draws on here, see G. Bareille, *Dictionnaire de théologie catholique*, 1 (1903), cols. 1195–1200.

rightly say, "The world is mine" (Ps 49:12). Or certainly, because he knows what is the best means for his purpose he does not look to the capacities of the creature for service, but its suitability.

Agreed then that bodily instruments are often and appropriately used in God's works, as, for example, rain to make seeds sprout or cause crops to grow or fruit to ripen, what need has he, I ask, for a body of his own when at his bidding all bodies in heaven and on earth do his will? A body of his own would be superfluous to him when all bodies are his to use. Truly, if I were to include all that occurs to me in this connection this sermon would go on for too long and would outrun your patience. We will come to them on another occasion.

SERMON 7

I.1. I see that when I invited your questions I brought a good deal of work on myself! I tried to explain about the spiritual feet of God, with their descriptions and their names, under the heading of the first kiss. You are now asking about the hand to which the second kiss is given. I give in; I will do what you ask. I will also show you not the hand but both hands, and give them their names. One is called "generosity" because it gives freely. The other is called "strength" because it powerfully defends what it has given. He who is not ungrateful will kiss both, in gratitude to God who is the giver of all good things and recognizing and trusting him as protector.

I.2. I think enough has been said about the first two kisses. Let us examine the third. "Let him kiss me," she says, "with the kiss of his mouth" (Sg 1:1). Who is speaking? The Bride. But why "Bride"? She is the soul which thirsts for God. I set out the different affections so as to make it clearer which properly belongs to the Bride. If someone is a slave, he fears his master's face. If he is a hireling, he hopes for payment from his master's hand. If he is a pupil, he bends his ear to his master. If he is a son, he honors his father. But she who asks for a kiss feels love. This affection of love excels among the gifts of nature, especially when it returns to its source, which is God. For no names can be found as sweet as those in which the Word and the soul exchange affections, as Bridegroom and Bride, for to such everything is common, nothing is the property of one and not the other, nothing is held separately. They share one inheritance, one table, one house, one bed, one flesh. For this she leaves her father and her mother and clings to her husband and they two are one flesh (Gn 2:24). She is also commanded to forget her people and her father's house so that he may desire her beauty (Ps 44:1).

So then love especially and chiefly belongs to those who are married and it is not inappropriate to call the loving soul a Bride. For she who asks a kiss feels love. She does not ask for freedom or payment or an inheritance or learning, but for a kiss, in the manner of a most chaste bride, who sighs for holy love; and she cannot disguise the flame which is so evident.

It is a great thing which she will ask of the Great One, but she does not flirt with him as others do, and she does not beat about the bush. She tells him clearly what she desires. She uses no preliminaries. She does not try to win him round. But with an open face she bursts out suddenly from a full heart (Mt 12:34), "Let him kiss me," she says, "with the kiss of his mouth." Surely it seems to you as though she said, "Who have I in heaven but you and who but you do I want upon earth?" (Ps 72:25).

III.3. She loves most chastely who seeks him whom she loves and not some other thing which belongs to him. She loves in a holy way, because she does not love in fleshly desire but in purity of spirit. She loves ardently, because she is drunk with love so that she cannot see his majesty. What? He it is "who looks on the earth and causes it to tremble" (Ps 103:32). And she asks him for a kiss? Is she drunk? Indeed she is! And perhaps then when she burst forth thus she had come out of the wine-cellar (Sg 1:3, 2:4). She said afterward that she had been there, glorying in it. For David, too, said to God concerning such, "They shall be intoxicated with the plenty of your house, and you will give them the torrents of your pleasure to drink" (Ps 35:9). Oh, what force of love! What great confidence of spirit! What freedom! What is more evident than that perfect love casts out fear? (1 Jn 4:18).

III.4. But modestly she does not speak directly to the Bridegroom himself, but to others, as if he were not present. "Let him kiss me," she says, "with the kiss of his mouth." She asks a great thing, and it is necessary that such prayer should be accompanied by modesty, to commend the request. And so through servants and intimates one seeks to be allowed to enter a house and reach one's desire.

Who are these? We believe that the angels stand by in prayer, to offer God the prayers and vows of men, where they can see that the prayer is offered with clean hands upraised, without anger or deceit. This angel speaking to Tobias demonstrates it, "When you prayed with tears and buried your dead and left your table and hid the dead by day in your house for burial at night, I bore your prayer to the Lord" (Tb 12:12). I think you are sufficiently persuaded by this and other testimonies of Scripture. For the Psalmist shows clearly that the holy angels are accustomed to mingle their songs with ours. "The princes went before with the singers in the midst of young damsels playing the timbrels" (Ps 67:26). He also said, "I will sing praise to you in the sight of the angels" (Ps 137:1).

IV.4. I grieve to find some of you deep in sleep during the night office; showing no respect for the criticisms of heaven you appear before these princes like dead men; yet they are deeply moved when you show eagerness, and they delight to be present at your solemn services. I fear that sometimes they may be horrified by our casualness and go away indignantly, and then when it is too late each of us will begin to groan aloud and say to God, "You have put my friends far from me; they have found me an abomination" (Ps 87:9). Or, "You have turned my friend and my neighbor against me, those who know me will not share my misery" (Ps 87:19). Again, "Those who were close to me stand far off and those who sought my soul were violent" (Ps 37:12ff.).

If the good spirits stand far away from us, who will bear the attack of the wicked? I say then to those who behave in this way, "Cursed is he who does the work of God negligently" (Jer 48:10). He says, too, not I but the Lord, "Would that I found you hot or cold. But because I find you lukewarm, I spit you out of my mouth" (Rv 3:15–16ff.). For that reason, think of these princes when you stand up to pray or sing; stand with reverence and discipline, and glory that your angels daily see the Father's face (Mt 18:10). Sent to serve for our sake, who are heirs of salvation (Heb 1:14), they carry our devotion to the heights and bring us grace in return. Let us make use of their help, we who share their destiny, so that praise may be made perfect by the mouths of babes in arms (Ps 8:3). Let us say to them, "Sing praises to God, sing praises." And let us hear them responding in turn, "Sing praises to our King, sing praises" (Ps 46:7).

IV.5. Singing praises then with the heavenly singers, sing wisely (Ps 46:8), as fellow-citizens with the saints and members of God's household (Eph 2:19). Food tastes sweet in the mouth, a psalm in the heart. But the faithful and wise soul will not neglect to tear at the psalm with the teeth of its understanding. If you swallow it whole without chewing it the palate will miss the delicious flavor which is sweeter than honey from the honey-comb (Ps 18:11). Let us with the apostles offer the honey-comb in the heavenly banquet at the Lord's table (Lk 24:42). The honey in the wax is the devotion in the words. Otherwise, the letter kills (2 Cor 3:6), if you eat it without the condiment of the spiritual meaning. But if, with the Apostle, you sing with the spirit and with the mind, too (1 Cor 14:15), you will know as he did the truth of Jesus' saying, "The words I have spoken to you are spirit and life" (Jn 6:64) and also, "My spirit is sweeter than honey" (Sir 24:27).

IV.6. In this way your soul will be delighted in fatness (Is 55:2); in this way your sacrifice will be full of richness (Ps 19:4). In this way you will please the king, if you please the princes and make all his court well-disposed toward you. And when they smell this sweet scent in heaven they will say of you, too, "Who is this who comes up from the desert like a column of smoke, fragrant with myrrh and frankincense and with all the spices of the merchant?" (Sg 3:6).

V.6. "The princes of Judah," says the Psalmist, "are their leaders, the princes of Zebulun, the princes of Naphtali" (Ps 67:28), the angelic leaders of the faithful, the continent, those in contemplation. These princes know how acceptable to our king is the confession of those who sing psalms, the fortitude of the continent, the purity of those in contemplation. And they are anxious to make us show those firstfruits of the spirit which are nothing but the first and purest fruits of wisdom. For you know that in Hebrew Judah means someone who praises or makes acknowledgement, Zebulun a fortified dwelling, Naphtali a swift hind (Gn 49:21),[1] which by its agile leaps signifies the ecstasies of the soul in contemplation.

The hind also finds its way into the dark woods, as the contemplative soul sees into the hidden meanings of things. We know who said, "The sacrifice of praise honors me" (Ps 49:23).

V.7. If truly, "Praise is ugly in a sinner's mouth" (Sir 15:9), you will see how absolutely necessary is the virtue of continence, through which sin is prevented from ruling in your mortal body (Rom 6:12). But continence will gain you no merit before God if you practice it to win glory among men. And so the most important thing is purity of intention, by which your mind seeks to please only God, and is able to cling

---

1. See Jerome on the interpretation of Hebrew names, ed. P. de Lagarde (1827), pp. 94.27–28 and p. 39.26.

to him. For to "cling to" God is nothing but to see God, and that is given as a special happiness only to the pure in heart (Mt 5:8). David had a pure heart (Ps 50:12). He said to God, "My soul clings to you" (Ps 62:9), and again, "My joy lies in being near to God" (Ps 72:28). By his vision, he clung to him; by clinging he beheld him.

Souls exercised in these heavenly ways show themselves to be intimates of the angels and fellow-members of their family, especially if the angels often come upon him in prayer. Who will grant, O kind princes, that my petitions may be made known before God? It is not that they need to be made known to God (Phil 4:6), who knows all the thoughts of men (Ps 75:11), but before God, that is, to those who are with God, the blessed virtues and those souls which are separated from their bodies.

Who will raise me up in my poverty from the earth and lift this poor man from the dung-hill, that I may be seated with the princes (Ps 112:7) and be given a seat in glory (1 Sm 2:8)? I do not doubt that they will gladly welcome into their mansions him whom they did not disdain to visit on the dung-hill. And if our conversation pleased them will they not welcome us when we join them?

VI.8. And so I think that it was to these, her companions and members of her household, that the Bride spoke when she opened up her heart and said, "Let him kiss me with the kiss of his mouth." See the familiar and friendly conversation which the longing soul still in the body has with the heavenly powers. She desires to be kissed and she asks for what she desires. But she does not name him whom she loves, because she has so often spoken of him to them. Therefore she does not say, "Let him, or him, kiss me," but just, "Let him kiss me," just as Mary Magdalene did not say the name of him whom she sought, but she spoke to the man she thought was the gardener, "Lord, if you have taken him away . . . " (Jn 20:15). Who is "him"? She does not say. She takes it for granted that everyone knows who it is, who is never for a moment out of her thoughts. And so then she, speaking to the Bridegroom's companions, takes it that they know what she means, and she speaks no name when she bursts forth about her beloved. "Let him kiss me with the kiss of his mouth."

I do not want to keep you longer today to talk of the kiss, but in tomorrow's sermon you will hear from me whatever your prayers can draw from him whose teaching is the source of all we know (1 Jn 2:27). For flesh and blood do not reveal such a secret (Mt 16:17), but only he who sees into the depths of God (1 Cor 2:10), the Holy Spirit, who, proceeding from the Father and the Son (Jn 15:26),[2] lives and reigns equally with them forever.

I.1. You will remember that yesterday I promised that I would speak today about the supreme kiss, the kiss of the mouth. Listen the more carefully to that which tastes the sweeter, is enjoyed the more rarely, and is the more difficult to understand.

I think I should begin by speaking briefly about that highest kiss which is beyond description and which no creature has experienced, that kiss which was referred to in these words, "No one has known the Son except the Father and no one has known the Father except the Son, or him to whom the Son has chosen to reveal him" (Mt 11:27). For the Father loves the Son and embraces him with a special love. He who is supreme embraces his equal; he who is eternal embraces him who is eternal; the One embraces his only Son. But the Son is bound to him by no less a bond. For his love he even dies, as he himself bears witness when he says, "So that all may know that I love the Father, rise, let us go" (Jn 14:31). He went, as we know, to his Passion. And so that mutual love and knowledge between him who begets and him who is begotten, what is it but that sweetest and most mysterious kiss?

I.2. I myself am sure that no creature, not even an angel, is admitted to such and so holy a secret of divine love. Does not Paul say from his own knowledge that that peace surpasses all understanding, even that of the angels (Phil 4:7)? That is why the Bride, although she is bold in many things, does not dare to say, "Let him kiss me with his mouth," for that is reserved for the Father alone. But she asks something less. "Let him kiss me," she says, "with the kiss of his mouth." See the new Bride receiving the new kiss, not from the Bridegroom's mouth but from the kiss of his mouth.

"He breathed on them," it says, and that certainly means that Jesus breathed on the apostles, that is, the primitive Church, and said, "Receive the Holy Spirit" (Jn 20:22). That was the kiss. What was it? A

---

2. Bernard adds "and the Son" as in the creed of Western Christendom. The schism of 1054, which had divided Greek and Latin Christians over the *filioque* clause, was the subject of heated debate in Bernard's day. Anselm of Canterbury's *De Processione Spiritus Sancti* (*Opera Omnia*, II) was published at the beginning of the twelfth century.

breath? No, but the invisible Spirit, who is so bestowed in the breath of the Lord that he is understood to have proceeded from the Son as well as from the Father (Jn 15:26).

The kiss is truly common to him who kisses and to him who is kissed. And so it satisfies the Bride to receive the Bridegroom's kiss, although it is not a kiss from his mouth. For she thinks it not a small or light thing to be kissed by the kiss, for that is nothing but to be given the Holy Spirit. Surely if the Father kisses and the Son receives the kiss, it is appropriate to think of the Holy Spirit as the kiss, for he is the imperturbable peace of the Father and the Son, their secure bond, their undivided love, their indivisible unity.

II.3. It is he who prompts the Bride's boldness, and it is he whom she trustingly asks to come to her when she asks for a kiss. She has a reason to be bold which never fails. For the Son, when he said, "No one has known the Son except the Father and no one has known the Father except the Son," added, "or him to whom the Son has chosen to reveal him" (Mt 11:27). The Bride has no doubt that if he is willing to reveal him to anyone, it is to her. Therefore she asks boldly to be given the kiss, that is, the Spirit in whom the Father and the Son will reveal themselves to her. For one of them cannot be known without the other. That is why Christ said, "He who has seen me has also seen the Father" (Jn 14:9). And John, "He who denies the Son does not have the Father. He who believes in the Son has the Father, too" (1 Jn 2:23).

From this it is clear that the Father is not known without the Son and the Son is not known without the Father. The supreme happiness consists in the knowledge not of one but of both, as, "This is everlasting life, to know that you are the true God and to know Jesus Christ whom you have sent" (Jn 17:3). So those who follow the Lamb are said to have his name and that of the Father written on their foreheads (Rv 14:1–4), and that is to be glorified by the knowledge of both.

II.4. But someone is saying, "Therefore it is not necessary to know the Holy Spirit, for when he said that eternal life is to have known the Father and the Son, he made no mention of the Holy Spirit. That is so, but where Father and Son are known fully, how can their goodness, which is the Holy Spirit, not be known? For no man really knows another, as long as he does not know whether he is a man of goodwill or not. So although it has been said, "This is everlasting life, to know that you are the true God and to know Jesus Christ, whom you have sent" (Jn 17:3), that sending shows the good pleasure both of the Father who kindly sends and of the Son who willingly obeys; there is an implied reference to the Holy Spirit where mention is made of such grace on the part of both. For the Holy Spirit is the love and goodness of both.

II.5. So when the Bride asks for a kiss she begs to be flooded with the grace of this threefold knowledge as much as mortal flesh can bear. She asks it of the Son, for he is to reveal it to whom he wills (Mt 11:27). Therefore the Son reveals himself to whom he wills and he reveals the Father when he does so. It is undoubtedly through the kiss that he makes this revelation, that is, through the Holy Spirit. The Apostle bears witness to this when he says, "But God revealed himself to us through his Spirit" (1 Cor 2:10). But in giving the Spirit through whom he reveals, he reveals him as well. In giving he reveals him; in revealing he gives him. The revelation he makes through the Holy Spirit does not only illuminate the understanding; it also fires with love, as the Apostle says, "The love of God is diffused in our hearts through the Holy Spirit which has been given us" (Rom 5:5).

III.5. That is perhaps why we do not read that those who know God but do not give him glory (Rom 1:21) do not know him through the revelation of the Holy Spirit, for although they know him they do not love him. Thus you have, "God has revealed himself to them" (Rom 1:19), but Paul does not add, "through the Holy Spirit," lest those wicked minds should think themselves to have received the kiss of the Bride. They were content with a knowledge which puffed them up, but they did not know about that which builds up (1 Cor 8:1). The Apostle tells us how they knew. "They perceived him in the things he had made" (Rom 1:20).

It is clear from this that they did not fully know him, for they did not love him. For if they had fully known him they could not have been ignorant of the goodness which made him willing to be born and to die for their redemption. Hear what was revealed to them about God, "his everlasting power and divinity" (Rom 1:20). You see that in their presumption of spirit (their own spirit, not the Spirit of God) they considered his sublimity and majesty, but they did not understand that he was meek and lowly of heart (Mt 11:29). That is not surprising, for their leader Behemoth sees everything that is high (Jb 41:25), nothing that is humble. But David did not walk in great things, nor in wonders above himself (Ps 130:1). He was not a peerer into majesty, in case he should be dazzled by glory (Prv 25:27).

IV.6. You, too, always remember the words of the wise, so that you may be cautious in stepping into mysteries. "Do not try to understand things that are too difficult for you, or try to discover what is beyond your powers" (Sir 3:22). Walk in such things in the Spirit (Gal 5:16) and not by your own senses. The teaching of the Spirit does not sharpen curiosity; it inspires love. The Bride rightly, when she seeks him whom her heart loves (Sg 3:1), does not trust her senses or rely on the vain speculations of human curiosity; she asks for a kiss. That is, she calls on the Holy Spirit, through whom she will receive at the same time both the taste of knowledge and the savor of grace. And that knowledge which is given in a kiss is received with love, for a kiss is the sign of love. The knowledge which puffs up (1 Cor 8:1) does not come from a kiss, for it is loveless. But they who have a zeal for God but not by knowing him (Rom 10:2) cannot in any way lay claim to it. For the grace of the kiss brings with it a double gift, both the light of knowledge and the wealth of devotion. He is the Spirit of wisdom and understanding (Is 11:2). Like a bee carrying both wax and honey he has the power to kindle the light of knowledge and to pour out the savor of grace. Neither he who understands the truth without love, nor he who loves without understanding, then, can think himself to have received this kiss. This kiss leaves no room for error or apathy.

V.6. Therefore let the Bride who is about to receive the twofold grace of this holy kiss prepare her two lips, her reason for the gift of understanding, her will for the gift of wisdom, so that rejoicing in the fullness of the kiss she may deserve to hear, "Your lips are moist with grace, for God has blessed you forever" (Ps 44:3).

VI.6. And so the Father, kissing the Son, pours into him in full the mysteries of his divinity, and breathes the sweetness of love. Scripture says so when it remarks that "day to day pours forth speech" (Ps 18:3). As we have said, no creature has been given the privilege of witnessing this eternal unique and blessed embrace. Only the Holy Spirit is witness, and able to share their mutual knowledge and love. "For who has known the mind of the Lord, or who has been his counsellor" (Rm 11:34)?

VI.6. But perhaps someone will say to me, "What thunderous voice, then, told you what you say no creature knows?" I reply, "It is the only-begotten Son, who is in the bosom of the Father. He has made him known" (Jn 1:18). He has made him known, I say, not to me, unworthy wretch that I am, but to John, the Bridegroom's friend (Jn 3:29), for these are his words; and he made him known to John the Evangelist, too, the disciple Jesus loved (Jn 13:23). For his soul was pleasing to the Lord (Wis 4:14), and worthy both of the dowry and the name of a Bride; deserving the Bridegroom's embraces and worthy to recline on the

Bridegroom's breast (Jn 13:25). John learned from the heart of the only-begotten what he had learned from his Father. Not he alone, but all those to whom the Angel of Great Counsel (Is 9:6) said, "I call you friends, for all that I have heard from my Father I have told you" (Jn 15:15). Paul imbibed it, for the Gospel he preached is not of men, not did he receive it through men, but by the revelation of Jesus Christ (Gal 1:11).

VII.7. All these could say happily and with truth, "The only-begotten who was in the bosom of the Father, he has told" us (Jn 1:18). And what is that telling but a kiss? But it is the kiss of a kiss, not of the mouth. Hear about the kiss of the mouth, "I and the Father are one" (Jn 10:30), and again, "I am in the Father and the Father in me" (Jn 14:10). This is a kiss from mouth to mouth which no creature can receive. It is a kiss of peace and love. But that love surpasses all knowledge (Eph 3:19) and that peace passes all understanding (Phil 4:7). Truly what eye has not seen nor ear heard, and what has not entered the mind of man (1 Cor 2:9), God revealed to Paul through his Spirit, that is, by the kiss of his mouth. Therefore, the kiss of the mouth is the Son in the Father and the Father in the Son (Jn 14:10). As we read, "Instead of the spirit of the world we have received the Spirit that comes from God, to teach us to understand the gifts he has given us" (1 Cor 2:12).

VII.8. But let us distinguish more clearly between the two. He who receives of the fullness receives the kiss of the mouth. He who receives of the fullness (Jn 1:16) receives the kiss of the kiss.

Paul was great. But however high he lifted up his mouth, even to the third heaven (2 Cor 12:2), he could only remain at a distance from the mouth of the Most High. He must be content to stay within the limits of his nature, and since he could not reach the face of glory, he humbly asked for the kiss to be given him from above.

He who did not think it robbery to be equal with God (Phil 2:6) dared to speak thus, "I and the Father are one" (Jn 10:30), because he was united to him as an equal and embraced him as an equal. He does not beg a kiss from below, but his mouth meets the Father's mouth directly and by a unique privilege he kisses him on the mouth. Therefore the kiss Christ receives is fullness, that of Paul a participation. Christ gloried in the kiss of the mouth, and Paul only in the kiss of the kiss.

VII.9. This kiss is a joy, however, through which not only is God known but the Father loved, who is never fully known unless he is loved. Is there not a soul among you who sometimes hears the Spirit of the Son crying in his inmost heart, "Abba, Father" (Gal 4:6)? Let him who feels himself loved by the Father realize that he is moved by the same Spirit as the Son. Trust without reserve. Be of good courage (Jas 1:6). Know yourself to be the Father's daughter in the Spirit of the Son. Know yourself to be the Bride, or sister of the Son, for you will find both these names given to her who loves the Son. Here is a text to prove it—I need not labor the point. The Bridegroom says to her, "Come into my garden, my sister, my Bride" (Sg 5:1). She is a sister because she is of the one Father, a Bride because she is in one spirit with him. For if carnal marriage makes two one flesh (Gn 2:24), why should not spiritual union make two one spirit (1 Cor 6:17)? But hear, too, of the Father, how lovingly he calls her "daughter" to honor her, and nevertheless invites her as his own daughter-in-law to the sweet caresses of his Son, "Hear, daughter, and see, and listen; forget your people and your father's house and the King will desire your beauty" (Ps 44:11ff.). See from whom this bride demands a kiss. O holy soul, be reverent, for he is the Lord your God (Ps 94:6ff.), who perhaps ought not to be kissed, but adored with the Father and the Holy Spirit, world without end, Amen.

Sermon 50

I.1. Perhaps you are waiting for me to go on and finish talking about the verse we have been considering. I have a better idea; for I have still some crumbs of yesterday's feast to set before you, which I have gathered up so that they may not be lost (Jn 6:12). They will perish if I do not offer them to anyone. If I want to keep them to enjoy for myself, I myself shall perish! I am unwilling to cheat your throat, which I know well, especially as they come from the dish of love, the sweeter because they are delicate, the more full of flavor because they are tiny. It is quite contrary to love to cheat in love. So here I am; "He has ordained love in me" (Sg 2:4).

I.2. Love is expressed in action and in feeling. As to love in action, I believe men have been given a law, a settled commandment (Dt 5:6). But what need has love of commandment? You are commanded to show love in action so that you may have merit; the sensation of love is its own reward. We do not deny that this present life can, by divine grace, give experience of its beginning, and of its progress, but we stoutly maintain that it is fully known only in the happiness of the life to come. How then were things which could not in any way be fulfilled made commandments? Or, if you would rather say that it is the sensation of love which is commanded, I do not disagree, so long as you agree with me that it can never and never will be possible for any man to fulfill it. For who dares to claim for himself what even Paul owned he did not understand (Phil 3:13)? The Lawgiver knew that the burden of law was greater than men could bear, but he judged it to be useful for this very reason to advise men that they were not able to fulfill it, so that they might know clearly to what end of righteousness they ought to strive as far as their powers permit. So by commanding what was impossible he made men, not prevaricators, but humble, so that every mouth may be silent and all the world made subject to God, for no one will be justified in his sight by keeping the law (Rom 3:19–20). So accepting that command and aware of our insufficiency, we shall cry to heaven and God will have mercy on us (1 Mc 4:10). And we shall know on that day that God has saved us not by the just works we have done, but because he is merciful (Ti 3:5).

I.3. This is what I should say if we were agreed that the sensation of love is commanded by law. But it seems to fit love in action much better, for when the Lord said, "Love your enemies" he spoke immediately afterward of actions, "Do good to those who hate you" (Lk 6:27). Scripture also says, "If your enemy is hungry feed him; if he is thirsty give him drink" (Rom 12:20). Here you have a reference to actions, not to feeling. But hear also what the Lord commands concerning love of himself. "If you love me," he says, "keep my commandments" (Jn 14:15). And here, too, by telling us to keep the commandments, he presses us to action. There would have been no point in his saying that we were to be active if love were nothing but feeling. That is why it is necessary for you also to accept the commandment to love your neighbor as yourself, even if it is not put as clearly as this (Mt 22:39). Do you think, then, that you do enough to fulfill the command to love your neighbor if you observe perfectly what natural law tells every man to do: "Do not do unto others what you would not wish done to yourself" (Tb 4:16; RB 61), and "Do to others as you would wish others to do to you" (Mt 7:12).

4. I do not say that we should be without feeling, acting with our hands only and with cold hearts. I read among other things that the Apostle, describing the many great and heavy troubles of mankind, numbers among them being without feeling (Rom 1:31; 2 Tm 3:3).

II.4. But there is an affection born of the flesh and another ruled by reason; and one seasoned by wisdom. The first is that which the apostle describes as not subject to the law of God—as it cannot be (Rom 8:7). The second, by contrast, he shows to be in accord with the law of God because it is good (Rom 7:16). There can be no doubt that the contentious and the harmonious differ. The third is very different from both, because it tastes and experiences the sweetness of the Lord (Ps 33:9); it dispatches the first and rewards the second. The first is certainly pleasing, but it is vile; the second dry but strong; the last is rich and sweet. Through the second, therefore, works are done and love is there, not the love of feeling, which, growing richer with the condiment of wisdom's salt (Col 4:6), fills the mind with the manifold sweetness of the Lord (Ps 30:20), but rather that which is practical. It does not yet refresh sweetly with the sweetness of that love, but it kindles a fierce desire for it. "Do not love," he says, "in word or speech, but in deed and in truth" (1 Jn 3:18).

II.5. Do you see how cautiously he makes his way between flawed and feeling love, while distinguishing both from the love which is active and saving? He does not find room in this love for the pretending of a lying tongue, nor does he demand as yet the taste of loving wisdom. "Let us love in deed and in truth," he says, because we are moved to good works more by the lively impulse of truth than by feeling the enjoyment of love. "He ordained love in me" (Sg 2:4). Which of these do you think he meant? Both, but in the opposite order. For love in action prefers what is humble; feeling, what is lofty. For instance, there is no doubt that the mind which feels rightly loves God more than men, and among men the more perfect is preferred to the weaker, heaven to earth, eternity to time, soul to body. In well-ordered action, on the other hand, often, or even always, the reverse is the case. For we are more often and more urgently moved to help our neighbor, and we do so with the more care, in the case of our weaker brothers. By human right and very necessity, we think more of peace on earth than peace in heaven (Lk 2:14). While we worry about temporal things we can scarcely attend to things eternal. In attending perpetually to the weaknesses of our bodies, we forget to take care of our souls. Lastly, as the Apostle says, we give greater honor to our weaker members (1 Cor 12:23), and thus fulfill in a way the Lord's words, "The last shall be first and the first last" (Mt 20:16). Who will doubt that a man speaks to God when he is praying? But how often are we drawn, even snatched away for love's sake, to help those who need our actions or words? How often does holy peace give way to the hurly-burly of business? How often is a book set aside with a good conscience, so that we may sweat at manual labor?

How often do we quite rightly omit even the solemn celebration of Mass for the sake of the duties of this world? A preposterous order, but necessity is subject to no law. Love in action imposes its own order, according to the command of the Head of the family, putting the last first (Mt 20:8). That is certainly holy and right, which is not a respecter of rank, and does not consider price but human need (Acts 10:34; Jb 32:21).

II.6. But not so the sensation of love, which takes its order from the first. It is the wisdom by which everything is experienced as it is. So, for example, the more deserving the nature, the greater the love it evokes; the less, the less; the least, very little. The order which the truth of love imposes, the love of truth makes its own. Now true love is found in this, that those who are in greatest need receive first (1 Jn 4:10), and once more loving truth is apparent, if we keep the same order in feeling as in reason.

III. But if you love the Lord your God with all your heart, with all your mind, and with all your strength (Mk 12:30), and, leaping in desire beyond that love of love with which love in action is satisfied to the divine love to which it is a stepping stone, you will be wholly on fire with the fullness of what you have received by the Spirit and you will taste God, not as he really is, for that is impossible for any creatures, but certainly to the limit of which you are capable. Then you will love yourself as you are, since you will know that there is nothing to love in you except insofar as you are his. He is all your reason for loving, and you pour all your love out upon him. You will know yourself as you are, I say, when you discover by experience of your love of yourself that there is nothing in you worthy of love except for his sake, you who without him are nothing.

III.7. As for your neighbor, whom you ought to love as yourself (Mt 19:19): To experience him as he is, is the same as to experience yourself, for he is as you are. You do not love yourself except as you love God, so love as you do yourself all those who love him likewise. But you who love God cannot love an enemy as you love yourself, for he is nothing, because he does not love God (1 Jn 4:20). Nevertheless, you will love him, so that he may love. For to love someone so that he may love and to love him who loves are not the same. In order to experience him as he is, then, you must experience him not for what he is, for that is nothing, but for what he may become, itself almost nothing, for it is not certain. Him who will obviously not return to the love of God you must regard not as almost nothing, but as absolutely nothing, for he will be nothing forever. There is only this exception: not only is he not to be loved; he is even to be regarded with hatred, according to these words, "Lord, do I not hate those who hate you, and loathe those who are your enemies?" (Ps 138:21). Open-hearted love does not, however, allow us to refuse to feel anything at all to any man, even the greatest enemy. Who has wisdom to understand this (Ps 106:43)?

III.8. Give me a man who above all loves God with all his heart, himself and his neighbor in that they love God; but his enemy as one who will one day love perhaps; his parents who begot him with a warm natural love, but his spiritual teachers the more because of grace. Let him deal similarly with the other things of God in an orderly, loving way, despising the earth, looking up to heaven, using this world as if not using it (1 Cor 7:31), and discriminating between what is used and what enjoyed, by the experience of his mind. Let him treat transitory things as passing, as necessary for the moment; let him cling to eternal things with an enduring desire. Give me such a man, I say, and I will boldly call him wise, because he recognizes things for what they really are, because he can truly and confidently claim, "He has ordained love in me" (Sg 2:4). But where is he, and where will he be found? I ask in tears (Phil 3:18), how long shall we scent and not taste, seeing our homeland far off, not possessing it but sighing for it. O Truth, fatherland of exiles, end of their exile! I see you, but imprisoned in flesh, I may not enter. Muddy with sins, I cannot be admitted. O Wisdom, stretching from end to end, establishing and ordering everything (Wis 8:1), and arranging all things sweetly by enhancing feeling and making it orderly, guide what we do as your everlasting truth requires, so that each of us may securely glory in you and say, "He ordained love in me" (Sg 2:4). For you are the strength of God and the Wisdom of God (1 Cor 1:24), Christ, the Bridegroom of the Church and our Lord, God blessed forever. Amen (Rom 1:25).

SERMON 62

"My dove, in the clefts of the rock, in the crannies of the wall" (Sg 2:14). The dove finds safe refuge not only in the clefts of the rock, but also in the crannies of the wall. If we take the "wall" to be not an assembly of stones but the communion of saints, perhaps the crannies of the wall can be seen as the gaps left empty by the angels when they fell, and which are to be filled by men, like ruins to be mended by living stones. That is why the Apostle Peter says, "Come to him, to that living stone, and like living stones be yourselves built into spiritual houses" (1 Pt 2:4–5).

I do not think it is inappropriate to understand the guardianship of angels as being like a wall in the Lord's vineyard (which is the Church of those who are predestined), for Paul says, "Are they not all ministering spirits sent forth to serve, for the sake of those who receive the inheritance of salvation?" (Heb 1:14). And the prophet says, "The angel of the Lord hovers round those who fear him" (Ps 33:8).

And so if we take it in that sense, it will mean that two things console the Church in her exile: the memory of the Passion of Christ in the past and in the future the contemplation of what she both thinks and believes will be her welcome among the saints (Col. 1:12).

In these glimpses of the past and the future she is filled with deep longing. Each is wholly pleasing to her. Each is a refuge from the evils which trouble her and from her sorrow (Ps 31:7, 106:39). Her consolation is complete, for she knows not only what she is to expect, but the source from which it is to come. It is a joyous expectation with no hesitation in it, because it rests on the death of Christ.

Why should she be awestruck at the greatness of the reward when she weighs the price that was paid for it? How joyously she thinks of the clefts in the wall through which the ransom of his most precious blood flowed upon her. How joyously she explores the crannies, the many and varied resting-places and mansions which are in her Father's house (Jn 14:2), in which he lodges his children according to the deserts of each! And indeed she does the only thing she can for now, and rests there in memory, entering in imagination into the heavenly home which is above.

In time, she will mend the ruins (Ps 109:6) and dwell in both body and mind in those crannies, when she will light up with the presence of all her members the empty habitations deserted by those who once dwelt there. Then no cranny will be seen in the wall of heaven. It will be happily restored again to perfection and wholeness.

II.2. But if you prefer, let us say that those crannies are not found but rather made, by studious and pious minds. How is that, you ask? By thought and desire. The wall crumbles like soft stone before the holy desire of the soul (Is 26:8). It falls to pure contemplation and yields to frequent prayer. For "the just man's prayer pierces the skies" (Sir 35:21).

It does not enter the spacious heights of this bodily air, in the way that a bird in flight does when it beats its wings, or pierce the dome of high heaven like a sharp sword. But there are holy heavens, living, rational, which tell of the glory of God (Ps 18:1), and they will look on us lovingly and gladly hear our prayers; and when they recognize our devotion, take us to their hearts whenever we come to them with good intentions. For "to him who knocks, it will be opened" (Mt 7:8).

So each of us is able, even while we live this mortal life, to hollow out a place for himself in this heavenly wall, wherever he likes. We can go and see the patriarchs now, greet the prophets now, now mingle even with the assembly of the apostles, now join the chorus of martyrs. Now we can even, with the quickness devotion gives us, run up and down the dwelling-places and ranks of the blessed orders of the angels up to the cherubim and seraphim. And if we stand and knock wherever we are drawn, moved inwardly by the Spirit's will (1 Cor 12:11), the door will be opened to us at once (Lk 12:36). It will be as though a cranny has been made in the holy mountains, or rather, in the minds of the holy ones, and they take us to themselves so that we may share their rest for a time.

God is pleased by the face and voice of every soul which does this: the face because of its candor; the voice because it is lifted in praise. "For praise and beauty are in his sight" (Ps 95:6). It is to the man who is like this that he says, "Show me your face. Let your voice sound in my ears" (Sg 2:14). This is the voice of wonder in the mind of the contemplative, the voice which gives thanks. God takes delight in crannies like this, from which rings out the sound of thanksgiving, the sound of wonder and praise.

II.3. Happy is the mind which is often at work making a hollow for itself in this wall. But how much happier is he who makes it in the rock! For it is good to make hollows in the rock, too, but to do that the mind must have a very keen edge of purity, and a wholehearted purpose, and it must have greater merits. "Who is equal to such a calling" (2 Cor 2:16)? Surely he was who said, "In the beginning was the Word, and the Word was with God and the Word was God" (Jn 1:1–2). Does it not seem to you that he had penetrated to the very depths of the Word, and drawn forth from his innermost breast the holiest essence of divine wisdom? What of he who spoke wisdom among the perfect, wisdom veiled in mystery, which none of the princes of this world knew (1 Cor 2:6–8)?

Surely this holy gazer, who passed through the first and second heavens by his keen but devout curiosity, gained this wisdom at last from the third? He tells us himself, as faithfully as he can, in the most exact words he can find. But he also heard words which cannot be spoken, which he is not allowed to speak to men, for he spoke them to himself and to God (2 Cor 12:4). Perhaps God says to him, as if to console his anxious love, "Why are you troubled because human hearing cannot capture your thought? Let your voice sound in my ears" (Sg 2:14). If what you feel cannot be revealed to mortals, be comforted nevertheless, for your voice can seek to delight the ears of God. Do you see the holy soul of Paul, now solemn for love of us, transported in the purity of its love for God (2 Cor 5:13)? See Holy David, too, whether he himself is not the man of whom he says to God as though he were speaking of someone else, "For the thought of a man will offer you praise, and the rest of his thoughts will be a feast-day for you" (Ps 75:11). So as much as could come through the medium of the prophet's thought, word, and example, he spoke aloud at once in praising the Lord before the people; and the rest he kept between himself and God. They hold festival together "in joy and exultation" (Ps 44:16). This, then, is what he wanted to tell us in this verse. He passed on whatever he could of all he saw and understood of the mystery of wisdom, by preaching it fully to the people. The remainder, which the people could not understand, he expressed in praise to God in a festivity of joy. See, there is nothing lost in holy contemplation, when what cannot be shared with the people for their edification becomes a sweet and lovely praise of God (Ps 146:1).

III.3. It is clear, then, that there are two sorts of contemplation. One is concerned with the life and happiness and glory of the heavenly city, where a great multitude of heavenly citizens is busy with activity, or at rest. The other is directed toward the majesty, eternity, and divinity of the King himself. The first is of the wall, the other of the rock.

The more difficult the hollowing out, the sweeter the taste of the reward. Do not be afraid of Scripture's warning about gazing upon majesty (Prv 25:27). Just bring a pure and single eye (Lk 11:34). You will not be dazzled by the glory, but allowed to look into it (Prv 25:27)— unless it is not God's glory but your own that you are seeking. Otherwise, each is overwhelmed not by God's glory but his own. When you bend down toward your own glory, you cannot lift up your head to look at his, because you are weighed down by greed.

With that out of the way, let us tunnel confidently in the rock, in which the treasures of wisdom and knowledge are hidden (Col 2:3). If you are still not convinced, hear what the Rock himself says. "Those who do things in me shall not sin" (Sir 24:30). Who will give me wings like a dove so that I may fly away and be at rest (Ps 54:7)? The meek and simple find rest (Mt 11:29) where the deceitful man is oppressed, and the man who is puffed up and desirous of vainglory (Gal 5:26). The Church is a dove, and so she rests. She is a dove because she meekly receives the Word which enters her (Jas 1:21). And she rests in the Word, that is, in the Rock, for the Rock is the Word.

And so the Church is in the clefts of the Rock, and she gazes through them and sees the glory of her Bridegroom. But she is not overwhelmed by glory because she does not claim it for herself. She is not overwhelmed because she is not peering into the majesty of God but seeking to know his will. She does sometimes dare to contemplate what belongs to his majesty, yet in wonder, not curiosity. But if ever she is carried away in rapture, it is because the finger of God deigns so to raise man up (Ex 8; Lk 11:20), not the rashness of man insolently pushing its way into the depths of God. For when the Apostle recalls that rapture, he makes excuse for his daring (2 Cor 12:2). What other mortal man would be so presumptuous as to attempt by himself to make a fearful scrutiny of the divine majesty? What insolent contemplative would try to burst into those awesome mysteries? I think that although those who scrutinize majesty are called "invaders," that applies not to those who are carried away but to those who push their way in. And so it is they who are overwhelmed by glory.

III.5. Scrutinizing God's majesty, then, is something to regard with awe. But it is safe and devout to seek to know his will. Why should I not devote myself wholeheartedly to studying the mystery of his holy will when I know that I must obey it in all things? Sweet is the glory whose only source is the contemplation of his sweetness, the riches of his goodness, the multitude of his mercies (Ex 34:6; Rom 2:4). "We have seen his glory, the glory as of the only-begotten of the Father" (Jn 1:14). Whatever glory is seen in this way is kindly and fatherly. That glory will not overwhelm me (Prv 25:27), even if I bend all my energies upon it; rather, it will impress itself on me. And "with faces unveiled, beholding the glory of the Lord, we are being transformed into his likeness from one degree of glory to another; for this comes from the Lord, who is the Spirit (2 Cor 3:18).

We are transformed when we become like him. God forbid that a man should presume to be conformed to the glory of his majesty rather than the modesty of his will. This is my glory (2 Cor 1:12), to hear it said of me one day, "I have found a man after my own heart" (Acts 13:22). The heart of the Bridegroom is the Father's heart. What is it like? Be merciful, even as your Father is merciful (Lk 6:36). This is what he wants to see when he says to the Church, "Show me your face" (Sg 2:14), a look of love and gentleness. Let her raise such a face in perfect faith to the Rock she resembles. "Come to him and be enlightened," says the Psalmist, "and your faces shall never be ashamed" (Ps 33:6). How can the humble be put to shame by the humble, the devout by the holy, the modest by the meek? The Bride's pure face will no more shrink back from the purity of the Rock than virtue from virtue or light from light.

IV.6. But because up to now the whole Church has not been able to make a cleft in the Rock—for it is not possible for everyone in the Church to search out the mysteries of the divine will (Eph 1:9) or penetrate the depths of God for himself (1 Cor 2:10)—the Church is shown to dwell not only in the clefts of the rock but also in the crannies of the wall. Therefore she dwells in the clefts of the rock through those who are perfect, who dare to explore and penetrate into the secrets of wisdom in purity of conscience, and who are able to do so because of the keenness of their understanding.

As for others, those who either cannot hollow out the rock for themselves or do not have the courage to do so, let them be content to dig in the wall and see the glory of the saints in their minds. If anyone cannot do even this, let him set before him Jesus and him crucified (1 Cor 2:2), so that without any labor of his own he may dwell in the clefts of the rock he has not made for himself (Jn 4:38). The Jews labored at them, and such a man will take advantage of the labors of unbelievers in order to be a believer himself. Let him not fear that he will suffer a rebuff. "Enter into the rock," says Isaiah, "and hide in the hollowed ground from the face of the fear of the Lord, and from the glory of his majesty" (Is 2:10). To the soul which is still weak and sluggish, who confesses in the words of the Gospel that he is unable to dig and ashamed to beg (Lk 16:3), is shown here a hollow in the ground where he may gather strength until he grows strong and vigorous enough to make a cleft in the rock for himself to enter the inwardness of the Word.

IV.7. And if we understand a reference to this hollow in the ground in the words "they have dug my hands and my feet" (Ps 21:17), we can be in no doubt that the wounded soul which lies there will rapidly be restored to health. For what can be so effective a cure for the wound of conscience and so purifying to keenness of mind as steady meditation on the wounds of Christ? Indeed I do not see how anyone can apply the words "Let me see your face; let me hear your voice" (Sg 2:14) until he is wholly purified and healed. How can anyone dare to show his face or raise his voice if he is told to hide? He was told to "hide in the hollowed ground" (Is 2:10). Why? Because he was so ugly he was not fit to be seen.

He was not fit to be seen as long as he was not fit to see. But when he has made such progress in the healing of his inner eye by hiding in the hole in the ground that he can look on the glory of God with his face uncovered (2 Cor 3:18), then, pleasing in voice and face alike, he will confidently say what he will see. The face must be pleasing which can look on the brightness of God. Nor could it do this if it was not itself clear and pure, and wholly transformed into the likeness of the brightness it gazes on. Otherwise it would fall back through sheer unlikeness, recoil at the splendor it is not accustomed to. When a pure soul can gaze on the pure truth, then, the Bridegroom himself will want to look at his face and then to hear his voice.

IV.8. He shows how much he is pleased by the pure mind's preaching of the truth when he says at once, "For your voice is sweet" (Sg 2:14). He shows that an ugly face makes the voice displeasing to him when he says next, "And your face is lovely." What is the inner loveliness of the face but purity? A lovely face is pleasing in many who do not preach. But without it, preaching pleases no one. Truth does not reveal itself to the impure; wisdom does not entrust itself to such. How can they speak of that which they have not seen? We speak of what we know and we bear witness to what we have seen (Jn 3:11).

Go, then, and be bold to bear witness to what you have not seen, to preach what you do not know.

Do you ask whom I call impure? Anyone who seeks for human praise, who preaches for money (1 Cor 9:18), for a living, who sees godliness as a means of gain (1 Tm 6:5), who works not for the fruit of the Spirit but for financial reward—these are the impure; and although because they are impure they are not able to perceive the truth, they presume to preach it.

Why do you act so hastily? Why do you not wait for light? Why dare to do the work of light before the light comes? "It is vain for you to get up before it is light" (Ps 126:2). The light is purity, a love which does not want its own way (1 Cor 13:15). If that takes the lead, the tongue will not go astray.

The proud eye does not see the truth. To the sincere the truth is obvious (Ps 100:5). Truth does not withhold itself from the pure in heart and thus fail to be told. "God says to the sinner: what right have you to recite my statutes and speak of my covenant?" (Ps 49:16). Many, having nothing of this purity, try to speak before they see. They have gone badly wrong; knowing nothing of what they are saying or of what they claim, they deserve to be mocked when they teach others what they themselves have not learned (Rom 2:21).

Pray that we may always be preserved from these two evils by the Bridegroom of the Church, our Lord Jesus Christ, who is God over all, blessed forever. Amen.

Sermon 74

I.1. "Return," she says (Sg 2:17). It is clear that he whom she calls to come back is not present. But he was there, and not long before. Indeed, she seems to be calling him back as he is leaving. She calls him back urgently, and that is a sign of the great love she bears him and of his great loveliness. Who are these who are so wrapped up in love, these unwearying lovers who are driven on by a love which will not let them rest?

It is my task to carry out my promise and to show how these words apply to the Word and the soul (Sc 73:10). But to do so worthily—or indeed at all—I tell you that I need the help of the Word himself.

That Word ought to be expounded by someone far, far more experienced, who knows more about that holy and mysterious love than I. But I must do my duty—and what you ask. I see the danger, but I ignore it because you force me to (2 Cor 12:22). You oblige me to walk in great things and in wonders which are beyond me (Ps 130:1). Oh, how I fear that I shall suddenly hear, "Why do you speak of my delights and let my secret out in your talk?" (cf. Ps 49:16). Hear me then, as a man who is afraid to speak, but is not able to be silent. That fear of mine may perhaps excuse my boldness; and if you are perhaps edified, that will excuse me further—as perhaps, too, will these tears I shed.

"Return," she says. Good. He was going away; he is called back. Who will explain to me the mystery of this change? Who will give a worthy account of the Word's coming and going? Surely the Bridegroom is not inconstant? Where can he come from or go to, he who fills heaven and earth (Jer 23:24)? How can he who is spirit (Jn 4:24) move from place to place? How can you say that there is any movement of any kind in God? He is unchanging.

I.2. Let him who is able understand (Mt 19:12). But let us go on carefully (Eph 5:15) and with pure hearts (Prv 11:20) to expound this holy and mysterious utterance (Is 23:3), and do as Scripture does, in speaking of the wisdom which is hidden in the mystery (1 Cor 2:7); it speaks of God in images we can understand; in comparisons with things familiar to the senses; by putting what is precious, the unknown and unseen things of God (Rom 1:20), in common vessels (2 Cor 4:7), it brings them within the grasp of human minds.

Let us, then, follow the way of this pure Word (Ps 11:7) and say that the Word of God, God himself, the soul's Bridegroom, comes to the soul as he wishes and leaves it again (1 Cor 12:11). But let us understand that this is only how it feels to the soul; there is no movement of the Word. When the soul is aware of grace, she knows that the Word is with her. When she is not, she seeks him who is absent, and begs him to come to her, saying with the prophet, "My face has sought you; your face, Lord will I seek" (Ps 26:8). How could she not? For when so sweet a Bridegroom leaves her, she cannot desire or even think of any other. So she longs for him in his absence, and calls him back as he leaves. So then, the Word is recalled, and by the soul's desire, by that soul which has once tasted his sweetness (Is 26:8).

Is longing not a cry? It is a loud one! Then, "The Lord has heard the desire of the poor," says Scripture (Ps 9:38). When the Word goes away, then, the one and continuous cry of the soul, its endless desire, is a repeated "Return," until he comes.

I.3. And now give me a soul which the Word, the Bridegroom, often visits, to which familiarity has brought courage, which hungers for what it has tasted, and whose contempt for all but him has freed it from all other preoccupations. I will unhesitatingly attribute to her the voice and name of Bride, and I shall consider everything this passage says to be applicable to her. For that is how the speaker is portrayed. For she proves that she has deserved the presence of him whom she calls back, even if not his constant presence. Otherwise she would call him, not recall him. For the word "return" is a word of recall.

And perhaps he has withdrawn so that he might the more eagerly be called back and embraced more closely. For once he made as if to go further not because he wished to do so, but because he wanted to hear them say, "Stay with us till morning for the evening draws on" (Lk 24:28–9). And again, when the Apostles were in a boat and were laboring at the oars, he walked on the water, and seemed to be passing them by; yet he was not going by, but only testing their faith and encouraging their prayers (Mk 6:48). Then, as the Evangelist says, they were troubled and cried out, thinking he was a ghost (Mk 6:49). This holy pretense, this saving contrivance, which the incarnate Word then showed, the same Word still makes as spirit, in his spiritual way, when he wants to stir the soul which loves him. He pretends to pass by, but he goes only to be recalled, for the Word is not irrevocable. He comes and goes as he pleases, as if visiting the soul at dawn (Jb 7:18), and suddenly putting it to the test. His going is part of his purpose; his return is at his will. Both are in perfect wisdom. Only he knows his reasons.

II.4. Now it is agreed that his comings and goings are the alterations in the soul of which he speaks when he says, "I go away and come to you again" (Jn 14:28), and "A little while and you shall not see me and again a little while and you shall see me" (Jn 16:17).

Oh, little and little! Such a long time! Dear Lord, you say it is only for a little while that we do not see you. What you say must be true, yet it is too long, far too long. Both are true: It is a little while in terms of our deserts, and a long time in terms of our desire. You can find both in the prophet. "If he delays, wait for him; for he will come and not delay" (Hb 2:3). How can he not be long, if he delays, unless he comes more quickly than we deserve and yet more slowly than we desire? The loving soul is carried away by longing, swept away by desire; she does not think what she deserves. She closes her eyes to his majesty and sees only the pleasure he brings; she trusts in his saving grace (Ps 11:6), and puts her faith in him. Boldly and without shame she calls the Word back, and trustingly she asks to have his delights again. She calls him with the freedom we associate not with a Lord but with a lover. "Return, my Beloved." And she adds, "Be like a fawn or a doe on the mountains of Bethel" (Sg 2:17). We shall come back to that later.

II.5. Now bear with my foolishness for a little while (2 Cor 11:1). I want to tell you, for I promised, about my own experience. It is not important (2 Cor 12:1). But I do so in the hope that it may benefit you, and if it does I shall be content in my foolishness. If not, my foolishness will be plain enough.

I tell you that the Word has come even to me—I speak in my foolishness—and that he has come more than once (2 Cor 11:17). Yet however often he has come, I have never been aware of the moment of his coming. I have known he was there; I have remembered his presence afterward; sometimes I had an inkling that he was coming. But I never felt it, nor his leaving me (Ps 120:8). And where he comes from when he enters my soul, or where he goes when he leaves it, and how he enters and leaves, I frankly do not know. As it says, "You do not know where he comes from, nor where he goes" (Jn 3:8). That is not surprising, for of him was it said, "Your footsteps will not be known" (Ps 76:20). He did not enter by the eyes, for he has no color; nor by the ears, for he made no sound; nor by the nostrils, for he is not mingled with the air, but the mind. He did not blend into the air; he created it. His coming was not tasted by the mouth, for he was not eaten or drunk; nor could he be touched, for he is impalpable. So by what route did he enter?

Or perhaps he did not enter at all, because he did not come from outside? For he is not one of those who are without (1 Cor 5:12). Yet he does not come from within me, for he is good (Ps 51:11), and I know that there is no good in me. I have climbed up to the highest that is in me, and see! The Word is far, far above. A curious explorer, I have plumbed my own depths, and he was far deeper than that. If I looked outward, I saw him far beyond. If I looked inward, he was further in still. And I knew that what I had read was true, that "in him we live and move and have our being" (Acts 17:28). But blessed is he in whom he has his being, who lives for him and is moved by him.

II.6. You ask then how I knew he was present, he whose ways cannot be traced (Rom 11:33). He is life and power (Heb 4:12), and as soon as he enters in he stirs my sleeping soul. He moves and soothes and pierces my heart (Sg 4:9), which was as hard as stone and riddled with disease (Sir 3:27; Ez 11:19, 36:26). And he begins to root up and destroy, to build and to plant, to water the dry places and light the dark corners (cf. Jer 1:10), to open what was closed, set what was cold on fire, to make the crooked straight and the rough places smooth (Is 40:4), so that my soul may bless the Lord and all that is within me praise his holy name (Ps 102.1).

And so when the Bridegroom, the Word, came to me he never made any sign that he was coming; there was no sound of his voice, no glimpse of his face, no footfall. There was no movement of his by which I could know his coming; none of my senses showed me that he had flooded the depths of my being. Only by the warmth of my heart, as I said before, did I know that he was there, and I knew the power of his might because (Eph 1:13) my faults were purged and my body's yearnings brought under control. And when my secret faults were revealed (Ps 18:13) and made visible, I have been amazed at the depth of his wis-

dom (Sir 7:25). At the slightest sign of amendment of life, I have experienced the goodness of his mercy. In the remaking and renewing of
the spirit of my mind (Eph 4:23), that is, the inner man, I perceived the
excellence of his glorious beauty (Ps 49:2); and when I contemplate all
these things I am filled with awe of his manifold greatness (Ps 150:2).

II.7. But when the Word has left me, and all these things become
dim and weak and cold, as though you had taken the fire from under a
boiling pot, I know that he has gone. Then my soul cannot help being
sorrowful until he returns, and my heart grows warm within me, and
I know he is there.

With such an experience of the Word, is it surprising if I speak the
words of the Bride and call him back when he absents himself, when
even if I do not burn with an equal desire, I burn with a desire like hers?
It will be natural to me as long as I live to speak "Return," the word of
recall, to call back the Word.

As often as he slips away from me, so often will I seek him, and I
shall not cease to cry, as if after someone who is leaving (Jgs 18:23),
begging him, with a burning desire of the heart, to return (Ps 20:3); I
will beseech him to give me the joy of his salvation (Ps 50:14) and return
to me.

III.7. I tell you, children, nothing else gives me joy when he is not
with me, who alone is the source of my joy. And I pray that he may
not come empty-handed (Is 55:11) but full of grace and truth (Jn 1:14),
as is his way, as he did yesterday and the day before (Gn 31:3). In this
he is like a roe or a faun (Sg 2:17), for his truth is like a roe's clear eyes
and his grace like the gaiety of a faun.

III.8. I need both: truth, so that I cannot hide from him, and
grace, so that I do not wish to hide. If either were lacking, his severity
might seem heavy without the one and his gaiety frivolous without the
other. Truth without grace is bitter; and without the restraint of truth,
devotion can be capricious, immoderate, and overconfident. How
many people have received grace and not benefited, because they did
not accept the truth at the same time to temper it? As a result they have
been too complacent in their possession of it (Is 42:1), without regard
to the truth. They have not imitated the full-grown roe, but behaved
like gay and giddy young fauns. So it is that they have lost the grace
they wanted to enjoy by itself. It could be said, too late, to them, "Go
then, and learn what it is to serve the Lord in fear, and rejoice in him
with awe" (Ps 2:11).

The holy soul once said in her abundance, "I shall never be

moved" (Ps 29:7–8), when suddenly she felt the Word turn his face away from her, and she was not only moved but thrown into confusion. And so she sadly learned that she needed not only the gift of devotion but also the gravity of truth. Therefore the fullness of grace lies not in grace alone, nor in truth alone. What profit is it to know what you ought to do if you cannot do it? I have known many who were sadder for knowing the truth, for they did not have the excuse of ignorance when they knew what the Truth wanted them to do and did not do it.

III.9. So neither is sufficient without the other. I have not put it strongly enough. Neither is of any use without the other. How do we know that? Scripture says, "If anyone knows what is good and does not do it, it counts as sin in him" (Jas 4:17). And again, "A servant who knows his master's will and does not do it as he should will be soundly beaten" (Lk 12:47). That is said of truth. What is said of grace? It is written, "And after the sop Satan entered into him" (Jn 13:27). The reference is to Judas who, having received the gift of grace, did not walk in the truth with the Lord of truth (or rather, with truth as his mistress), but let the devil find a foothold in him (Eph 4:27). Hear again, "He fed them with the finest wheat and satisfied them with honey from the rock" (Ps 80:16). Those he has fed with honey and the finest wheat have lied to him because they have not joined truth to grace. Elsewhere you can read of them, "The strange children have lied to me; the strange children have become feeble and limped off their paths" (Ps 17:46). Of course they limp when they walk on one foot, of grace, and do not use the other foot, of truth. Their destiny will be eternal, like that of their prince (Ps 80:16), who himself did not stand fast in the truth, but was a liar from the first (Jn 8:44), and for that reason heard the words, "You have lost your wisdom through your beauty" (Ez 28:17). I do not want a beauty which can rob me of wisdom.

III.10. Are you asking what this harmful and dangerous beauty is? It is yours. Do you perhaps still not understand (Mt 15:16)? Let me put it more plainly. It is a beauty which is exclusive and selfish. It is not the gift that is to blame for the use to which it is put. For if you notice, it is not because of his beauty but because of his *own* beauty that Satan is said to have lost his wisdom. And unless I am mistaken, the beauty of an angel and the beauty of a soul are the same. Either is a rough, shapeless mass without that wisdom. But with it, there is not only shapeliness but beauty (Wis 10:1). But he lost it because he kept it for himself, so that he lost his wisdom not only through his own beauty but through his own wisdom. Possessiveness is the reason.

It is because he was wise in his own eyes (Prv 26:5), not giving the glory to God (Jn 9:24), not returning grace for grace (Jn 1:16), not walking in grace in pursuit of truth (2 Jn 4), turning it to his own purposes; that is why he lost it. Scripture says, "And if Abraham was justified by his works, he has his glory, but not before God" (Rom 4:2). And I would say, "I am not safe." Whatever I have which is not before God, I have lost. For what is as lost as that which is separated from God? What is death but the deprivation of life? There is no loss which is not separation from God. "Woe to you who are wise in your own eyes, and prudent in your own estimation" (Is 5:21). It is said of you, "I will destroy the wisdom of the wise and the prudence of the prudent I will frustrate" (1 Cor 1:19). They have lost wisdom, because their own wisdom has caused them to be lost. What have they not lost, who are themselves lost? Surely those whom God does not recognize are lost (Mt 12:12)?

III.11. Now the foolish virgins (whose foolishness I think consisted in their thinking themselves wise) (Mt 25:2), have been made foolish (Rom 1:22). They hear God saying, "I do not know you" (Mt 25:12). Those who have used grace to perform miracles to give themselves glory will also hear, "I do not know you" (Mt 7:23). It is perfectly clear that grace is not profitable where there is no truth in the intention; in fact, it is a stumbling-block.

Both grace and truth are found in the Bridegroom. "Grace and truth came by Jesus Christ" (Jn 1:17), says John the Baptist. If the Lord Jesus knocks at my door with one but not the other—for he is the Word of God, the soul's Bridegroom—he will enter not as a Bridegroom but as a judge. Perish the thought! "Do not enter into judgment with your servant" (Ps 142:2). Let him enter as a bringer of peace, joyous and glad; but may he come grave and adult, too, to purify my joy and restrain my overconfidence with the stern face of truth. Let him enter as a leaping faun and a sharp-eyed roe, to pass over my blameworthiness at a bound, and look on my faults with pity. Let him enter as one coming down from the mountains of Bethel, full of joy and radiance, descending from the Father (Jn 15:26), sweet and gentle (Ps 85:5), deigning to become the Bridegroom of the soul that seeks him and to be known as such (Lam 3:25), he who is God, blessed above all forever (Rom 9:5).

SERMON 80

I.1. I gather that some of you are disturbed that for several days my sermon, lingering in delight with awe and wonder at the mysteries of God, has been spiced with nothing, or only the merest trace, of the salt of practical advice on the living of the Christian life (Col 4:6). That is indeed not my usual way. But let me put it right. I cannot go on unless I cover everything fully. Tell me then, if you can remember, from what point I began to make this omission, so that I may start again there. For I must make good these losses—or rather, it is for the Lord to do, on whom we depend in everything. So where shall I begin again? Perhaps from here, "In my little bed by night I sought him whom my soul loves" (Sg 3:1). I think that is the place. From there I had only one anxiety, to bring to light from the dense obscurity of these allegories the secret delights of Christ and the Church. So let us go back and look for the moral sense. What is for your benefit cannot be wearisome to me. And we shall do this appropriately if we look at the Word and the soul as we were looking at Christ and the Church (Eph 5:32).

I.2. But someone says to me, "Why do you join these two together? What connection is there between the soul and the Word?" A great deal in every way (Rom 3:2). First, there is the kinship of nature, for one is the Image and the other made in his image (Col 1:15). Second, their kinship indicates an affinity. Surely the soul is made not only in the image of God but also in his likeness (Gn 1:27). In what does this likeness consist, you ask? Hear first about the image. The Word is truth and wisdom and righteousness; these are the Image. Of what? Justice, wisdom, and truth. For this Image is righteousness from righteousness, wisdom from wisdom, truth from truth, as he is light from light, God from God (Nicene Creed). The soul is none of these things, for it is not the Image. But it is capable of these things, and it desires them, and that perhaps is why it is said to be made in the Image. It is a supreme creature, in its capacity for greatness and in its desire to be visibly upright. We read that God made man upright (Qo 7:30) and great. As we have said, his capacity proves that. For what is made in the Image ought to conform to the Image and not bear his name in vain; for the Image himself is not so-called for nothing. You have the saying of him who is the Image that "although he was in the form of God, he did not think it robbery to be equal with God" (Phil 2:6). You see that his uprightness is implied in saying that he is in the form of God, and in the reference to his equality in majesty, so that when uprightness is compared with uprightness and greatness with greatness each is clearly seen to match the other, Image and he who is in his Image, Image with Image. For he is the one of whom you have heard holy David sing, "Great is the Lord and great is his power" (Ps 146:5), and again, "The Lord our God is upright and there is no wickedness in him" (Ps 91:16). He is the Image of this upright and great God, and the soul has it in her because she is in his image to be upright and great too.

II.3.   But I ask, is there nothing more of greatness and uprightness in the Image than in the soul which is made in his Image? A great deal! For the Image is equal with God, but the soul has these things according to her capacity. Is there more than this? Listen to something else. The soul has both these things by creation and because God makes it worthy; the Image has them by begetting. And there is no doubt that that is more glorious. If anyone wants to deny that, he should remember that the soul receives both from God by his gift, but the Image has them from God directly, that is, from his very substance. For God's Image is of one substance with him, and everything which he is seen to share with him is of their common substance, not accidental. There is still one thing to consider, in which the Image is no less supreme. It is obvious to everyone that greatness and uprightness are different; but in the Image they are one. And not only that, they are one with the Image himself. For the image, it is not merely the same to be great as it is to be upright, but it is the same to be great and upright as to be. It is not thus for the soul. Her greatness and her uprightness are other than herself and different from each other. If, as I said before, the soul is great because it has a capacity for things eternal, and upright in desiring heaven, then the soul which does not seek or taste what is above but what is earthly (Col 3:2) is not upright at all, but bowed; yet it does not cease in this way to be great; it remains forever capable of enjoying things eternal. For even if it never attains to heaven it never loses its capacity to do so, as it is written, "Truly man passes as an image" (Ps 38:7), but only in part, so that the supremacy of the Word may be clear in its fullness. For how can the Word fail to be great and upright, since he possesses these as his very self? Man has these in part, because if he lacked them completely there would be no hope of salvation (Acts 27:30); for if he were to cease to be great he would not be capable of greatness, for as I have said, it is in its capacity for greatness that the soul's greatness lies. What hope could he have who could not receive it?

II.4.   And so by the greatness which he still has even when he has lost his uprightness, "Man passes as an image," but it is as though he were limping on one foot and has become an estranged son. I think it is of such that it is said, "The estranged sons have told me lies; they have grown weak and limped away from the path" (Ps 17:46). They are appropriately called "estranged sons" for they are "sons" because they still have their greatness, "estranged" because they have lost their righteousness. If they had lost their image altogether the Psalmist would not have said "limped," but "fallen away" or something of the sort. Now, then, man "passes as an image" because of his greatness, but as far as his uprightness is concerned, he is troubled, and torn from the image as though limping. Scripture puts it like this, "Truly man passes as an image; he is troubled in vain." Wholly in vain, for it follows, "He piles up treasures and knows not for whom" (Ps 38:7). Why does he not know, unless it is because he is bending down to the ground, and putting his treasure there (Jn 8:6)? More, he does not know for whom he is piling up these treasures on the earth, which may be eaten by moths, dug up by a thief (Mt 6:19), stolen by a foe (Dt 9:3), devoured by fire (Is 30:27). And so it is to the wretched man, bowed down and brooding over earthly things, that the voice of one who weeps speaks in the Psalm, "I am wretched, and bowed down to the earth; I go in sadness all the day long" (Ps 37:7). He has experienced the truth of Wisdom's saying: "God made man upright but he is bowed down by many sorrows" (Qo 7:30). And just afterward he is mocked and told, "Bow down and let us walk over you" (Is 51:23).

III.5. But how have we got here? Was it not by way of showing that uprightness and greatness, both of which we had found in the Image as his defining characteristics, are not one in the soul, nor one with the soul, in the way that, as we showed in our statement of faith, they are one in the Word and with the Word? It is clear from what we have said that uprightness is distinct from the soul and from the soul's greatness, for even when it is lost, the soul still exists and has its greatness. But how can it be shown that there is a distinction between the soul and its greatness? It cannot be shown in the same way as we employed in the case of the soul and its uprightness, for the soul cannot lose its greatness as it can its uprightness. Yet the soul is not its greatness. For even if the soul cannot be found without its greatness, yet that greatness is found outside the soul. Where, you ask? In the angels, for the greatness of the angels comes from the same source as the greatness of the soul, that is, from a capacity for what is eternal.

If we agree that the soul can be separated from its uprightness, because it can lose it, is it not equally clear that it can be distinguished from its greatness, which it cannot claim as its own? And since one is not found in every soul and the other is not found in the soul alone, it is obvious that both alike are distinct from the soul. Again, no form is that of which it is the form. But greatness is the form of the soul. It must be, if it is inseparable from it. All differences between substances are like this, both those with forms which are unique to one thing and those which have many varied forms. The soul is not itself its greatness, any more than a crow is its blackness or snow its whiteness, or a man his capacity for laughter, or his power of reasoning. Thus the soul and its greatness are not to be separated, but they are distinct from one another. They must be inseparable, since one is the subject and the other its substance. Only the supreme and uncreated Nature, which is God the Trinity, possesses this unique simplicity and purity of essence, in which there is not to be found one thing and another, nor one place and another, nor one time and another. God dwells in himself; he is what he possesses and what he is, always and changelessly. In the Trinity many are one, difference is alike, so that no plurality arises from number nor change from variety. God contains all places, and orders all things, being contained in nothing. All time is subject to him, not he to time. He does not look to the future or back at the past, or live in the present.

IV.6. Keep away, beloved, keep away from those who teach innovations, who are not logicians but rather heretics, who impiously argue that the greatness by which God is great (2 Ch 2:5), the goodness by which he is good, the wisdom by which he is wise, the righteousness by which he is righteous, and finally the divinity by which he is God, are not God.[1] "God is by divinity," they say, "but divinity is not God." Perhaps it does not deign to be God because it is that by which God is what he is? But if it is not God, what is it? It is either God, or something which is not God, or else nothing. You will not concede that it is God; nor, I think, will you grant that it is nothing. But you say that it is so necessary to God that not only can God not be God without it, but by it he is God. But if it is something which is not God, it must be greater

---

1. On the controversy over the teaching of Gilbert of Poitiers to which Bernard is referring, and which came to a head in Gilbert's trial at Rheims in 1148, see N. M. Häring, "The Case of Gilbert de la Porrée, Bishop of Poitiers (1142–54)," *Mediaeval Studies* 13 (1951): 1–40.

than God, or lesser, or his equal. How can that by which God is be less than he? So you must postulate that it is greater or equal. If it is greater, it is itself the highest Good, yet not God. If it is equal, there are two highest goods, not one. But the Christian shrinks from both interpretations. Now we hold the same faith about his greatness, his goodness, his righteousness, his wisdom, as we do about his divinity, that they are one in God and with God. His goodness does not have a different source from his greatness, or his righteousness or his wisdom a different source from these. All these have no other source but God. And that is no other than himself.

III.7. But the heretic says, "What? Do you deny that God is God by his divinity?" No, but I hold that the divinity by which God is God is itself God, in case I should regard anything as more excellent than God. For I hold that God is God by his greatness, but is himself that greatness. Not to believe that is to set something else above God. And I say that he is good by his goodness, which is nothing else but himself. Otherwise I might appear to have discovered something better than he is. And so for the rest. I go on in freedom and security, without stumbling, as they put it, keeping before me the vision of him who said, "God is great with the greatness which is himself, otherwise the greatness would be greater than God." It was Augustine who said so, that most powerful hammer of heretics. If this can properly be said of God, more correctly and appropriately may it be said, "God is greatness, goodness, righteousness, wisdom" than "God is great, good, just or wise."

III.8. [Omitted.][2]

III.9. I have thought it worthwhile to go into this since the opportunity occurs, because we are examining the difference between the Image and the soul. Then if any of you had ever drunk the forbidden waters which seem to have a sweeter taste (Prv 9:17), you might drink the antidote and vomit them up. Then, with minds purged, you may come to what I have promised to tell you about the likeness of the Word and the soul, and may drink with joy (Is 12:3), not of what I say but of the fountain of the Savior, the Church's Bridegroom, Jesus Christ our Lord, who is God above all, blessed forever. Amen (Rom 9:5).

---

2. The omitted section refers to the trial.

SERMON 2

1. Our earlier inquiry into the affinity of the soul for the Word was essential. For what can such majesty and such poverty (cf. 2 Cor 6:15) have in common that such sublimity and such humility should be thought to meet as equals? If we say truly that they do, that is a most joyous confidence. If we say it falsely, it is an audacity which deserves severe punishment. That is why we had to look into their affinity; and we have found many ways in which they are alike, but not all. No one can be so obtuse as not to see the likeness between the Image and that which is made in its image (Col 1:15; Gn 1:27). Yesterday, if you remember, our sermon dealt with their likeness and their difference. And not the image alone, but also the similitude was shown to be close (Gn 5:3). But we have not yet examined that similitude to see in what it chiefly consists. Come, let us now look into that, so that the soul, understanding her origin more thoroughly, may be the more ashamed to lead an unworthy life, and will indeed strive to reform by hard effort the damage she perceives that sin has done in her nature, so that, with God's assistance, she may govern herself in a way befitting her kind and faithfully enter the Word's embrace.

2. Let her take note, then, that because she is made in God's likeness she has herself a natural simplicity of substance, by which for her to exist is to live, even if not in blessedness. Thus it is a likeness, not an equality. It is near in degree, but still it is lowlier. It is not the same as living in a state of endless blessedness by nature, which is the case with the Supreme Excellence. If, then, life is the prerogative of the Word, because his nature is sublime, and of the soul because of her likeness to him, except that the Word is supreme, the affinity of nature between the soul and the Word is evident, and the soul's prerogative clear. And so that what I have said may be plainer, it belongs to God alone that being is blessedness; this is the first and purest simplicity. The second is like it (Mt 22:39), that is, that to be is to live; this is the prerogative of the soul. Even if it is a lowlier prerogative, it can be lifted up, not only to living well, but also to living in blessedness: not that then it will be like God, whose being is blessedness, but it will be glorified by its likeness to him by whom it was raised up. Yet because of the difference it will always have reason to say, "Lord, who is like you?" But there is in this a degree of uplifting for the soul, by which, and only in this way, it rises to blessedness of life (Ps 34:10).

3. For there are two kinds of living things, those which feel and

those which do not. Those which have feeling are higher than those who do not, and above them both is life, by which comes living and feeling. Life and living things are not equal; much less life and lifeless things. Life is the living soul, but it does not have its life from any but itself. And so this is more properly called "life" than "living." That is why when it is infused into the body it gives it life, so that the body of this present life is not "life" but "living." From this it is plain that, even for the living body, to be is not the same as to live. How much less do things which have no life rise to this level. But not everything which is called "life," or is in fact life, will be able to continue thus. There is a life of beasts and of trees, the first a feeling life, the other without feeling. But for neither is their being life, for, as many think, they have existed in their elements before they had bodily parts or branches. But according to this opinion, when they cease to be filled with life, they cease to live, but not to be. They are dissolved and broken up, as though they had not only been brought together but mingled. For they are not one simple thing, but made up of many. And so such a creature is not reduced to nothing (Jb 16:8, 17:7, 30:15), but separated into parts, so that each may return to its beginning, for example, air to air, fire to fire, and the rest in their own ways. For life such as that to be is not the same as to live, for they exist when they do not live.

4. None of these things, to which to be is not the same as to live, will ever progress or rise, for they cannot reach even the lowest degree. Only the soul of man is created with this dignity, which is inseparable from it, of being life from life, simple from simple, immortal from immortal, so that it is not far from the highest degree, where to be is to live in blessedness, in which dwells the blessed and only powerful King of kings and Lord of lords (1 Tm 6:15). The soul has received in its creation, not blessedness, but the potential for blessedness, and it approaches that highest degree as far as it can, although it does not reach it. For as we have already said, even when it attains blessedness, that will not be the same as being blessed by nature. We affirm the likeness, but we do not claim equality. God is life; the soul is life; like, indeed, but different. She is like him because she is life, because she lives in herself, because she is not only living but life-giving, just as he is all these things; she is unlike him as the creature is unlike its Creator, for unless he had created her she would not have existed, and unless he had given her life she would not have lived. She would not live, I say, but I am speaking of spiritual life, not a natural one. The soul must necessarily live immortally, by nature, even if it does not live spiritually.

But what kind of life would it be in which it would be better not to have been born than not to leave it by death? It is more death than life, and the worse a death because it is thus by sin and not by nature. For, "The death of sinners is very the worst" (Ps 33:22). So then the soul which lives according to the flesh (Rom 8:13) experiences a living death, for it would have been better for her never to have lived at all than to live in such a way (1 Tim 5:6). And she will never ever arise from that living death except by the Word of life, or rather, through the Word which is Life, living and life-giving (Eph 5:26).

III.5. But the soul is also immortal, and in this she is like the Word, but not his equal. For the immortality of God so excels hers, that the Apostle was able to say of God, "He alone has immortality" (1 Tm 6:16). I think this was said of him because God alone is immutable in his nature, he who says, "I am the Lord and I do not change" (Mal 3:6). It is a true and complete immortality to have neither change nor end, for all change imitates death. Everything which changes dies in a sense when it alters from one thing to another, for that is to begin not to be. If there are as many deaths as changes, where is immortality? "For the creature was made subject to vanity not of its own will but of him who made it and gave it hope" (Rom 8:20). Yet the soul is immortal, for, since she is her own life, there is no way in which she can fall from life, for she cannot cease to be herself. But we all know that she changes in her feelings, and she recognizes that she is so like God in her immortality that she knows she lacks no small part of immortality. She sees absolute and perfect immortality in him alone with whom there is no change, nor any shadow of alteration (Jas 1:17). But it has been settled in the present disputation that the soul has no small dignity, in that she seems to come close to the Word in her nature in two ways, in simplicity of essence and perpetuity of life.

6. But one further point arises, which I shall certainly not pass over: and which does not make the soul any less noble and similar to the Word, and perhaps makes her more so. This is freedom of choice, something clearly divine, which shines in the soul like a jewel in a setting of gold. From this the soul derives her power to judge and to choose between good and evil, life and death, and no less between light and darkness, and to make any other choices which present themselves to her. The eye of the soul, a critical judge, discriminates and discerns, a judge in discriminating, free in her choice. That is why it is called free choice, because the will can exercise its judgment in making it. For this a man is rightly praised; not only he who is able to do wrong and does

not do it (Sir 31:10), but he who cannot do good and does it, and so
merit is as much his who could do evil and does not do it as his who
could have done good and did not do it. But where there is no freedom
there is no merit. Animals which do not have reason have no merit, for
just as they lack the power of thought, so they lack freedom of choice;
they are moved by their senses, carried away by impulse, led on by
appetite. They do not have judgment by which they may discriminate
or govern themselves, not even the instrument of judgment, which is
the reason. That is why they are not judged, for they cannot exercise
judgment. Would it not be unreasonable to expect reason of those who
have not received it?

IV.7. Only man is not subject by nature to this limitation, and so
only he is free. Yet when he sins he feels the force of it in himself to
some extent, but by will not by nature, and he does not thereby lose
his inborn liberty. What is voluntary is also free. By sin the body which
is corrupted burdens the soul (Wis 9:15), but by love not force. For although the soul fell by her own act she cannot rise by herself, because
her will, weak and cast down by her depraved and flawed love of the
corrupt body, cannot feel a love of righteousness at the same time. So,
in some wicked and surprising way the will makes itself a slave of the
sin into which it has fallen and actually changes for the worse, so that
necessity cannot excuse the will because it acted freely, and the will,
since it is in chains, cannot avoid necessity. For this "necessity" is in
some sense voluntary. It is a pleasant bondage which flatters while it
captures and captures while it flatters, so the will makes itself guilty by
once consenting to sin, and cannot escape by itself, nor find any excuse
for itself by reason. Then, like the voice of one complaining under the
burden of necessity, there comes, "Lord, I am oppressed; answer for
me" (Is 38:14). But again, knowing that he has no just cause for complaint against the Lord, for his own will was the cause, hear what he
says next: "What am I to say? Who will answer for me, for I have
brought this on myself?" (Is 38:15). He was burdened by the yoke, but
the yoke of a voluntary servitude, and it was a wretched servitude, but
he could not be excused from it for he had chosen it. For it is the will
which, though it is free, has been made the slave of sin in consenting
to sin; nevertheless, it is its will to place itself under the yoke of sin,
and it serves voluntarily.

8. "Look what you are saying," someone says to me. "You say that
something is voluntary which is agreed to be necessary." It is indeed
so, because the will has brought itself to this necessity. But it does not

keep itself there; it is, rather, kept there against its will. You must agree that it is being held. But hold onto the fact that it is the will which you say is being held. And so you say that the will is unwilling? The will is not held against its will. For the will is what wills, not what is against will. If it is held willingly, it holds itself. What then will a man say, or who will answer for him, when he has done this himself (Is 38:15)? What has he done? He has made himself a slave. That is why it is said, "He who sins is a slave of sin" (Jn 8:34). So when he sins—and he has sinned when he has decided to obey sin—he has made himself a slave. But he would be free if he did not continue to sin. However, he goes on, holding himself in this servitude. For the will is not held unwillingly; it is the will. Therefore, because he does it willingly, he has not only made himself a slave, but he continues to do so. Rightly then— and this must be often remembered—is it asked who will speak for him, when his slavery was and is his own fault (Is 38:15).

9. "But," you say, "you will not force me to deny that I am in an entrapment which I feel in myself and against which I struggle hard?" "Where do you feel this constraint?" I ask. "Is it not in your will?" So you do not will the less because your will is enslaved. Your will wills much that you cannot refuse to will, however much you resist. Now where there is will, there is freedom. "I am talking of natural not spiritual freedom, by which, as the Apostle says, Christ sets us free" (Gal 4:31). For of that he himself says, "Where the spirit is, there is freedom" (2 Cor 3:17). So in a strange and evil way, the soul is held as a slave in this willing and yet irresistible bondage, and is also free. She is at the same time a slave and free, and what is more strange and wretched still, guilty in proportion to her freedom and a slave in proportion to her guilt, and in this was a slave in that she is free. Wretched man that I am, who will free me from the shame of this slavery (Rom 7:24)? Wretched I am, but free: free because I am a man, wretched because I am a slave; free because I am like God, wretched because I go against God. "O guardian of men, why have you set me in opposition to you" (Jb 7:20)? For you placed me thus when you did not prevent me from falling. Otherwise it is I who am against you, "and I have become a burden to myself" (Jb 7:20). It is very just indeed that your enemy should be my enemy, and he who sets himself against you should oppose me. It is I who do so, I who have opposed myself and in myself I find that which is enemy both to my mind and to your law (Rom 7:23).

V. Who will free me from my own hands? "I do not do what I wish to do" and it is I not someone else who is preventing me. "And what I hate I do" (Rom 7:24, 15–6), but it is I not someone else who compels me. But would that this prohibition and this compulsion were so strong that it was not voluntary. Then, perhaps, I might be excused. If it were so much a matter of will that there was no compulsion, then I could be corrected. But as it is, nowhere does a way of escape lie open to this wretch, whom his willingness denies excuse and necessity makes impossible to correct, as I said. Who will snatch me from the hand of the sinner (Ps 70:4), from the hand of him who breaks the law and is wicked?

10. "Who do you complain of?" someone asks. Myself! I am that sinner, that outlaw, that wicked man. I am a sinner because I have sinned, an outlaw because I deliberately and persistently go against the law. For my will rules my members, denying the law of God (Rom 7:23). And since the law of the Lord is the law of my mind, it is written, "The law of God is in his heart" (Ps 36:31), my very will is seen to be against me; and this is the greatest iniquity. To whom am I not wicked, when I am wicked to myself? If a man injures himself, how can he do good to anyone (Sir 14:5)? I tell you: I am not good because good is not in me. But I shall find comfort in the words of the saints, "I know that there is no good in me" (Rom 7:18). But the Apostle makes a distinction when he puts it like this, explaining that he speaks of the flesh because it is there where the perverse law rules. For he has a law in his mind, and that is a better law. Surely the law of God is good? If wickedness comes from evil law, surely good comes from good law in a man? If the law in a man's flesh is evil and that is why he is wicked, will he not be good because of the good law? It is so. The law of God is in his mind (cf. Ps 36:31), and it is there in such a way that it is the law of his mind. He himself is witness who says, "I find a law in my body warring against the law in my mind" (Rom 7:23). Can what is in his flesh be his and not what is in his mind? It is certainly his own; even more. I will use the Apostle's words. "With my mind I obey God's law, but in my flesh I obey the law of sin" (Rom 7:25). He makes it plain that he regards it as his own when he calls the evil in his flesh foreign to him, saying, "And so it is not I who act but the sin that is in me" (Rom 7:20). And so perhaps he said that he found "another" law in his members because he thought this which came as if from outside him to be foreign to him. So I am bold to go a little further, but not rashly. Paul was not evil because of the evil in his flesh as much as he was good because of the good which he had in his mind. Is not a man good when he consents to the law of God, for that is good? Even if he admits that he is a slave to

the law of sin, that is in the flesh, not in the mind. So since he serves the law of God in his mind and the law of sin in his flesh, you can see which is rather to be considered his. I am readily persuaded that the law of the mind is greater than the law of the flesh, and not only I but Paul himself, as has already been said, when he claims, "I do what I do not wish to do, but it is not I who do so, but the sin which dwells is me" (Rom 7:20).

11. Let that be enough about freedom. In the little books I have written about grace and free will, you will find more reflections on image and likeness, but, I think, nothing which contradicts what I have said. You have read it; you have heard what I have said. I leave it to you to judge which is better put. If you find anything in either to your taste, I am glad and shall be glad (Phil 1:18). Whatever you choose, remember that I have made three points especially here: bear in mind the simplicity, immortality, and liberty of the soul. I think it must be obvious to you that through its inborn and built-in likeness, which shines in these three most clearly, the soul has no little affinity with the Word, the Bridegroom of the Church, Jesus Christ our Lord, who is God above all, blessed forever. Amen (Rom 9:5).

Sermon 83

1.1. For three days I have set out as fully as the allotted time permits the affinity between the Word and the soul. What profit has there been in all that labor? Surely this: We have learned that every soul, even if it is loaded down with sins (1 Tm 3:6), ensnared in vices, trapped by the enticements of pleasure, a captive in exile, imprisoned in the body, stuck in mud (Ps 68:3), caught in the mire, bound to its members, enslaved by cares, distracted with business, shrinking with fear, afflicted with griefs, astray in errors, troubled by anxieties, disturbed by suspicions, and, lastly, a stranger in a hostile land (Ex 2:22) and, as the prophet puts it, sharing the pollution of the dead, counted with those who go down to hell (Bar 3:11)—we have learned that every soul, even thus condemned and thus despairing, can turn back and find that it can not only breathe the hope of forgiveness and mercy, but even dare to aspire to be the Bride of the Word, when it is not afraid to make alliance with God and to take on the sweet yoke of love with the King of the angels (Mt 11:30). For what can it not safely dare with him in whose image it sees it is honored to be created and in whose glorious likeness it recognizes itself made glorious? Why should it be fearful of majesty, when it has confidence that it is Majesty's creation? It has only to preserve purity of nature by innocence of life; or, rather, to strive to beautify and adorn the heavenly beauty of its creation with its actions and affections.

2. Why, then, does it doze in idleness? There is a great gift in our nature; and if it is not used to the full the rest of our nature will become ruined, as though it were gnawed away by rust. That would be an affront to the Author of our being. And indeed that is why that Author, God himself, has desired divine glory and nobility to remain in the soul always, so that it may have within it that which may be touched by the Word, and moved to stay with him, or to return to him if it has slipped away. It does not slip away by moving to another place, or by actually walking; it slips away as a spiritual substance does, in its affections— or we should say defections; and it grows unlike itself when it becomes unlike him in its wickedness of life and actions. But this unlikeness is not a destruction of its nature, but a flaw; for natural goodness grows by returning to itself just as much as it is damaged by its dealing with what defiles it. So the soul comes back to itself and turns back to the Word, to be made new by him and to be made like him. In what? In love, for he says, "Be imitators of God, like beloved children, and walk in love, as Christ also has loved you" (Eph 5:1).

3. This "making like" marries the soul to the Word. It is like him in nature, but it shows that it wants to be like him by loving as it is loved. Therefore, if it loves perfectly, it "weds" him. What is more joyous than this union? What more to be desired than love, by which it comes about that, not content with a human master, you approach the Word with confidence, O soul, and cling to him with constancy, talk to him as a close friend about everything, with as clear a grasp as your desire is bold. Truly, that is the contract of a holy and spiritual marriage. I have not put it strongly enough in calling it a "contract." It is an embrace, a full embrace, where both are at one in will and which makes one spirit of two (1 Cor 6:17). Nor is it to be feared that inequality between the persons will prevent this coming together in one will, for love knows nothing of such distance. It is loving, not paying respect, that gives love its name. Let someone else be horrified, stupefied, terrified, amazed; he who loves feels nothing of these. His love fills him; love takes all other affections captive when it comes. Therefore what it loves it loves, and it knows nothing else. He who is feared, honored, regarded with awe, and admired would rather be loved. They are bride

and Bridegroom. What other bond and commitment do you seek to find between those who are betrothed than to love and be loved?

II. This bond is stronger even than the firm tie nature makes, the bond of parents and children. That is why it says, "For this a man will leave his father and mother and cleave to his bride" (Mt 19:5). You see the love between bride and bridegroom is not only stronger than other affections, but even stronger than itself.

4. Add to this that the Bridegroom is not only loving. He is Love. Is he not honor, too? It has been said that he is, but I have not read it. I have read that God is love (1 Jn 4:16), but not that he is honor. It is not that God does not want honor, for he says, "If I am a Father, where is my honor?" (Mal 1:6). Here he speaks as a Father. But if he shows himself to be a Bridegroom, I think he will speak differently and say, "If I am a Bridegroom, where is my love?" For he spoke differently before, "If I am the Lord where is my fear?" (Mal 1:6). God then demands to be feared as Lord, honored as Father, and loved as Bridegroom. Which of these is first? Which is supreme? Surely love. Without love, fear is a source of pain (1 Jn 4:18), and honor is thankless. Fear is servile until it is set free by love. And the honor which does not proceed from love is not honor but adulation. And indeed "honor and glory belong to God alone" (1 Tm 1:17), but God will accept neither if they are not sweetened with the honey of love. That is enough on its own; it pleases by itself and on its own account. It is its own merit and its own reward. Love needs no cause, no fruit besides itself; its enjoyment is its use (Augustine, *De Doctrine Christiana* I.1). I love because I love; I love that I may love. Love is a great thing; as long as it returns to its beginning, goes back to its origin, turns again to its source, it will always draw afresh from it and flow freely. In love alone, of all the movements of the soul and the senses and affections, can the creature respond to its Creator, if not with an equal, at least with a like return of gift for gift. For example, if God is angry with me, can I return his anger? Not at all; I shall be afraid and tremble and beg for his pardon. If he accuses me, I shall not return his accusation, but concede that he is right. If he judges me, I shall not judge him but adore him; and in saving me he does not seek to be saved by me in return, nor does he need to be set free by anyone in return when he frees all. If he commands it is for me to obey; if he gives me orders it is for me to do what he says and not ask service or obedience from the Lord in return. Now you see how different it is with love. For when God loves, he wants

nothing but to be loved; he loves for no other purpose than to be loved, knowing that those who love him are blessed by their very love.

5. Love is a great thing, but there are degrees of love. The Bride stands at the high point. For children love, but they are thinking of their inheritance, and as long as they fear they may lose it in some way they honor more than love him from whom they hope to have it. I am suspicious of love which seems to be prompted by hope of gain. It is weak if when hope is gone it either vanishes or diminishes. It is impure when it desires something else, other than the beloved. Pure love does not hope for gain. Pure love does not draw its strength from hope; nor is it weakened by mistrust. Love is the very being of the Bride. She is full of it, and the Bridegroom is satisfied with it. He asks nothing else. That is why he is the Bridegroom and she the Bride. This love belongs only to them; no one else can share it, not even a child.

III. Thus he says to his children, "Where is my honor?" (Mal 1:6), but he does not say, "Where is my love?" for he protects the Bride's prerogative. He commands a man to honor his father and his mother (Dt 5:16), but he says nothing of love, not because children ought not to love their parents, but because most children are inclined to honor rather than to love their parents. It is true that the King's honor loves judgment (Ps 98:4). But the Bridegroom's love, or rather the Bridegroom who is Love, asks only the commitment of love and faith. Let the beloved love in return. How can the Bride not love, the Bride of Love himself? How can Love not be loved?

6. So, rightly renouncing all other desires, she gives herself up wholly to Love, for it is in responding to Love that she is able to return love. For though she pours herself out completely in love, what is that in comparison with the inexhaustible flow of love from his spring? Love does not flow in equal measure from her who loves and Love himself, the soul and the Word, the Bride and the Bridegroom, creature and Creator, any more than a thirsty man is like a fountain. What then? Will the marriage vow come to nothing because of this, the desire of her who longs, the ardor of her who loves, the trust of her who is confident, because she cannot run step for step with a giant, rival honey in sweetness, the lamb in mildness, the lily in whiteness, the sun in brightness, or match in her love him who is Love (1 Jn 4:16)? No. For even if the creature loves less because it is lesser, yet if she loves with all her heart (Mt 22:37), nothing is lacking where all is given. So, as I have said, to love in that way is to be married, for a soul cannot love like this and not

be loved in return. Full and perfect marriage consists in this (Mt 18:16). No one can doubt that the soul is both first loved and loved most by the Word. He both goes before her in love and outruns her in love. Happy is she who has deserved to be anticipated in the blessing of such sweetness (Ps 20:4)! Happy is she to whom it is given to know the embrace of such tenderness! For it is nothing other than holy and chaste love, love sweet and tender, love as tranquil as it is true, mutual, close, deep love, which is not in one flesh, but which joins two in one spirit, making two no longer two but one (Mt 19:5). As Paul says, "He who is united to God is one spirit with him" (1 Cor 6:17). On this subject let us listen to her who by his anointing (1 Jn 2:27), and by frequent experience, has become our mistress before all others.

But perhaps we had better keep this for the starting-point of another sermon, rather than compress something important into the short time before we finish. If you approve, I will end here before the end, so that we may come early tomorrow, eager to taste the sweets which are the reward of the holy soul, which the souls of the blessed deserve to enjoy with the Word and from the Word, the Bridegroom, Jesus Christ our Lord, who is God above all, blessed forever. Amen (Rom 9:5).

SERMON 84

"All night long in my little bed I sought him whom my soul loves" (Sg 3:1). It is a great good to seek God; I think nothing comes before it among the good things the soul may enjoy. It is the first of its gifts and its ultimate goal. None of the virtues approaches it, and it yields place to none. What could be better when nothing has a higher place? To what could it yield place, when it is the consummation of all things? What virtue can be attributed to him who does not seek God? What limit is there for him who seeks him? "Always seek his face," it says (Ps 104:4). I think that even when it has found him the soul will not cease to seek him. God is sought not on foot but by desire. And the happy discovery of what is desired does not end desire but extends it. The consummation of joy does not consume desire, does it? Rather, it is oil poured on flames, which itself catches fire. Thus it is. Joy will be fulfilled (Ps 15:11). But there will be no end to desire, and so no end of seeking. Put from your mind, if you can, the absence of God as the cause of this eagerness to seek him, for he is always present; and anxiety in the search, for you cannot fail to find his abundance.

2. Now see why I have said this as a preliminary. It is so that every soul among you which is seeking God will know that he has gone before and sought you before you sought him. Otherwise you may turn a great good into a great evil for yourself. For from great goods can arise evils no less great, when we treat as our own the good things God gives and act as though they were not gifts, not giving God the glory (Lk 17:18). So it is that those who seem greatest because of the gifts they have received count for nothing before God because they do not give thanks for them. I am putting it mildly (1 Cor 7:28), using inadequate words, "great" and "little," which I know do not say exactly what I mean. I have been obscure; I will make it plain. I ought to have said "good" and "evil." For truly and undoubtedly, the best of men, if he claims the credit for his goodness, is as evil as he seemed good. This is very evil. If someone says, "Perish the thought, I know that it is by the grace of God that I am as I am" (1 Cor 15:10), yet is eager to take even the smallest credit for the grace he has received, surely he is a robber and a thief (Jn 10:1)? Let such a man hear this, "Out of your own mouth I judge you, wicked servant" (Lk 19:22). What is more wicked than for a slave to usurp his master's glory?

3. "All night long in my little bed I sought him whom my soul loves" (Sg 3:1). The soul seeks the Word, but she has first been sought by the Word. Otherwise, once she had gone out from before his face, or been cast out, her eye would not look to see good again, if the Word did not seek her (Jb 7:7). Our soul is no different from a wandering spirit which does not return (Ps 77:39) if she is left to herself. Hear a fugitive and a wanderer who grieves and pleads, "I have gone astray like a lost sheep. Seek your servant" (Ps 118:176). O man, do you wish to return? But if it is a matter of will, why do you plead? Why do you go begging for what you have in plenty in yourself? It is clear that she wishes but cannot; she is a wandering spirit which does not return (Ps 77:39). And he who does not want to return is still further away. If a soul wants to return and seeks to be sought, I should not say she was wholly lost and abandoned. For where does she get this will? Unless I am mistaken, it is from the visitation of the Word who has already sought her. That seeking has not been in vain, because it has made the will active, without which there can be no return. But it is not enough to be sought once. The weakness of the soul is great and great is the difficulty of the return. For what if she wills? Willing is idle, where

there is no power to act upon it. "For the will is in me," says Paul, "but I have no power to do good" (Rom 7:18). What does the Psalmist whom we quoted ask? Nothing but to be sought, for he would not seek unless he was sought, and he would not seek if he had been satisfied with the seeking. So he asks more, "Seek your servant," he says, so that he who has given the will may also give the power to act, at his good will (Ps 118:176; Phil 2:13).

4. But I do not think that this passage can be speaking of such a soul, which has not yet received the second grace, willing, but not yet able to approach him whom her soul loves (Sg 3:1). For how can the words which follow apply to such a soul? She rises and goes about the city, seeking her beloved in the streets and squares (Sg 3:2), and she could not do that if she herself needed to be sought. Let her do what she can, so long as she remembers that she was first sought, and first loved, and that it is because of this that she seeks and loves. And let us pray, beloved, that his mercies may quickly go before us (Ps 78:8), for we are only too poor. I do not say this of everyone (Jn 13:18). For I know that many of you walk in the love with which Christ has loved us (Eph 5:2), and seek him in simplicity of heart (Wis 1:1). But there are others, I am sad to say, who have not yet given us any sign of this saving and prevenient grace, men who love themselves, not the Lord, and who seek their own good, not his (2 Tm 3:2; 1 Cor 13:5).

5. "I have sought," she says, "him whom my soul loves" (Sg 3:1). This is what the kindness of him who goes before you urges you to do, he who both sought you first and loved you first (1 Jn 4:10). You would not be seeking him or loving him unless you had first been sought and loved. You have been forestalled not only in one blessing (Gn 27:28) but in two, in love and in seeking. The love is the cause of the seeking, and the seeking is the fruit of the love; and it is its guarantee. You are loved, so that you may not think that you are sought so as to be punished; you are sought, so that you may not complain that you are loved in vain. Both these sweet gifts of love make you bold and drive diffidence away, and they persuade you to return and move you to loving response. Hence comes the zeal, the ardor to seek him whom your soul loves, for you cannot seek unless you are sought and now that you are sought you cannot fail to seek.

6. But do not forget whence you came. Now, to apply what I say to myself (1 Cor 4:6)—for that is the safest course—is it not you, my soul, who left your first husband (Sir 23:32), with whom you were happy, and broke your faith (1 Tm 5:12) by going after your

lovers (Hos 2:5, 13)? And now that you have perhaps fornicated with them and been despised by them, do you dare, impudent and shameless, to return to him whom you proudly despised? What? Do you seek the light when you deserve to be hidden, run to your Bridegroom, when you deserve blows rather than kisses? It will be surprising if you do not come face to face with the judge when you expected the Bridegroom. Happy he who hears his soul answering in these words, "I do not fear because I love, which I should not do if I were not loved. And so this is love." She who is loved has nothing to fear. Let those who do not love be afraid. Must they not constantly fear hostility? I love, and I cannot doubt that I am loved, any more than that I love. Nor can I fear his face whose love I experience. In what? In that he not only sought but loved me, and made me bold in seeking. How can I not respond to his seeking since I respond to his love? How can he be angry with me for seeking him, when he overlooked my contempt for him? He will surely not thrust away the seeker whom he sought when he despised? Kind is the Spirit of the Word, and he greets me kindly (Wis 1:6), whispering to me and coaxing me to recognize the ardor and longing of the Word, which he knows well (Mt 5:14). He sees into the mysteries of God (1 Cor 2:10), and knows his thoughts, thoughts of peace and not of vengeance (Jer 29:11). How can I not be roused to seek him when I have experienced his mercy and been assured of his peace?

7. Brothers, to understand this is to be sought by the Word; to be assured is to be found. But not all receive this Word (Mt 19:11). What shall we do for our little ones? I speak of those among us who are beginners, but not fools, for they have the beginning of wisdom (Ps 110:10) and are subject to one another in the fear of Christ. How shall we bring them to believe that they may be his brides, when they do not yet perceive that this is how he deals with them? But I send them to him whom they should not fail to believe. Let them read in the book what they do not see in another's heart, and because they do not see it, do not believe. It is written in the prophets, "If a man puts away his wife and she leaves him and takes another husband, will he go back to her? Will she not be dishonored and in disgrace? You have committed fornication with many lovers. But return to me, says the Lord, and I will receive you" (Jer 3:1). These are the Lord's words. You cannot disbelieve them. Let them believe what they do not know from experience, so that by their faith they may in the future have the reward of experience. I think it has been

made plain enough what it is to be sought by the Word, and that this is a need not of the Word but of the soul. It only remains to say that the soul which has experienced this knows it more fully and more happily. It remains for us in what follows to teach thirsty souls how to seek him who seeks them, or, rather, we ought to learn it from her who is spoken of in this passage as seeking him whom her soul loves (Sg 3:3), the soul's Bridegroom, Jesus Christ our Lord, who is God, blessed above all, forever (Rom 9:5).

LETTERS

LETTER 64

About 1129 Bernard wrote to the bishop of Lincoln on behalf of Philip, who had become a monk at Clairvaux, and who held a benefice for whose disposition the bishop was responsible. Philip was anxious that his family should not suffer financially as a result of his action. Bernard asked the bishop to allow his mother to keep the house he had built for her. He takes the opportunity to paint for the bishop a picture of the foretaste of the heavenly Jerusalem that is to be enjoyed at Clairvaux. Bishop Alexander (1123–1147) was notorious for his self-indulgence and injustice, and Bernard adds a personal note of exhortation to him.

To Alexander, bishop of Lincoln c. 1129

To the honorable Lord Alexander, by the grace of God bishop of Lincoln.[1] Bernard, abbot of Clairvaux, wishes that he may desire to be honored more in Christ than in the world.

1. Your Philip, who wanted to go to Jerusalem, has found a short-cut and arrived there sooner than he expected. He crossed this great wide sea (Ps 103:25) quickly, and with a following wind he has now landed on the shore he was making for, and has dropped anchor in a safe harbor. Now he has his feet planted in the courts of Jerusalem (Ps 121:2) and him whom he heard of in Ephrathah he has found in the woodland plains, and he worships him gladly in the place where he now stands (Ps 131:6–7). He has entered the Holy City, and his lot is cast

---

1. On Alexander, bishop of Lincoln, see *Bernard de Clairvaux* (Paris, 1953), p. 637.

as a fellow heir with those to whom it is rightly said (Mt 27:53), "Now you are not guests and strangers, but citizens with the saints and members of God's household" (Eph 2:19). Going in and out with them (Act 9:28) like one of the saints, he glories with the others, saying, "Our home is in heaven" (Phil 3:20).

He has been made not a curious spectator but a loyal inhabitant and enrolled citizen of Jerusalem (Heb 12:23); and not of this earthly Jerusalem which has a border with Arabia at Mount Sinai, (Gal 4:25–26) and which is in slavery with her children, but of that free Jerusalem which is above and mother of us all.

2. And if you want to know, this is Clairvaux! Clairvaux is itself Jerusalem; it is one with the Jerusalem which is in heaven, in whole-hearted devotion of the mind and in similarity of life and in spiritual kinship. Here, as Philip promises himself, he will find rest forever (Ps 131:13–14). He has chosen it for his dwelling-place, because here is, if not yet a clear sight of it, certainly the expectation of true peace, that peace of which it is said, "The peace of God which surpasses all that we know" (Phil 4:7). He wishes to be able to enjoy with your good wishes this good of his which he has received from above. Indeed, he trusts that he has it, for he knows that you are aware of that wise saying that a wise son is his father's glory (Prv 10:1).

But he asks your fatherly kindness, and we ask it, too, with him and on his behalf, to allow the arrangement which he has made to continue, so that his creditors may have his prebend. He does not want to cheat anyone and be found (perish the thought!) a debtor and a breaker of promises. For the gift of a contrite heart, which he offers every day, will not be accepted as long as any brother has anything against him (Mt 5:23). He also asks that the house which he himself built for his mother on church lands may be granted to his mother as long as she lives, with the land he gave with it. So much for Philip.

3. And now a few words for you yourself. I thought I would add something, prompted by God, and perhaps inspired by him, to presume to exhort you lovingly not to take the glory of the world seriously as something which will last, and so lose that glory which will never pass away. Do not love your possessions more than yourself, or for your own sake, and so lose both your possessions and yourself. Do not let the pleasure of your present prosperity hide your end from you, or endless adversity will follow. Do not let the joy of this world bring about while concealing from you, and conceal

from you while bringing it about, the grief which is everlasting. Do not think death is a long way off, for it may catch you when you are not ready, and when you think life will go on and on, it may suddenly come to an end when you are in the wrong frame of mind, as it is written, "When they are saying, 'Peace and security,' then suddenly death will come, like the pains of a woman in labor, and they will not escape it" (1 Thes 5:3).

LETTER 144

In the autumn of 1137, when he would have liked to return to Clairvaux, Bernard was forced to go to Apulia to try to bring an end to the sack of the Campania by Roger of Sicily and his Saracen forces. He had been working for a long time to heal the schism that had been dividing the Church under Pope and Antipope and bring Western Christendom together under the papacy of Innocent II. Southern Italy and Sicily were among the last areas to be settled. He writes with longing to his brothers at Clairvaux of the pain of his exile from them and the sweetness of life among them. He asks them to pray for the Pope, and for a number of those who are with him in Italy: Haimeric, cardinal deacon of Santa Maria Novella and chancellor, a man who had been influential in the election of Innocent II, and the same Aimeric who asked Bernard to write his treatise On Loving God; Cardinal Lucas, cardinal priest of St. John and St. Paul; Cardinal Chrysogonus, cardinal deacon of St. Mary in Porticu; Cardinal Ivo, who was a former Victorine canon; and two of their own number, Bruno, who was later abbot of Chiaravalle, and Bernard's brother Gerard.

To the Brothers at Clairvaux[1]

My soul is sorrowful (Mt 26:38) until I can return to you, and it will not be comforted until I am with you again (Ps 76:3). For what consolation is there for me, "In this evil time" (2 Mc 1:5) "and in the place

---

1. September 1137, *Bernard de Clairvaux* (Paris, 1953), p. 590.

of my exile" (Ps 118:54)? Surely only you in the Lord? Wherever I go
the sweet thought of you never leaves me; but the sweeter the memory,
the more grievous the separation. "Alas for me that my exile" is not only
"prolonged" but piled up (Ps 119:5)! And indeed, according to the
prophet, "They added to the pain of my wound" (Ps 68:27) who separated me from you in the body for a time. There is a common exile
which is hard enough to bear, in which, "as long as we are in this body
we are in exile from the Lord" (2 Cor 5:6).

To this is added the further circumstance, which makes me almost impatient, that I am forced to live without you. It is a long tribulation and a tedious waiting, to remain so long a slave to the affairs
of this empty life, and to be shut up in the rottenness of the body,
and to be bound still by the chains of death, and not to be with Christ
all this time (Phil 1:23). More: I had one remedy for all this, a gift
truly given from heaven. Instead of the face of glory (Is 53:2) which
is still hidden from me, I was able to see you who are the holy temple
of God. The way seemed easy to me from this temple to that glory
for which the prophet sighed, saying, "I have asked one thing of the
Lord, and this I require, that I may dwell in the house of the Lord
all the days of my life, so that I may see the Lord's will and visit his
temple" (Ps 26:4).

2. What can I say? How often has that solace been kept from me!
And now my heart is torn for the third time, if I reckon correctly. My
children are snatched from my breast before it is time. Those whom I
have "begotten" in the Gospel (1 Cor 4:15) I am not allowed to rear. I
am forced to leave my own and take care of strangers and I do not know
which hurts me more, to be taken away from the one or to be burdened
with the other. Good Jesus, surely my life is not to be passed in sorrow
and my years in grief (Ps 30:11)? O Lord, it is better for me to die than
to live but not among brothers, intimates, those who are dearest. That
is sweeter, safer, and more manly as everyone agrees. It would be an
act of love to give me a period of refreshment, before I go away and am
no more (Ps 38:14).

If it please my Lord, let my sons be allowed to close with their own
hands the eyes of him who is a kind of father to them, although he is
not worthy to be called "father," so that they may see his end and console him at his death and lift up his soul on the wings of their desire to
join the company of the blessed (if you judge him worthy); let them
bury this poor man's body with the bodies of the poor, and if "I have
found favor in your eyes" (Gn 18:3) grant this great desire of mine for

the sake of the prayers and merits of those same brothers of mine. But "not my will but yours be done" (Lk 22:42). I do not wish to live or to die for myself (Rom 14:7).

3. But since you have listened to my sorrow, you must know of my consolation, if I can be said to have any. First, all the labor and trouble (Jb 6:2) which I suffer is I think in the cause of him for whom all things live (Lk 20:38). Whether I will or not, it is necessary for me to live for him who has bought my life by laying down his own, the merciful and just judge who is able to recompense us for anything we suffer for him, on that day when the world ends (2 Tm 4:8; 1 Cor 9:17). If I fight for him unwillingly, his dispensation will allow for that, and I shall be an unprofitable servant (Mt 18:32). If I fight for him willingly, that is my glory. I find some rest in that thought. Then, often he has caused my work to prosper by his heavenly grace (Wis 10:10) through no merit of my own, and that grace will not be profitless in me (1 Cor 15:10) as I have often experienced; you know something of that. But how necessary to the Church my presence is and has been I should tell you personally for your consolation, if it did not sound like boasting. But for now it is better that you should hear of it through others.

4. At the most pressing request of the Emperor and at the Pope's command, and that of some of the princes and leaders of the Church, I have given way, sorrowfully and reluctantly. Weak and ill, and, to tell you the truth, pale with fear of death, I am forced to go to Apulia. Pray for the peace (Ps 121:6) of the Church. Pray for my safety, and that I may see you again and live and die with you. And live so that your prayer may be granted.

I have written this under pressure of time, with tears and sobs, as our dear brother Baldwin[2] will tell you, for I dictated it to him. The Church has called him to another office, and another dignity. Pray for him, too, as my only comfort and one in whom my spirit (II Kgs 2:15) finds great refreshment (2 Kgs 2:15). Pray for the Lord Pope, who has a fatherly affection for me and for all of you too. And pray for the Lord Chancellor,[3] who is like a mother to me, and for Luke[4] and

---

2. Baldwin, monk of Clairvaux, was later a cardinal, and from October 1137 he was archbishop of Pisa (*Bernard de Clairvaux*, p. 702).

3. On chancellor Aimeric, to whom Bernard wrote Letter 15 and others, see *Bernard de Clairvaux*, p. 624.

4. Cardinal Lucas, *Bernard de Clairvaux*, p. 625.

Dom Chrysogonus,[5] and Master Ivo,[6] who are like our brothers. Our brothers Bruno[7] and Gerard[8] greet you, and they, too, ask for your prayers.

LETTER 523

Ailred, abbot of Rievaulx (1147–1167), was one of the major authors of the Cistercian Order in the twelfth century. He grew up at the Court of the King of Scotland, but he was English born, and he returned to England to enter the monastic life as a young man. In this letter, written at the beginning of the 1140s, Bernard is encouraging him to write the book that was later published as Speculum Caritatis (The Mirror of Love), *to feel it not a presumption to write it, but an act of charity. Ailred had never attended the schools of northern France where so many of his contemporaries got a university education, and Bernard reassures him that he need not regard that as a disqualification for his task. God has given him a good mind and the Holy Spirit has educated him. Ailred's books show him to have been deeply read in the Bible and the Fathers, especially Augustine. He brought to his writing, as Bernard did, a vivid personal experience of the spiritual life. His treatise* On Spiritual Friendship *makes Christian Cicero's* On Friendship, *and everything he wrote reflects both a distinctively Ailredian and a Cistercian spirituality.*

To Ailred of Rievaulx[1]

The greatest virtue of the saints is humility, but a humility which is real because it is discreet. True humility has nothing to do with deceit; the sacrilege of disobedience destroys it.

---

5. On cardinal Chrysogonus, see *Bernard de Clairvaux*, p. 624.
6. On cardinal Ivo, see *Bernard de Clairvaux*, p. 625.
7. Bruno, monk of Clairvaux, later abbot of Chiarvalle; see Letters 164, 165, 209, and *Bernard de Clairvaux*, p. 705.
8. Bernard's brother; see *Bernard de Clairvaux*, p. 717.
1. C.1141–2. On Ailred, abbot of Rievaulx, see A. Hoste, *Bibliotheca Aelrediana* (Steenbrugge, 1962).

I have asked your brotherly love; more, I have ordered you; more, I have commanded you in the name of God, to write me a little something to help those who are entangled in grievances and who are following the narrow way of self-indulgence.

I do not condemn or reprove you for excusing yourself, but I accuse you of obstinacy. It was humility to excuse yourself. But is it humility to disobey? Is it humility not to give way? More: "It is the sin of the soothsayers to refuse, and to be stubborn is wickedness and idolatry" (1 Sam 15:23).

But you claim that it would be too heavy a burden for your girlish shoulders to carry and that it would be wiser not to take it on, than to fall down under the weight when you have undertaken it. What I command is, indeed, heavy. It is difficult. It is impossible. But that gives you no excuse. I persist in my view. I repeat my command. What will you do? Surely he in whose words you make your vow says, "Let the junior know that it is best for him, and obey, trusting in God's help."[2] You have done as much as you ought, if not more, to excuse yourself. You have gone as far as you can. You have shown why it is impossible for you, saying you are not a learned man, indeed you are almost illiterate, that you come to the monastic life not from a school but from a kitchen,[3] and that you have been leading the life of a country bumpkin among rocks and hills, and laboring for your daily bread in the sweat of your brow with axe and mallet (I Kgs 6:7). You say that in those circumstances it is easier to learn silence than skill in speaking and that an orator's rhetoric scarcely graces a poor fisherman's clothes.[4]

I accept your excuses very gratefully; but I am aware that they fan the flame of my desire rather than extinguish it. For knowledge got not from the school of some grammarian but from the school of the Holy Spirit will taste the sweeter to me. And if perhaps you have this treasure in an earthenware vessel, "so that the excellence may come from God's power and not your own" (2 Cor 4:7), what a joyful thing, what a foretaste of the future, that you should be carried from the kitchen to the monastery. For perhaps one who has been entrusted in his time with the responsibility of providing bodily food in a royal household will be procuring spiritual food and feeding those who are hungry with the Word of God in the house of our King.

---

2. RB 68.5.
3. Ailred was once a steward in the household of the king of Scotland.
4. RB 14.12.

I am not put off by what you say about the steepness of the mountains or the cragginess of the rocks or the plunging valleys, for in those days the mountains will drop sweetness and the hills will flow with milk and honey (Jl 3:18) and the valleys will stand thick with corn (Ps 64:14), and honey will drip from stone and oil from the hardest rock (Dt 32:13). Christ's sheep (Ps 99:3) will feed among the crags and peaks. So I think that that mallet of yours will be able to strike something from those rocks that you have not taken from the books of the masters by using your sharp wits in study, and that you will have experienced something under the shade of the trees in the heat of the day that you would never have learned in the schools.

Therefore give the glory not to yourself but to his name (Ps 113:9), who not only snatched you from the lake of wretchedness and the filth of the mire (Ps 39:3), when you were in despair, from the house of death and the cesspit, but also remembering his mercies the merciful and compassionate Lord (Ps 110:4) gave the sinner hope that he would be raised up, gave light to the blind, instructed the ignorant, taught the inexperienced (Ps 145:8). So then, since everyone who knows you knows that what you give is not yours, why do you blush and tremble and hesitate? Why do you refuse to give it even at the command of his voice who gave you that which you have to give? Do you fear to be presumptuous or to be the envy of others? As if anyone ever wrote anything useful without being envied, or as though you could be called presumptuous when you are a monk obeying his abbot.

And so I order you in the name of Jesus Christ and in the spirit of our God, that whatever thoughts about the excellence of love, its fruits, its ordering, have come to you in your daily meditations, you will not put off writing them down, so that we can see as in a mirror what love is and how sweet it is to possess; and how great an oppression there is in greed, which is its opposite; and that outward affliction does not diminish that sweetness of love as some think, but rather increases it; and lastly, with what discretion it should be exercised. Indeed, to spare your modesty, let this letter be copied at the beginning of the book, so that whatever may displease the reader in *The Mirror of Love*[5] (for that is the title I give it) may be blamed not upon you who obey, but upon me, who forced you to write it against your will.

Farewell in Christ, beloved brother.

_____

5. On the writing of Ailred's *Speculum Caritatis*, see the edition of C. H. Talbot, *Opera Omnia, CCSL, Continuatio Medievalis*, I (Turnholt, 1971), pp. 3–161.

Selected Bibliography

Background Studies

Butler, C. *Western Mysticism*. 2nd ed. London, 1926.

Châtillon, F. "Regio Dissimilitudinis." *Mélanges E. Podéchard*. Lyon, 1945, pp. 85–102.

Chenu, M. D. *La théologie au douzième siècle*. Paris, 1957.

Constable, G. "Twelfth Century Spirituality and the late Midde Ages." *Mediaeval and Renaissance Studies* 5, ed. O. B. Hardison. North Carolina, 1971, pp. 27–60.

James, W. *Varieties of Religious Experience*. Edinburgh, 1901–1902. Reprinted with introduction by A. D. Nock. London, 1960.

Lubac, H. de. *Exégèse médiévale*. 2 vols. Paris, 1959.

Smalley, B. *The Study of the Bible in the Middle Ages*. 3rd ed. Oxford, 1983.

Ward, B. "St. Bernard and the Anglican Divines." *Bernard of Clairvaux*, Cistercian Studies 23. Washington, 1973.

Bernard and his Contemporaries

Evans, G. R. *The Mind of Bernard of Clairvaux*. Oxford, 1983.

Gilson, E. *The Mystical Theology of St. Bernard*. Tr. A. H. C. Downes. London, 1940.

—. "Sub umbris arborum." *Mediaeval Studies* 14 (1952):149–51.

Haillier, A. *The Monastic Theology of Ailred of Rievaulx*. Tr. C. Heaney. Shannon, 1969.

Hugh of St. Victor. *Six opuscules spirituelles*. Ed. R. Baron. Paris, 1969.

Leclercq, J. *Recueil d'études sur S. Bernard*. 3 vols. Rome, 1962–1969.

—. "L'attitude spirituelle de S. Bernard devant la guerre." *Collectanea Cisterciensia* 36 (1974):195–222.

Matter, E. Ann. "Eulogium Sponsi de Sponsa: Canons, monks and the Song of Songs." *The Thomist* 49 (1985):551–74.

Richard of St. Victor. *Spiritual Writings*. Tr. and introd. G. A. Zinn. Classics of Western Spirituality. New York, 1979.

INDEX TO INTRODUCTION

INDEX TO TEXT